HOMOAFFECTIONALISM

MALE BONDING
From Gilgamesh To The Present

HOMOAFFECTIONALISM

MALE BONDING
From Gilgamesh To The Present

PAUL D. HARDMAN

GLB Publishers   San Francisco

Published in the United States by
ℜ𝔲𝔣 Division, GLB Publishers
P.O. Box 78212, San Francisco, CA 94107 USA

Cover Design by Curium Design
Cover line art from:
Thomas Hope, *Costumes of the Greeks and Romans*
Dover Publications, New York

Publisher's Cataloging in Publication
(Prepared by Quality Books Inc.)

Hardman, Paul D., 1923-
    Homoaffectionalism : male bonding from Gilgamesh to the present / Paul D. Hardman.
    p. cm.
    Includes bibliographical references and index.
    1-879194-13-9 (casebound)
    1-879194-11-2 (pbk.)
    1. Men--Social life and customs--History. 2. Homosexuality, Male--History. 3. Gay men--Social life and customs--History. I. Title. II. Title: Male bonding from Gilgamesh to the present.

HQ1090.H37 1993   305.3'2
                                             QBI93-20066

First printing, April, 1993
10 9 8 7 6 5 4 3 2 1

DEDICATED TO

WARREN

whose warm friendship, infinite patience,
and encouragement through the years
contributed significantly to the creation
of this book

TABLE OF CONTENTS

PREFACE

Words and the manipulation of meanings and connotations of words are the principal tools of biased writers. Over the centuries, religious and politically motivated individuals have used the written and the spoken word to attack, condemn, and persecute those who differed.

Religious polemicists became experts; as exegetists, they could and did find any meaning they sought in the Bible or, more correctly, in selected bibles. With such a variety of translations to accommodate the preconceived purposes of the compilers, it is hardly surprising that they were tempted to meddle with the meanings.

The same process affected the writing of the laws in the development of Western culture. Therefore, to analyze the attitudes of various groups who contributed to the formulation of laws and religious beliefs regarding homosexuality in Western culture, certain words are used here with definite meanings:

Homosexual: The coinage of the word which deals with same–sex erotic behavior is credited to Karoli Kertbeny (Karl Maria Benkert, 1824–1882). He was a literary scholar and a Hungarian who wrote in German under the name Benkert. The word may have been coined in response to the need for a term other than "unnatural indecency" used in the repressive laws of Prussia at the time.

Homoerotic: The word is usually defined as relating to homosexual expression. In this text, the word will be used to describe conduct involving same–sex activity regardless of sexual orientation. The connotation here includes lust, and not necessarily affection.

Homoaffectionalism: As coined by the author, the word means same–sex relationships which do not necessarily involve homosexual sex acts, but do involve strong emotional bonding, which may or may not include sexual conduct. The emphasis is on affection and bonding regardless of any carnal involvement. As defined, it recognizes the phenomenon of mutual altruism between individuals of the same gender and recognizes the basis of mutual support, loyalty, and cooperation needed (in our view) to allow civilization to develop. It would be difficult to imagine a military organization that does not rely on homoaffectionalism for maintaining loyalty among its members. The term also allows for a recognition of the phenomenon of opposite gender subjugation, particularly manifested in heterosexual, patriarchal societies, and especially apparent in early Christianity and Judaism.

While the conclusions reached in this study are my own, the paths which led to them were made easier by a number of scholars who read the text and made valuable suggestions. Wayne Dynes was of great help in locating sources. Walter Williams patiently reviewed the data and made his insights available, particularly regarding the influence of the Crusades on attitudes toward sexual conduct in medieval Europe. Many facets of sexual conduct have not been included in this study, to concentrate more specifically on the theme of homoaffectionalism. Selected periods were used to trace the course of events. In Europe the main emphasis is on the ancient and early medieval periods, while the influence of Islam is centered on the Mamlukes from the later middle ages to early modern times. Again this method was used to focus on homoaffectionalism as it relates to the development of Western Civilization. A special chapter is devoted to military homoaffectionalism from ancient to late twentieth century times.

The word "homosexual" is used, in the latter chapters particularly, especially in its modern sense. The word "gay" is used for discussion of the more contemporary periods.

CHAPTER I

MANIFEST HOMOAFFECTIONALISM

Section 1

Gilgamesh

It is difficult enough to explore the nature of ancient peoples, but the problem is made worse when we superimpose modern concepts through the use of emotionally–charged words. "Homosexual", "lesbian", "gay" and "bisexual" are words which automatically trigger ingrained conditioned responses. We cannot avoid the overtly sexual connotations evoked by such words. The emphasis in this study is on same–sex bonding, and there is no denying homoeroticism.

As we begin this closer scrutiny of ancient laws for attitudes toward homosexuality, it must be borne in mind that there are recognizable evolutionary factors that apply to *homo sapiens* and other primates. The observable sexual behavior of primates and other mammals in particular cannot be ignored, and must be recognized as having a place in nature.[1] However, we are confining this study to the written record and to inferences drawn from tangible evidence left as artifacts of human beings.

Recognizing the acceptance of male homoaffectionalism among the cultures of ancient Mesopotamia may explain the lack of concern expressed in their laws regarding homoerotic behavior. Therefore, we will look for homoaffectionalism.

"Homoaffectionalism" is a term fashioned by the author to identify a particular phenomenon. Using the prefix "homo–", from the Greek meaning "same," and joining it to the English word "affection," which describes tender feelings of fondness toward another, we produce a word devoid of immediate sexual connotations, which more accurately accounts for mutual altruism and mutual nurturing observed between individuals of the same gender. The word also recognizes the friendship, comradeship and bonding which is manifested by human beings of the same sex. Same–sex eroticism is not precluded, but it is not the focus of the phenomenon. Thus emotionally–charged, erotically–based terms can be avoided. It is then possible to analyze the relationships depicted in ancient laws and customs without the burden of modern religious and legal

1

prejudices. Individuals whose lives are closely associated in terms of close bonding need not be identified as homosexual, even if they are. It is the capacity of same sex individuals to manifest mutual affection that is the issue, not their actual sexual conduct; thus we can recognize heterosexual comradeship as part of the same phenomenon which produces romantic homophilia and which ultimately allows for the development of civilization.

Even the Old Testament relates the legend of David and his homoaffection for Jonathan: "I grieve for thee, my brother Jonathan: exceedingly beautiful and amiable to me above the love of women as the mother loveth her son, so did I love thee..." [2] What does this strange quotation mean?

The word "brother" is a translation from the ancient Hebrew which describes a friend for whom there is a strong emotional attachment.[3] A quite different relationship, more social than emotional, is described between Chusai and David in II Samuel 15:37, wherein Chusai is described as the "friend" of David but not "brother." [4] This difference is significant. Since we will be scrutinizing the words of the ancient laws and legends to find clues to homoaffectionalism, we must keep in mind the shades of meaning designated by words like "brother" and "friend." In Semitic languages, including Hebrew and Babylonian, there is a word *ra'u'* or sometimes *ru'u* which describes the kind of "friend" to whom one is emotionally bound.[5] It is the very word used in the Akkadian Gilgamesh epic.

The Gilgamesh epic serves not only as the model for male bonding and homoaffectionalism in the ancient world, it is in some respects the precursor to the Biblical book of Genesis. For example, the legends of creation and the flood are found in the epic.[6]

The epic is the longest and perhaps the most beautiful of the Babylonian poems yet discovered. One of the oldest versions of the poem was incised onto twelve large tablets in the seventh century B.C. and unearthed in 1853 by Austen H. Layard, Hormud Rassan, and George Smith near the site of Nineveh. George Smith of the British Museum presented the first arrangement and translation of the epic on December 3, 1872, before the Society of Biblical Archaeology.[7] Other fragments containing the Gilgamesh epic have been discovered from time to time, providing scholars with a rather complete version.[8]

The epic's central figure, Gilgamesh, was a youthful ruler

assigned by researchers to the second dynasty of Uruk (2700–2500 B.C.). Originally a historical figure, he apparently became a hero of myths and legends. Ultimately he became the god of the lower world.[9] Depicted as a man of great wisdom who knew of the world before the flood, he went on a great quest to learn the secret of life. What is of major interest for this study is that the quest for the secret of life was prompted by the death of his lover–friend, Enkidu. Enkidu is described as a wild–looking hairy man of great strength. His friendship with Gilgamesh is termed *ra'u'* and their emotional bonding is referred to as *ibru*.[10] Much is made of his hair which covered his whole body, and much is made of the fact that he was wild, that is, uncivilized.

Gilgamesh had heard of the hairy wild man, and sent out a courtesan to seduce Enkidu into coming into the town to meet him. They meet at the entrance of a community house which was the scene of a nocturnal orgy. Enkidu is repulsed by the orgy, and attempts to block Gilgamesh from participating. Thus began the struggles and encounters which mark their relationship. It was during this first encounter that Gilgamesh bested his newfound friend. They fought like infuriated bulls so that even the walls shook. Enkidu was eventually pinned to the ground. Each then admires the other's strength, and they form a strong bond with each other. Together they seek adventure. They become inseparable.

Gilgamesh is so handsome, the legend tells us, that Ishtar, the goddess of love, asks him to be her husband. Gilgamesh refuses, leading her to invoke her wrath against Gilgamesh and his preferred companion, Enkidu. A great bull is fashioned by the god Anu, father of Ishtar. In a rage she sends it against Enkidu.

Enkidu seizes the bull and holds it until Gilgamesh enters and slays it with his sword. Then Enkidu taunts the goddess Ishtar with vulgar curses, and he tosses at her the right thigh of the "bull of heaven."

Because of this defiance, Enkidu becomes the object of the wrath of the gods, and is killed by an illness. Gilgamesh is heartbroken; he then leaves Uruk to roam the world to seek the secret of immortality. Eventually Gilgamesh obtains the secret, only to have it stolen from him by a snake. The epic reveals the degree of passion engendered between the pair. Male bonding is the basic theme, coupled with contemplation of death and the meaning of life itself. The character of Gilgamesh is mapped out in the clay fragments: "Gilgamesh leaves no son to his father; day and night his outrageousness continues unrestrained;" then the sexual theme is repeated in other lines: "Strong, handsome (and) wise... Gilgamesh leaves no virgin to her lover." [11]

Gilgamesh's sexual appetite for both boys and girls indicates bisexuality. However, the bisexuality depicted before his bonding with Enkidu is the mere satisfaction of carnal lust which is essentially uncivilized and disturbing to the population of Uruk. In contrast, as we will see, the relationship between Gilgamesh and Enkidu involved deep emotional responses not found in the earlier bisexual conduct. The brutish sexual dominance suggested by the bisexual behavior yields to the civilized mutuality of respect and affection between equals. The manifest homoaffectionalism found in the epic replaces the pattern of sexual abuse depicted before Gilgamesh met Enkidu. These factors should be considered when analyzing the epic.

Apparently in an effort to obtain some relief from the unruly sexuality of Gilgamesh, the people pray to Aruru:

> Great Aruru, they called: 'Thou, Aruru, did create Gilgamesh; now create his equal; to the impetuousity of his heart let him be equal; let them strive with each other, and let Uruk thus have rest;' when Aruru heard this she conceived in her heart an image of Anu: Aruru washed her hands, pinched off clay, and threw (it) on the steppe... Valiant Enkidu she created.

What we have here is an especially–created mate for Gilgamesh, the someone who would be his equal and satisfy his appetites, thus keeping Gilgamesh away from fathers' sons and virgins. The juxtaposing of the sons and virgins is significant in the comprehension of Gilgamesh, his friend Enkidu, and the social attitudes toward male bonding at the time. What we see is a pair of super–masculine heroes who were homoaffectional, who were designed by the gods to satisfy each other's passions.

Gilgamesh was fascinated when he heard tales of a great hairy wild–man seen on the steppe.[12] It is indicative of the way people thought of sex when the epic relates that Gilgamesh selected a prostitute to lure the wild–man to him.

It is interesting to observe that Alexander Heidel translates the section in Tablet 1, lines 8 to 21, in Latin rather than English: that

4

segment describes the carnal encounter with the prostitute in detail. Enkidu copulates with her for "six days and seven nights," after which he was "sated with her charms." [13]

The prostitute then tells Enkidu of Gilgamesh who "seeks a friend, one who understands the heart." Enkidu is interested and says, "Come, oh prostitute, take me to... the one perfect in strength, who prevails over men like a wild ox..." [14]

Whether the description of Gilgamesh was intended to rearouse the satiated Enkidu is a matter of conjecture. The prostitute extols the charms of Gilgamesh: "I will show you Gilgamesh, a joyful man. Look at him, behold his face; comely is his manhood, endowed with vigor is he, the whole of his body is adorned with pleasure...." She went on to relate that "Shamash (the great god) has conferred a favor upon Gilgamesh... Before you will arrive from the open country, Gilgamesh will behold you in his dreams...." [15] Enkidu agrees to go.

Then Gilgamesh dreams of Enkidu before he meets him, and he relates his dream to his mother:

My mother, last night I saw a dream. There were stars in the heaven; as if it were a host of heaven, (one) fell down to me. I tried to lift it, but it was too heavy (too strong) for me; I tried to move it away, but I could not remove (it)... The men trudged around it... while my fellows kissed its feet; I bent over it as over a woman (and) put it at your feet (and you yourself did put) it on a par with me.

The use of the neuter personal pronoun "it" refers to the man who is later known to be Enkidu.[16] His mother responds: "... I myself did put him on a par with you [over whom] you did bend as over a woman" (Column vi of Tablet I) and continues right after that by stating, "He is a strong companion, one who helps a friend in need; he is the strongest on the steppe; strength he has, and his strength is as strong as that of the host of heaven; that you did bend over him (as over) a woman means that he will never forsake you; this is the meaning of the dream." [17]

Gilgamesh then dreams that he bent over an ax "as over a woman." His mother explains that it was not an ax. "The ax you did see is a man. That you did bend over him as over a woman means that he is a strong companion, one who helps a friend in need; he is the strongest on the steppe; and his strength is as strong as the host of heaven."[18] In the Assyrian version, on Tablet II, the part which is related above as "bend over him as over a woman" is translated "I put my forehead firmly against it." This is followed by the line spoken by his mother: "When you see him, you will rejoice, as over a woman, the heroes will kiss his feet, and you will embrace him... and lead him to me."[19] The lines related above about the ax are translated from the Assyrian text as follows: "I looked at it and I rejoiced, loving it and bending over it as over a woman; I took it and put it at my side."[20]

The Assyrian text relates how the prostitute tore her garment in two to cover Enkidu.[21] From this it may be concluded that he was not only wild but also naked. He knew nothing of "eating bread." Lines 23 through 27 from Tablet II once again described his "hairy body" which he anointed with oil; "he put on a garment" and became like a human being, "and now he is like a man."[22]

When Enkidu arrives at Uruk, as was noted, he observes the orgy customs there and turns pale; would–be brides are tried in public first. The men of the town are enthralled at the sight of Enkidu: "The men rejoiced; 'a mighty one has arisen as a match for the hero whose appearance is so handsome; for Gilgamesh, an equal like a god has arisen... for Ishtar (the goddess of love), the bed is made...'"[23] On Column I of Tablet II it is related, "They kissed one another and formed a friendship." There is a break at this point in the text.[24]

Later, after it has become the will of the gods that Enkidu must die, he becomes ill and Gilgamesh watches his friend as he dies. "It is for Enkidu, my friend, that I weep, crying bitterly like unto a wailing woman," laments Gilgamesh.[25] In his lament Gilgamesh refers to Enkidu as "my friend, my younger brother." It is well to notice again that, in the Semitic language, close personal companions are described as "brother" implying a close emotional attachment. "On a couch of honor I let you recline. I let you sit on a seat of ease, the seat at my left, so that the princes of the earth kissed your feet," says Gilgamesh to the dying Enkidu.[26]

After Enkidu's death, Gilgamesh "weeps bitterly and roams the desert..."[27] He sets out to learn the secret of immortality. The god Shamash admonishes him that the life he seeks "... you will not find."[28] Gilgamesh pleads, however, "... May he who has died the death see the light of the sun. Enkidu, whom I loved so dearly...

has gone to the common lot of mankind. Day and night I have wept over him."

There is an ambiguous section in Tablet X, column iv, dealing with Gilgamesh's journey. He attempts to cross the waters of death and has only 120 wooden poles to use to push and propel the boat; soon all are used and gone. Then "he un–girdled his loins... pulled off his clothes... and with his hand raised the mast." No explanation is offered to describe his action.[29] This may suggest masturbation.

There can be no doubt that the epic of Gilgamesh deals with male bonding. We find homoaffectionalism clearly expressed. In a culture which matter–of–factly relates the idea that Gilgamesh would be involved sexually with boys as well as women, we may conclude that when Gilgamesh "bends over him as over a woman" the words are describing homoerotic sexual conduct. That means that one of the oldest epics ever written is a tale of homosexual love and homoaffectionalism, as well as male bonding.

In the Gilgamesh epic, Enkidu is the epitome of desirability to his lover, but the emphasis was not on the erotic aspects of their relationship. It was on the satisfaction each brought to the other through comradeship and the benefits each brought to the other. Gilgamesh was able to mend his sexually–aggressive behavior, which troubled his subjects, and divert that energy to constructive accomplishments. Enkidu was able to become civilized and, through the homoaffectionate relationship with Gilgamesh, contribute to the good of the community at large. Even the death of Enkidu is redeemed in the story; it permits Gilgamesh to be a better leader of his people.

George F. Held wrote an analysis of the Gilgamesh epic which deals with the relationship with Enkidu. He noted the vigorous sexual prowess of both men, and pointed out that the emphasis is not on homoeroticism but rather on their capacity for love. It is that capacity which we refer to as homoaffectionalism. Held also called attention to some extremely interesting puns which were used in the original texts. These puns are definitely homoerotic. For example, when Gilgamesh dreams of a falling star and an ax to presage his meeting with Enkidu, the words "falling star" and "ax" have double meanings: the ancient words *hassinu*, "ax," and *assinu*, "male prostitute," are revealing, just as the words *kisru* for "ball" (round object, meteorite) and *kerzru* meaning "male with curled hair" (male prostitute) make the same point. Despite these puns, which must have delighted ancient readers, the emphasis of the story remains homoaffectionate rather than homoerotic.[30]

Section 2
The Code of Hammurabi

The homoaffectionalism observed in the Epic of Gilgamesh obviously developed during the preliterate stages of Mesopotamian civilization. It was a legend which was told and retold for centuries before being written. Consequently, it reflects very ancient folk customs and beliefs. The attitudes and customs concerning human sexuality related in the legend must be kept in mind when analyzing subsequent codifications of law arising in the same region.

Modern discovery of Near Eastern law began during the second half of the 19th century and the early 20th century. Fragments of clay legal tablets were unearthed in 1854 at Tell Sifr by W. K. Loftus.[31] Other tablets were subsequently added to the growing collection. However, it was not until Dr. M. J. De Morgan discovered the original stelae of King Hammurabi in December, 1901, that scholars had enough material to discuss the laws of Babylon with certainty.[32]

The Code of Hammurabi, for example, says very little regarding sexual conduct, but what it does say is significant. Freedom of sexual expression is inferred in the Code of Hammurabi by the very lack of prohibitions it contains and by the specific privileges it creates to honor both male and female sacral harlots. No homophobia is expressed by Hammurabi. It is not negative evidence alone which makes this point, but specific laws set down to assure the privileges of the male harlots associated with the King and the gods, as well as religious personnel in the service of the temple.

As we shall see, the Code of Hammurabi inspired the Hittites and subsequently influenced the Hebrews who ultimately affected Western law through the Bible. Because various interpretations of biblical tradition have played a major role in the formulation of Western legal attitudes, their origins should be scrutinized to discern the rationale. We should determine what has made biblical tradition the source of contemporary negative attitudes towards homosexuals, as manifested in Western law.[33]

In tracing the sources of homophobia found in the Bible, we must pick up a thread which goes back at least 5,000 years. In doing this the Bible must be regarded as a collection of writings set down by human beings over a span of time.

Since we will be dealing with written words, which provide the internal clues, it is important to realize from the outset that the language of the Old Testament was Hebrew. If it is realized that there was no alphabetical form of the Hebrew prior to about 850 B.C., then it is safe to conclude that we are dealing with a set of writings of rather late developments. The Old Testament, therefore, can be dated from about 850 B.C. for the last entries.[34] The problem of exact dating will be left to others. These points are made to help dispel any delusions regarding greater antiquity and thereby demystify the books themselves. Their importance does not lie in their antiquity, but in their function as a transmitter of laws and customs older than the written books themselves.

Those who influenced the Hebrews were their neighbors and dominators, the Babylonians and the Hittites, in the region known as Mesopotamia. Semites and Indo–Europeans intermixed in this area very early, among them the Sumerians with traceable roots to the Indus Valley. It was the Sumerians who exerted the strongest civilizing impact on the people of the region, introducing cuneiform writing and religious customs. It was their language and customs which were the basis of what followed in Babylon.[35]

A continuum is assumed in tracing the evidence of attitudes found in the ancient laws which still influence Western law. Laws are not usually created *de novo* each time they are codified, not even the most ancient laws. For example, G. R. Driver and John Miles noted, "... Urukagina of Lagas (c. 2800 B.C.) says that 'he has established the ordinances of former times,' and Sardon of Accad (c. 2751–2695 B.C.) is called 'the King of Justice, one who speaks justice'; also Ur-Engur, King of Ur (c. 2450–2400 B.C.), leaves it on the record that 'according to the righteous laws of Samas he made... justice prevail'; Lipit-Ister of Isin (c. 2217–2207 B.C.) speaks of the time 'when I established justice in the land of Sumer and Accad,' using almost the same words as Hammurabi in the prologue to his laws; and Sinidinnam, also King of Isin (c. 2125–2120 B.C.), describes himself as a prince 'who restores the ordinances and the laws of Annunaki, the gods of the nether–world who determined the fates of the living and tried the dead'." [36]

From the beginning the concept of "sin" was too pervasive to ignore. However, it must be limited to its proper perspective. It was but one of the components of society's reaction toward homoerotic behavior, as it was expressed in laws and religious customs. There is another factor which must be considered. It is

10

observable that people often promulgate laws based on idealized concepts of their social norms. This phenomenon is particularly true of laws regarding sexual conduct.

In societies subject to autocratic rule, which had been the case for most state–level societies, the enactment of laws regarding homosexual conduct had a unique characteristic: prohibitions have generally been for political rather than for "moral" reasons. Irrationality, religiosity, greed and corruption have been responsible for the negative legal responses found in Western laws regarding homosexual behavior.

As sophisticated as people may see themselves, they are still subject to physiological urges. Hunger, thirst and the desire to engage in sexual activity are strongly influenced by the body. The rules devised by different societies as responses to these particular needs often form the basis of religious practices. Religious practices become customs and customs become laws.

There are other observable phenomena which occur with sufficient regularity to warrant special comment: religious and civil laws and the oral traditions which preceded them are the precursors of specific codes. The earlier laws were enforced by popular custom supported by an interpretation of the will of the gods. This allowed for little or no mercy and no humanitarianism. As society developed beyond a rudimentary state, the principle of *talio* manifests itself as in Mesopotamia.

Lex talionis is based on the concept "like for like," which is a fundamental approach easily understood as a practical solution to a problem. While primitive, it is a far more advanced concept than law based on the will of a god.[37] *Talio* describes the principle of "an eye for an eye" which is found in the Code of Hammurabi and in the Bible, and other written records of the Near East.

The main concern of the ancient laws was to settle arguments by compensating for the damages done by one party to another. Punishment was apparently a secondary consideration.[38] "Maintaining the equilibrium of mutuality," noted Neufeld, was the overriding consideration.[39] Decisions were made to reduce tensions and resolve the problem at hand. The records speak with no concern for "legal" issues; they speak of "right" or "wrong" with no reference to "legal" and "illegal."

The written records of Western civilization began on the banks of the Nile in Egypt, and between the Tigris and Euphrates rivers

11

in the region referred to as Mesopotamia. The development of writing appeared with the earliest builders about 5,000 years ago. The archaeologist Charles Breasted called that time the "dawn of conscience," a period during which concepts of "good" and "evil" were first written and preserved.

The Sumerians began building in Mesopotamia. The cities of Sumer and Akkad attracted the nomadic tribes to their outer walls as traders. Semitic people were attracted to the area, including the tribes of Abraham, according to tradition. Other people were also attracted including Indo–Europeans.[40] Each migration added to the developing culture which endured with vigor until about the time of Alexander the Great.[41] It continued with less fervor through the first century of the Roman Empire, fading as Christianity grew.

The earliest extant collections of laws come to us from the Sumerians of Ur-Nammu. They were apparently written during the Third Dynasty of Ur, about 2110 B.C. Those of Lipit-Ishtar of Isin were formulated about 1925 B.C.[42] The earliest written in a Semitic language are the laws of the town of Eshnunna, dated about 1800 B.C. These are the fragments whose importance in this study lies in their influence on the Code of Hammurabi, collected and published about 1700 B.C., which in turn obviously influenced those who compiled the Old Testament of the Hebrews.

Hittite laws written in Indo–European language also survive from about 1500 B.C., as do laws of the Assyrians in Semitic, from 1100 B.C. Each text influenced its successors, and ultimately the legal attitudes expressed in Western culture. The Hebrews, as we shall see, responded to and specifically rejected the traditions they had found in the laws of their neighbors, especially as they concerned homoerotic sexual conduct.

In reading various translations of the Code of Hammurabi, it will be noted that only one section concerned itself with men and women whose sexual proclivities were apparently homoerotic. None of the ancient legal texts were concerned with homoerotic relationships, but they did specifically condone male and female prostitution. However, the rules for married women were especially rigid, and the rights of the husband were carefully protected. The emphasis was on property rights in a wife and of an heir, and on the obligations which accrued as a result of marriage. Morality was not an issue. The laws of Hammurabi were designed to cover specific activities which affected the society, perhaps those not

12

effectively covered by oral tradition and family customs.

If it is assumed that the family had governed the conduct of family members and adjudicated problems under the authority of the family, then it might be argued that homosexual conduct would be dealt with in the family, and not be a matter for the government. While that may well have been the case, we should not assume that homosexuality was condemned simply based on modern attitudes. If there were hostile attitudes at the family level, we should not expect to find special privileges granted to homosexuals in the formal written laws, and we do.

There is a special privilege in the one section where homosexual conduct is described: Paragraph 187 of the Code. This was translated by Chilperic Edwards and published in 1904 as follows: "The son of a *Nersega*, an inmate of the palace, or the son of a devotee may not be reclaimed"[43] by the natural parents. The word *Nersega* was left untranslated with the suggestion that it represented a male "of unknown class."[44] C. H. W. Johns translated the same Paragraph 187, also published in 1904, as: "The son of a 'royal favorite,' of one that stands in the palace or the son of a 'votary' shall not be reclaimed."[45]

G. R. Driver and John C. Miles also analyzed and translated the Code of Hammurabi in 1952.[46] They identify the word for the male "royal favorite" as *girsegum* in Babylonian, asserting that the word was archaic to the Babylonians and derived from an even older source.[47]

Both categories of persons mentioned in Paragraph 187 are of similar status, one being a male, the other female. The female is described in more purely Babylonian terms as *sal-zikrum* which Driver and Miles render as "votary" or "devotee." The femaleness of *sal-zikrum* is confirmed by comparative analysis of the texts themselves. There is no question when the same word is used in Paragraph 187, wherein it says of the *sal-zikrum*: "Her father was given her dowry..."[48]

This is the same interpretation accepted by Edwards.[49] Johns referred to *sal-zikrum* as a "vowed woman." Driver and Miles give the most interesting interpretation, and declare that *sal-zikrum* was described by Dhorme as a masculine woman who was also a transvestite. Driver and Miles felt that Dhorme had gone "too far" and had reached his conclusion on slim evidence.[50] They used the Greek word *hierodule* in their description, which means "a temple

13

slave... used especially with reference to ritual prostitution."[51] Thus we can discern what the duties were of both males and females referred to in Paragraph 187. The word in Babylonian to describe them is *gudistum* which, like *kaddish* for prayer in Hebrew, implies something holy. There is also an obvious, philologically identical relationship with the Hebrew word used to describe a sacred prostitute, as used in the Canaanite religion: "There shall be no female harlot among the Israelite men" (Deuteronomy 23:16).

Thus we see a direct negative reference in the Old Testament responding to Babylonian laws and customs. There is also a confirmation in the Hebrew response that the male *girsegum* counterpart of the *sal-zikrum* was a male who prostituted himself as a respected aspect of religious worship in Babylon. Rabbi Dr. Charles Ber Chavel quotes the biblical text: "There shall be no *k'deishah* of the daughters of Israel (one who is devoted to and always prepared for illicit intercourse), nor shall there be a *kadeish* of the sons of Israel (one who is always prepared for pederasty)." There is no doubt that Chavel considered the temple boys to be catamites.[52] Archaeological evidence also supports that view, according to Donald Harden who viewed depictions on ancient artifacts which showed various professionals, including those who served: "The servers included religious prostitutes, both women and boys. Such a practice was common form in Phoenician sanctuaries, at least in the east." [53]

There is nothing in Babylonian law to prohibit the "votives" or "palace favorites" from having natural children. In addition, Paragraph 187 establishes a privilege, apparently unique, that permits *sal-zikrum* and *girsegum* to adopt sons and have that adoption finalized without ever allowing the natural parents to "redeem" their sons. This is expressly stated in the law.[54] Thus we can detect a practice which must have been fairly common: parents donated their sons to the temple for adoption, in this case irrevocably, without possibility of redemption.

Offering sons to god was also an Israelite tradition. The irrevocable nature of such an offering as depicted in Paragraph 187 of Hammurabi's code is refuted in the Old Testament (Numbers 18:15–16): "... that they give to the Lord as their first fruits... every living thing that opens the womb, whether of man or of beast, such as are yours; but you must let the first–born of man, as well as of unclean animals, be redeemed." This tradition among Jews permits

14

the redemption of a son from a priest. The ritual of "Pidyum ha-ben" is based on this tradition, and to this day the first born son of a Jewish mother may be offered to a priest or "cohen" to be redeemed by coins—five shekels of silver.

The historian Vern Bullough refers to the individuals described in Paragraph 187 (and in Paragraphs 178-9) as "eunuchs" and *hierodule*. He contends the Greek word *hierodule* is a term devoid of sexual characteristics, yet he admits that the term "has frequently been equated with homosexuality." Such an interpretation is "misleading." He contends that "homosexuals were not necessarily priests, and priests were not necessarily homosexuals."[55] However, the word in the Babylonian text is *girsegum*, not *hierodule* or "eunuch," and *girsegum* does appear to imply homosexual prostitution.

If it is also possible to infer from references to the *sal-zikrum* as identifying her male counterpart, *girsegum*, then it is logical to conclude that since both were apparently sacral harlots, both cross-dressed for religious reasons and both enjoyed the same privileges.[56] The *sal-zikrum* has been described as a "woman–man" with the duties of a "eunuch–chamberlain." Women in this situation were accorded a remarkable degree of equality not generally observed in the ancient world. It should be noted that transvestitism, as implied in the words *sal-zikrum* and *girsegum*, was common in the ancient East. Male religious personnel affected female attire while celebrating certain rites at Uruk, for example. Certain female religious figures in Babylon were represented by statues of women in men's clothing.[57]

The *girsegum* has also been described as *epicene*, which denotes the sexual ambivalence of either a eunuch or an effeminate man.[58] Thus, despite the obvious reluctance of scholars to admit it directly, the evidence clearly implies that the male *girsegum* was homosexual in practice, with duties in the palace corresponding to those of the female *sal-zikrum*.[59]

What is most important in Paragraph 187 is the fact that the only apparent reference to homosexuals in the Code of Hammurabi is an explicit grant of privilege. The *girsegum* quite probably engaged in transvestitism, and clearly engaged as sacral prostitutes with other men; yet they were highly respected and privileged officials of the palace.

Furthermore, the privileges granted in Paragraph 187 follow a logical pattern in the Code, especially with regard to the donation of a son to the priestly personnel, in the same way that a son is offered to a master craftsman as an apprentice. The irrevocable nature of the adoption suggests that the donated son is intended to be trained to perform the duties of the adopting parent. Under Babylonian law, apprentices who were adopted for training could not be redeemed by the natural parents. This would mean that parents who offered their sons to a *girsegum* knew that they would be trained to engage as sacral prostitutes with men. The priestly male prostitutes were regarded as men "whose manhood Ishtar has changed into womanhood."[60] Obviously, a society which regarded their priests as honorable must have regarded their homosexual conduct as honorable as well, at least in religious terms.

With reference to the Code of Hammurabi, then, we may conclude that homosexuality was certainly not forbidden; indeed, it was recognized and accepted and incorporated in the religion. Whatever the attitude may have been at the family level is not known, but officially, in the Code, there was no proscription against homosexual behavior in ancient Babylon.

NOTES

1. Desmond Morris, The Naked Ape (New York: McGraw Hill Book Co., 1967), p. 94.

2. II Samuel 1:26, New American Catholic Edition, The Holy Bible (New York): Benziger Bros., Inc., 1961).

3. Silvestro Fiore, Voices From The Clay (Norman: University of Oklahoma, 1965), p. 82.

4. Silvestro Fiore, p. 82.

5. Silvestro Fiore, p. 82.

6. J. Finegan, Light From The Ancient Past (Princeton: Princeton University Press, 1959), pp. 31–35.

7. Alexander Heidel, The Gilgamesh Epic and Old Testament Parallels (Chicago: University of Chicago Press, 1971), p. 2.

    According to N. K. Sandars, *The Epic Of Gilgamesh* (New York: Penguin Books, 1983), it was the eleventh tablet of the Assyrian version of The Epic of Gilgamesh which Smith discussed at The Society of Biblical Archaeology in 1872. Soon after, he published his Chaldean Account of the Deluge with an outline of the Gilgamesh narrative. The tablets were incomplete at that time.

8. Heidel, p. 224

9. Heidel, pp. 4–5
    Heidel had placed Gilgamesh in the First Dynasty of Uruk based on the qualified assignment of "researchers." More recent studies place him in the Early Second Dynastic period: John Gardner, John Maier, *Gilgamesh* (New York: Alfred A. Knopf, 1984), p. 4. They also note that fragments of the epic predate the reign of Gilgamesh (about 3000 B.C.).

10. Silvestro Fiore, p. 82.

11. Heidel, p. 18. See Tablet I, column ii, lines 16, 20, 27, 30 and 32.

12. Heidel, p. 20.

13. Heidel, p. 22.

14. Heidel, p. 22.

15. Heidel, p. 23.

16. Heidel, p. 24.

17. Heidel, p. 24.

18. Heidel, p. 25.

19. Heidel, pp. 25–26.

20. Heidel, pp. 26–27.

21. Heidel, p. 28.

22. Heidel, p. 29.

23. Heidel, p. 33.

24. Heidel, p. 33.

25. Heidel, p. 62.

26. Heidel, p. 63.

27. Heidel, p. 64.

28. Heidel, p. 69.

29. Heidel, p. 77.

30. George F. Held, "Parallels Between the Gilgamesh Epic and Plato's Symposium," Journal of Near East Studies (Chicago: University of Chicago, 1983), 42, No. 2, pp. 133–141.

Held explored the homoerotic parallels between the Gilgamesh epic and Plato's *Symposium* where he observed that the "seeds of a teleological ethical approach to male sexuality are found in the Gilgamesh Epic which are traceable to the Homeric poems and the Symposium."

31. Chilperic Edwards, The Hammurabi Code (Port Washington, N. Y.: Kenikat Press, Reprint, 1971, originally printed 1904), p. 1.

Fiore, pp. 3–43.

32. Edwards, p. 2.

33. Genesis 2:28.

34. Jack Finegan, Light From The Ancient Past (Princeton: Princeton University Press, 1959), pp. 10, 148–149.

Hebrew, like Phoenician, was not among the older forms of the Semitic family of languages. Again like Phoenician, Hebrew has an alphabetical form, which is a late development (p. 10). Prototype Semitic inscriptions dating from the beginning of the Late Bronze Age, about 1500 B.C., were found at Serabat el-Khaden, only about fifty miles from the traditional site of Mt. Sinai on the Sinai

Peninsula in 1904–1905 A.D. by Flinders Petrie. The script considered to be "normal alphabetic" grew out of these sources, including the English alphabet. A more accurate dating of events occurred during the Neo–Babylonian period (612–529 B.C.) when scribes added the constellation of the date to their texts: Silvestro Fiore, *Voices From The Clay* (Norman: University of Oklahoma Press, 1965) p. 41.

35. Silvestro Fiore, p. 20.

36. G. R. Driver and John C. Miles, The Babylonian Laws (Oxford: The Clarendon Press, 1952) p. 5.

37. N. E. Neufeld, The Hittite Laws (London: Luzac & Co., Ltd., 1951) p. 96.

38. Neufeld, p. 99.

39. Neufeld, p. 100.

40. Vern L. Bullough, Sexual Variance In Society And History (Chicago: The University of Chicago Press, 1976), p. 51.

41. Bullough, p. 52.

42. Bullough, p. 52.

43. Edwards, p. 60.

44. Edwards, p. 104.

45. C. H. W. Johns, Babylonian And Assyrian Laws (Edinburgh: T. & T. Clark, 1904), p. 61.

46. Driver, p. 369.

47. Driver, p. 369.

48. Driver, p. 57.

49. Johns, p. 59.

50. Driver, p. 369.

51. The American Heritage Dictionary (Boston: Houghton Mifflin Co., 1979).

52. Charles Ber Chavel, Commentary On The Torah (New York: Shilo Publishing House, Inc., 1976), p. 288.

53. Donald Harden, The Phoenicians (New York: Frederick A. Praeger, 1962), p. 103.

54. Edwards, p. 370.

55. Bullough, p. 53.

56. Driver, p. 369.

57. Driver, p. 368.

58. Driver, p. 392.

59. Driver, p. 369.

60. Bullough, p. 53.

   The author was quoting a number of sources for the quotation: W. G. Lambert, "Morals in Ancient Mesopotamia," Van Het Vooraziatisch–Egyptisch Genootschop, ex Oriente lux, Jaarbericht, XV (1957–1958), pp. 184–196, was his primary reference.

CHAPTER II

THE HITTITES — Laws and the Hebrew Bible

Semites settled in the fertile plain of the Tigris and Euphrates Rivers which cradled civilization. They also settled in the Palestine area where they developed the Hebrew language. Hebrew was essentially the *lingua franca* of the literate people of the Palestine area. A number of different peoples other than Israelites spoke Hebrew, including the Phoenicians. Semitic–Babylonian was akin to Hebrew. Indeed the linguistic relationship of Hebrew to Babylonian and the cultural relationship to Hittite and Assyrian cultures were important factors in the formulations of attitudes on sexuality by the Hebrews. The influence of Egypt may have been present, but not so directly as that of the civilizations of the Tigris–Euphrates, and therefore was not stressed.

Ancient Hebrew references to homosexuality in Egypt and in Canaan, where the tribes returned after enslavement, provide clues to the endemic nature of homosexuality in the ancient East. What we can observe in the Bible is the codifying of negative Hebrew reactions to the pre–existing Babylonian, Hittite and Assyrian laws. Their negative responses are important in analyzing the Holiness Code found in Leviticus.

The Babylonians, Hittites, and Assyrians wrote laws for their own purposes, to satisfy the needs of their dominant societies. The negative responses to these laws, recorded in the Old Testament, reflected the responses of a subjected people. The Old Testament begins as an objection to the customs and religions of others.

Unlike the sexual freedom expressed by Hammurabi, and as we will find in the Hittite laws, the attitude expressed in the Bible is rigid: procreate or perish. This is understandable if you consider that the Hebrews lived on the crossroads of conquest. In their case procreation was essential.

"Be fruitful and multiply" can be read, "be fruitful and copulate." To the dominant heterosexual males who wrote the Bible for the patriarchal Hebrew society, that could mean "subject females to the sexual demands of males," and it did. It rationalized lust as "God's law." [1]

The admonition to "multiply" was a demand to "beget." Thus we find in the Old Testament a major source of confusion regarding

21

human sexuality and its purposes. This narrow attitude has directly contributed to laws and customs which have repressed both women and homosexuals down through the ages. As written, however, the Old Testament reveals the attitudes of the ancient Hebrews toward the sexual customs and attitudes of those who were dominating them. As the Hebrews were affected when making their laws, so later is Western civilization affected by those laws.

Obviously the laws of Hammurabi were not new; they were compilations of existing laws and customs. However, the Code became the model for subsequent legal writings. Its influence is reflected in the Hittite laws, for example, and the laws of the Assyrians, and those of the Israelites as found in the Old Testament.

Like the Babylonians who had a settled urban lifestyle, the Hittites were at a more sophisticated cultural level than their contemporary nomadic Hebrew neighbors. They are credited with being the intermediaries who introduced Eastern culture into the West.[2] Although there is still much to be learned about the Hittites and their language, having access to their laws is revealing. Apparently the Hittite language is particularly difficult and requires laborious efforts to decipher. The study and translation of Hittite began in the twentieth century. Hittite law tablets were excavated by Neufeld and Hugo Winckler during 1906–1907 and 1911–1912 at Bogazkoy.[3] They were clay tablets with cuneiform writing incised. Their translation and the elucidation of the Hittite language is credited to Frederic Hrozny, a French citizen.[4] It is in these laws that we can find a clue to the Hittite attitude toward homosexuality.

If we look to the Hittite laws themselves, we see that justice did not mean "equal" rights—it simply guaranteed each man his "own" rights consistent with his status. They did not guarantee "liberty," only specific liberties. Importantly, justice was not dependent on any god, it was a function of men.

For example, homosexuality may be the issue in Law I # 36 of the Hittite laws as translated by E. Neufeld: "If a slave gives the bride–price to a free youth and takes him to dwell in his household as husband (of his daughter), no one shall surrender him."[5]

It is interesting to note that Neufeld could not accept the homosexual implication of his translation. He parenthetically adds "of his daughter" after the word "husband" to suggest that the slave was paying the bride–price to acquire a free youth as husband for his daughter. Other scholars, however, did find "the idea of pederasty is incorporated here." [6]

"It would seem that such a relationship among free men did not require any special legal provisions..." wrote Neufeld, based on the conclusions of others. Neufeld quotes Hrozny as the source for his parenthetical modification regarding the intent of Law I # 36.[7] It may have been that the custom of purchasing a male sexual partner by a free male was so common that no law was needed, but that granting the privilege to a male slave required a law.

Other explanations by some modern authorities of Law I # 36 attempt to deny the homosexual implications. The "husband for his daughter" theory requires parenthetical inclusions which the original text of the law does not contain. In any case, the last portion of the law, "no one shall surrender him," has been explained by some translators as words of art which prohibited anyone from releasing the youth from the contract. Others contend the last part should be translated: "no one shall change his social status." [8]

The attitude toward homosexuality in the Hittite laws is important. The influence of the Hittite laws on the Old Testament makes their understanding particularly significant. Whether emulated or rejected, the Hittite laws were transmitted to the Israelites who responded to them and passed them on. The close commercial contact and frequent migrations in the regions provided the means for this transmission of the form, if not the substance, of the laws.[9]

The differing explanations given to the translation of Law I # 36 by scholars is typical of the problems faced by any researcher considering the issue of homosexuality in ancient texts. Professor John Boswell, in his book *Christianity, Social Tolerance and Homosexuality*, criticizes those scholars who altered translations by inserting parenthetical comments not actually in the texts, or who, acting as censors, avoided actual translation and thus deliberately altered meanings. Specifically, Boswell took issue with E. Neufeld's translation of Law I # 36, "apparently regulating homosexual marriage," for "inserting words which completely alter its meaning."

Boswell is convinced that Law I # 36 regulated a kind of homosexual marriage. He lists J. B. Pritchard, D. S. Bailey, and D. R. Mace as supporting this view.[10]

Professor Ruggero Stefanini of the Department of Near Eastern Studies at the University of California, Berkeley, has reviewed various translations in English of Law I # 36, including that of

Neufeld. Stefanini singled out the English translation by A. Goetze quoted in J. B. Pritchard's *Ancient Near Eastern Texts Relating to the Old Testament*: "If a slave brings the bride price to the son of a free man and takes him as husband (of his daughter) no one shall change his social status," which is similar to that of Neufeld, and compared it to what he believes to be a "more modern and more understandable" translation rendered in Italian by Fiorello Imparati.[11] Imparati's translation avoids the issue of homosexuality and expresses the view of Stefanini and those whom Stefanini describes as the "greater and more reliable majority of Hittilogists." In Stefanini's view Law I # 36 "helps regulate the important institution of a person of male gender who joins the household of his bride and her parents." In Stefanini's view the situation described in Law I # 36 would be understandable only if the free youth were to join the family of his bride when the bride price is paid for the male youth who finds himself, paradoxically, in the role usually fulfilled by the bride.[12]

Stefanini contended that if the law really contemplated a homosexual "marriage," then the free youngster for whom the bride price had been paid should be referred to as the *ephebos*, the *Ganymedes*, and not as the "husband." The actual word in the text is given as *lu antiiant;* that word is rendered as "son–in–law" by the standard German lexicons, and not "husband."[13] Stefanini stated in his correspondence to me:

> ...I don't deny that homosexuality was a practice well–known to [the] Hittite world and culture... However, I don't think that Hittite laws ever took the trouble of regulating homosexual 'marriages' and I believe, with the greater and more reliable majority of Hittitologists, that Law I.36 rather helps regulate the important institution... [which involves a man] who joins the household of his bride and her parents.[14]

In considering Stefanini's explanation, we are suddenly confronted with another problem. He cited various experts who reject the translation of the Hittite word used in the text as "husband" by Neufeld and Goetze; they translated it as "eingeheirateter" (a married man), a "schwiegersohn" (son–in–law). Although various lexicons are quoted to make this point, the difficulty presents itself if we ask, "which interpretation is correct?" Are the lexicons reflecting a point of view or do they give the actual meaning as intended by those who wrote the original Hittite? Frankly, it cannot be known with certainty.

Furthermore, the fact that a price was paid implies a contract: whoever paid the money had a duty owed to him or her in exchange. If the money were theoretically provided to benefit a daughter, then the purchased "husband" would have had a legal duty to a third party beneficiary. In Neufeld's theory, then, the daughter would have a duty owed to her. To suggest that a male youth described as free would be made legally inferior to a female who was born of a slave seems inconsistent with the lower status of women in general, and a slave's daughter specifically, as reflected in the laws and customs of the time.

The assurance that the free youth would not lose his social status because of the legal transaction with a slave seems far more logical in the context of a legal relationship between the slave and the free youth directly, and less logical when the suggested legal relationship is extended to an implied third party beneficiary who is a female and of lower social status. Such a situation would be excessively demeaning to a free youth in a culture where status was significant.

What we appear to be considering is a purchased relationship like that in Roman times, a marriage in the form of *coemptio*.[15] Such a situation would obviously put the free youth under strong legal constraints under the control of the third party beneficiary. If we observe that females do not appear to have any legal right to seek divorce unilaterally under Hittite law, it would be odd if not inconceivable if a divorce were wanted by the free youth and he were prohibited by contract. This is mere conjecture, but it tests the theory by pushing its application to the limits. John Boswell's reasoning to accept the obvious rendering of Law I # 36 with its implied homosexual meaning appears convincing.

Under Hittite Laws I # 31–33, a marriage between a free man and a female slave can be dissolved by mutual agreement. The laws are clear and specific with no exceptions noted. The word "agree" in Hittite is specifically used. Where there is no agreement, Hittite law favors the will of the husband on the theory that possession of a woman by a man was the legal object of marriage. Providing husbands for daughters was not the object.[16]

In reading the translations of the Hittite laws, sections were sought out where the concept of sexual "sin" or wrongdoing was the issue. By determining what was considered sexually sinful, it was hoped to get a better understanding of the kind of conduct being prohibited. Law II # 187 states: "If a man sins with a cow, (it is) an abomination, he shall die..." The words *katta wastzi* in the Hittite text literally mean "sin together sexually," according to Neufeld. The expression is used in several laws where proscribed sexual conduct is regulated.[17]

Incest was clearly a taboo. Law II # 189 declares: "If a man sins with his mother, (it is) a sin, an abomination. If a man sins with a daughter, (it is) an abomination. If a man sins with a son, (it is) an abomination."[18] "Abomination" here in Hebrew could imply an offense deserving death, yet death is not specified in the Hittite law. Notice the equal treatment of a father's incestuous behavior with his son or daughter, which implies that the gender of the partner was not a factor.

Law II # 189 is concerned with incest, and while incest with a son may obviously be a homoerotic sexual act, it is not proscribed here because of its homosexual character, but rather because it is incest. The very fact that it is treated solely as incest suggests that only that aspect of the conduct is proscribed. The Hittite law obviously takes cognizance of homosexual conduct and confines the purview of the law to incest, a taboo.

If we look at the Laws relating to bestiality, Section II # 187–188, the phrase *katta wastzi* is used. The phrase denotes indecent carnal knowledge or exposure used as an idiomatic expression for wrongful sexual intercourse. The death penalty was applied to the man only and not the beast; the same situation in the Hebrew laws required the death of the beast also.[19] What is particularly interesting here is the fact that Hittite law prohibited sexual liaison with only specific animals and not all animals. This suggests that punishment was demanded only when bestiality involved totem animals associated with their ancestors. Sex with horses and mules, for example, was exempt from the death penalty; they were relative newcomers among animals. The crime then was not bestiality *per se*, but bestiality with a tribal totem. Thus we are again dealing with taboo and not morality. This is important to notice, since the negative moral connotations given the word "sodomy" in Western laws have also associated homosexuality with bestiality.

As the concept of taboo sex found its way into the Old Testament, the rationale based on totem–taboo was lost, and thus too the rationale for the death penalty, which was retained. By association, the Old Testament justifies the death penalty for all sexual "abominations."

If we scrutinize Law II # 189 and the penalty affixed for having incestuous carnal knowledge of a son, which is by definition homoerotic, it is extremely important that we notice that, while the act is reprehensible and condemned, it does not specifically call for the death penalty.[20] While the legal word used in Hittite is *hurkel*, for which the Israelites used a word we translate as an "abomination," implying the death penalty would be required, the death penalty is not in the law itself. What we see here is a form of homoerotic sexual misconduct involving incest and no specific demand for the death penalty. From this we may conclude that homosexual conduct, and especially nonincestuous homosexual conduct, in practice was not a serious concern of the Hittites.

There is a curious Hittite law which deals with sex induced by a ghost; Law II # 190 states: "If they come together (with the help) of a ghost, whether man or woman, (there shall be) no punishment..." The term "sin" is not used in this case, and "they," a third person plural, is used instead of the word "man." The choice of potential partners is either a "man or woman."[21] It suggests that this law may imply that, if a "spirit" or "ghost" moves two people to have sexual intercourse, one man with another man or with a woman, it is not punishable conduct.

Neufeld's suggested interpretation, based on Hronzy's translation, asserts that it "can be understood" to imply sexual intimacy with a ghost by either a man or a woman. Neufeld cited the notion of virgin birth and certain beliefs about the birth of twins among African tribes as examples justifying why he believes it "can be understood"; while it may be doubted, this interpretation must be considered. We also must consider the probability that Neufeld's interpretation may be an example of the translator's homophobia.

The same word for "sin" seems to be used to prohibit sexual intercourse with certain animals, as noted: cows, dogs, pigs, etc. Yet, as in Law II # 196, "If anyone's male–slaves and female–slaves practice (abomination) they shall bring them and make them live, one in this town and the other in that town. A sheep for the one and a sheep for the other shall be brought as a substitute."[22] The meaning of this law is vague in the translations, but it seems obvious that sexual intercourse with certain animals does not evoke the death penalty.

It should hardly be surprising that law and religion are so irretrievably enmeshed. The ancient scribes were more often than not priest–jurists or at least professional clerks associated with ecclesiastical functions. Legal development was in the hands of sacral functionaries. While the Hittite scribes were distinct from priests, they were nevertheless closely associated.

The Hittite law texts are not codes or law books, they are collections of judicial formulae of varying dates. It was in the 14th century B.C. that they seem to have been formulated, with some authorities suggesting the 13th century B.C.[23]

Although we have been discussing ancient laws, we must not think in terms of "legal" and "illegal" conduct; we are dealing with ethical principles by which human conduct is judged by the society in which the questions developed. Ethical development evidenced in tangible form began with the oldest civilizations in Mesopotamia, particularly in Babylon.[24] It was part of a continuum. The Babylonians, who contributed much, concerned themselves with good and evil. This is especially apparent in the totem devices used to animate these concepts. Evil is presented as a demon or group of demons, characterized as hideous creatures. Good is personified by sturdy, winged angelic beings.[25] These images were reiterated in the myths of the Old Testament and form the images of the devil and the heavenly hosts of angels and seraphim. The tales of the flood and the hymns found in the Old Testament of the Hebrews also preserve the religious beliefs and spirit of the more ancient Mesopotamian cultures, and the influence of Egypt.

It would be wrong to regard the other cultures of the Near East as less moral than the Israelites. The ethics reflected in earlier Mesopotamian cultures reveal a strong sense of justice; they recognized right and wrong in terms of good and evil. As a patriarchal society they believed in the power of the father over the family, who as head of the family meted out justice and set the moral tone of his family and the members of his household, including his slaves. There was a respect for goodness.

At the earliest stages of civilization the "justice of life's necessities" was enforced by the father or leader as an expression of the will of the gods. Mesopotamian civilization went beyond that: they wrote laws as men, for men, to be enforced by men.

As commerce and trade developed among various tribes, cities, and foreign neighbors, a strong concern for honesty developed. Indeed, mercantile enterprise necessitated that fundamental rules of fair play be developed. The perceived need for ethics and basic morality beyond the family gave rise to laws and the collection of legal opinions and customs. The Babylonian Sabbath or day of rest, for example, became standard among merchants of the Near Eastern world.

As we have seen, homoerotic conduct does not appear to have been of any concern to the originators of Western civilization. They left personal consensual sex to the individual when the act did not interfere with property rights or the obligations and duties of others. Heterosexual conduct, as related to a man's rights to his own wife and children, were of concern as they related to heirs, inheritance, and conjugal rights. Sexual conduct *per se* was not a question of morals. As noted, even the restrictions on bestiality seem to have been confined to totem animals and not all animals. What is apparent from studying the ancient Mesopotamian laws is that we are dealing with very materialistic societies, with a sense of right.[26]

Intellectualizing human ethics is a rather late development with the rise of Chaldean power (Neo–Babylonia) at a time when the pre–Israelites were developing their religious dogma.[27] The increased contact with the Greeks about the same time must have encouraged a mutual exchange, which bestowed benefits on both cultures. In the beginning, "truth and righteousness," not sexual conduct, were the criteria of morality.

It was the priestly art of writing which elevated words to magical heights. A hymn which Dr. James H. Breasted believed was part of the worship of Sin, the Moon–god of ancient Ur, declared: "The word bringeth forth truth and righteousness, so that men speak the truth."[28] This reverence for the "word" seems to have had an even more profound effect on the Hebrews. Perhaps the late development of writing among the Hebrews had put them in excessive awe of their more advanced neighbors once they perfected their alphabetical language, which must have occurred after about 850 B.C. It was modeled after forms developed by the Phoenicians to whom they were related.

The "word" became so holy that the very name of their god was unspeakable. Whether the symbol for their god (YHVH) could be pronounced as "yahveh," for example, or "jahoveh" may be questionable. The symbol for god, as with all Hebrew words, is written without vowels. The letters may be strictly symbols intended as an abstraction for the unknowable, the unpronounceable. Such reverence for words by the ancient Israelites engendered and encouraged the belief that their sacred writings, the Old Testament, were the actual words intended by their god to be written down. Thus interpretation of these words–of–god was the duty placed on the sages, the prophets and the scholars. It is their varying interpretations of the "word" which have posed so many difficulties for the Western world, and homosexuals in particular.

Hebrew literature flourished during the first millennium B.C. at a time of a concomitant decline in Egypt and Mesopotamia.[29] Hebrews appear in the notations of Tell–el–Amarna Letters dating after 1400 B.C., implying an even older period of Hebrew existence. They are identified as drifting nomads in the area of Palestine, then under Egyptian control. They apparently sold their skills and services as workers and mercenaries.[30]

According to C. Edwards, one of the earliest "Hebrew" inscriptions (c. 850 B.C.) was found in Moab; it was an inscription of Mesha, King of Moab.[31] Early Hebrew writing was found in Lebanon on the so–called Baal Lebanon Bronzes; it is in alphabetical form, not cuneiform. People called Habiru (Hebrew) were mentioned in a text of a First Dynasty Babylon tablet (c. 1800– c. 1500 B.C.) in which they were employed as soldiers and workers.[32]

The end of the second millenium was still a savage period for the Israelites who were at a rudimentary stage and who, as Breasted asserts, had "... rude and barbarous habits... even the half–savage practices of a primitive stage of life, like the slaying of first–born children as a sacrifice to the tribal god..." [33]

Since it is the interpretation of the Old Testament which has inspired so much of the later persecution of homosexuals, it is important that we have a clearer understanding of the people, the Israelites, who are too often blamed or credited with condemning homosexuality as against the will of God.

The very name "Israel" must be considered in any argument used to validate a condemnation of homosexuals. In Genesis 32: 22–23 there is a myth about Jacob and his encounter with an "angel" or spirit: "That same night he arose, took his two wives, the two maids... and sent them across the river Jaboc. Jacob stayed behind alone." Someone wrestled with him until break of dawn. "When (the spirit)... saw that he could not overcome Jacob, he touched the socket of Jacob's thigh so that it was dislocated... He said, 'Let me go; it is dawn.' But Jacob answered, 'I will not let you go until you bless me.' Then he asked Jacob, 'What is your name?' and he answered, 'Jacob!' He said, 'You no longer will be called Jacob, but Israel, because you have contended with god and men, and have triumphed'... to this day the Israelites do not eat the socket of the thigh because he touched the socket of Jacob's thigh on the hip muscle...."

At the time of Jacob's wrestling match in the desert south of Judea, his people believed in the existence of a local spirit called an *el*, which is not the same word in Semitic for "The One God." Thus the very name "Isra–el" which means "who is like *el*" is given to Jacob and consequently to his descendants, the Israelites. The name is in a similar form as the name "Michael." [34] The name "Israel" implies a belief in a multiplicity of gods. Jacob and his people were not monotheists. These names are important clues.

A popular myth found in Genesis 10:19 deals with two "cities in the plain," Sodom and Gomorrah. It is a tale about Lot, a nephew of Abraham who chose to live in the town of Sodom in the Jordan Valley. According to Jewish tradition, Lot was taken captive along with people from Sodom and Gomorrah during a campaign against the four kings of the Plain, and was rescued by Abraham. Lot presumably later returned to live in Sodom.

That city becomes the locus of a parable justifying the condemnation of the enemies of the Hebrews: "Because of grievous sins," God decides to destroy Sodom. "Will you destroy the good with the wicked?" Abraham asks in Genesis 18:23–24. This is the basic theme of the story.

In the standard interpretation, God sent two "angels" to Sodom. Lot encounters them at the city gate and offers hospitality. The "angels," with some reluctance, accept the hospitality. During the evening, after Lot prepares supper and washes the angels' feet, a mob "from every quarter, both young and old demand to know who the strangers are in Lot's home." [35] The word used in Hebrew is "know"; although most often used in the Old Testament simply as "to become acquainted with," it was sometimes used with a sexual connotation. For some reason the Catholic Church uses the word "abuse" for the action to be taken by the mob. Others who suspect that rape of the "angels" is intended are satisfied with the word "know" in Genesis 19:5 as used to imply sexual conduct.

31

Jewish tradition does not support the homosexual theory. The *Encyclopedia Judaica* notes: "The inhospitable behavior of the people of Sodom occurred on the occasion of their destruction." The fall of Sodom and Gomorrah is cited as an example of God's wrath; there is a warning in Deuteronomy 29:22 and Isaiah 13:19, and other places in the Old Testament give "inhospitality" as a cause of God's wrath.[36]

A rational analyst suggested in the *Encyclopedia Judaica* that the story of Lot, involving the destruction of the cities, is "related to the tectonic nature of the Dead Sea" region, which would account for violent earth movement and volcanic activity.[38] The *Encyclopedia Judaica* also notes that in the *Aggadah*, Sodom is the incarnation of wickedness of a special type, of "evil–mindedness," "hard–heartedness," and basing action on the "strict letter of the law." It also was noted that strangers were besieged and robbed. Each Sodomite took but a trifle, too small for the law to consider. When the victim complained, each had taken out a pittance, "less than a perutah," and were thus not subject to the law. If a stranger happened to wander into Sodom, lodging was offered; however, the Sodomites had a standard size bed in which strangers had to sleep. If the stranger was too long, they chopped off his feet; if he was too short, they stretched him. Obviously this is the same tale which was told in Greek mythology about the Procrustean bed. Bricks of gold and silver were given to strangers instead of food and water. Each donor had his name stamped on the metal, which was reclaimed when the stranger died of deprivation.[39]

According to Jewish tradition, there were four judges in Sodom named Liar, Awful Liar, Forger and Perverter of Justice. If a man assaulted his neighbor, the judges required the victim to pay for the medical "bleeding" he received. If a man waded across a stream rather than take the ferry, the man would be charged more than if he had taken the ride across. If a man accused another of stealing a rug, he was told that he only dreamed he owned a rug and would be made to pay for having his dream interpreted. An assaulted woman who had a miscarriage as a consequence would be given to her assailant so that he could impregnate her again. Charity was forbidden under penalty of death to discourage begging. Paltit, a daughter of Lot, was suspected of feeding a beggar, and reportedly was burned to death.[40]

Thus we see that those whose religion produced the story of

Sodom and Gomorrah cite inhospitality and insensitivity to strangers as the grievous wickedness for which the allegorical destruction of Sodom and Gomorrah took place. While some notice is taken of "Christian" versions of the Hebrew texts, there appears to be little to support the equation of Sodom with homosexuality in Hebrew tradition.

The word "sodomite" was used throughout the Middle Ages to refer to both heterosexual and homosexual conduct. Its strictly homosexual interpretation, John Boswell contends, is of relatively recent origin. Boswell, like D. S. Bailey and John McNeill, definitively attacks the inference that Sodom's grievous wickedness was homosexual in character.[41]

Boswell lists four inferences drawn from the destruction of Sodom: "1) The Sodomites were destroyed for general wickedness which had prompted God to send angels to investigate; 2) the city was destroyed because the people of Sodom had tried to rape the angels; 3) the city was destroyed because the men of Sodom had tried to engage in homosexual intercourse with the angels; 4) the city was destroyed for inhospitable treatment of visitors."[42]

In his conclusion, inhospitality, not homosexuality, was the issue, a position which apparently Jesus took as noted in Matthew 10:14–15: "Whosoever shall not receive you, nor hear your words... verily, I say unto you, it shall be more tolerable for the land of Sodom and Gomorrah in the day of Judgment, than for that city."

As John McNeill notes, the first explicitly sexual connotation given the Sodom story does not occur until the Palestinian apocrypha of the second century B.C., in the Book of Jubilees XVI:5–6. Implied in the Book of Jubilees is heterosexual misconduct, not homosexual: shameless promiscuity and gross sexual indiscretion between men and women were criticized. "They defiled themselves and committed fornication in their flesh... the uncleanliness of the Sodomites." Also in the Book of Jubilees VII:20–22, it was the heterosexual lusting after women that brought the flood: "a whoring after the daughters of men."[43]

The homosexual inference of the story of Lot does not appear until just before the Christian era during the Pharisaic period, about the second century B.C. Mixed marriages were also suggested as the sin of Sodom in the later interpretations; the incompatibility of sex with angels is not unlike Jews taking gentiles to wife. During the period 70–40 B.C., it was a transgression to marry "... the

33

daughter of the Gentiles... your union shall be like unto Sodom and Gomorrah." [44]

Homosexual condemnation appears to be a late response to the endemic nature of homosexuality in Hellenic cultures, once it was encountered by the Jews. *The Book of Secrets of Enoch* is a Hellenistic Jewish book based on *The Writings of Enoch*, which in II Enoch 34:2 indicated the homosexual lawlessness of the Gentiles. *Toevah ha-goyim*, which means the "uncleanliness of Gentiles," is a frequent phrase used by Jewish writers, as in Kings 14:24. By the second century B.C., Sodom's wickedness began to expand to include homosexuality, supporting the theory that, once again, Judaism responded negatively to the laws and customs of its dominant neighbors and codified those responses in its "Holy Writ." [45]

Homosexuality was flourishing in the ancient world and reached the pinnacle of respectability in that period of history when civilization was founded. It blazed most nobly just before the God of Israel was adopted as the God of Christians.

The *Midrash* provides scant references to homosexual conduct. Like the *Aggadah*, it encompasses oral tradition without reference to scriptures. The term *Midrash* is used in modern Hebrew as a technical literary term, a type of literature; however, there does not seem to be agreement on a precise meaning. Its authority derives from rabbinical usage and oral tradition. While there also is exegesis in the Talmud, that is not considered *Midrash* by rabbis. [46]

In the *Midrash* it is written: Kiddushin 4:14, Rabbi Judah (The Patriarch) says, "An unmarried man may not herd cattle, nor may two unmarried men sleep under the same cloak. But the sages permit it." Rabbi Judah took his position opposing two unmarried men sleeping together about 385 A.D. with an obvious reference to possible homoerotic sexual activity. What is significant here is the immediate refutation of his prohibition by "the sages." Thus the refutation of Rabbi Judah's prohibition is especially significant. [47]

Of Rabbi Judah, who prohibited two unmarried men from sleeping together, it was said that he was the son of Gamaliel V, little known in his time (c. 385–400 A.D.) and unpopular with other rabbis! Reports indicate that as a young man he was dissipated and consorted with "evil companions." There was a general decline under his patriarchate. The Roman emperors Arcadius and Honorius in 396 A.D. still permitted the Patriarch to decide judicial and religious matters in Jerusalem. Rabbi Judah was apparently also known as Judah IV and may have also been known as Nesiah. He was the father of Hillel, who fixed the Jewish calendar.[48]

In the early days, prior to the destruction of the Temple in Jerusalem, the scribes, or Soferim, and the repeaters of oral tradition, the Tannaim, supported the religious system of the Pharisees, opposed by that of the Sadducees.

After the destruction of the temple, the *Midrash* became a depository of four centuries of Jewish tradition, which was begun in Palestine at some uncertain date—possibly in the first half of the second century. The preservation of the Torah (the Pentateuch in the Christian Bible) became essential during this period: it was the scroll read in the synagogue, and still is. It is the body of traditional Jewish literature.

The lack of harsh condemnation, even by Rabbi Judah, and the disagreement of "the sages" regarding the prohibition of unmarried men sleeping together indicate a tolerance of homosexuality not indicated by later Christian religious leaders when they interpreted Jewish tradition.

Jewish dogma or *Ta'anit* is based on "the law" according to Rabbi Judah; Rabbi Johanan includes what is "adopted by the people." The law is taught; usage is not taught, and what is adopted shall not be nullified. Nowhere in these writings can be found specific condemnation of homosexuality.

The *Mishnah*, which is from the fourth century A.D. Roman period, as translated by Herbert Danby, quotes the Sanhedrin, the judges, in Sanh. 10:3: "The men of Sodom have no share in the world to come, for it is written how the men of Sodom were wicked and sinners against the lord exceedingly; wicked in this world and sinners in the world to come...." The quotation goes on to describe the crimes and greed of the men of Sodom; still nowhere is sexual misconduct mentioned! Aboth 5:10 is quoted as a source of *The Crime of Sodom*. Legal proscriptions against homosexuals had not yet penetrated civilized law. Jewish traditions had not yet been distorted to fit Christian purposes. While the base had been developed for later persecution of homosexuals, and while the whole foundation was in place at the time of the Christian era, the Jews cannot be blamed for the murderous Christian homophobia which eventually developed.[49] That trend will be discussed in the following chapters.

The spread of Greek culture in a Hellenized world held the tide against those who would deny the pleasures of the flesh, including homosexuality. Homosexuality continued to be beyond the purview of civil law as we enter the Golden Age of Greek culture.

NOTES

1.   Chilperic Edwards, The Hammurabi Code (Port Washington, N.Y.: Kenikat Press, Reprint, 1971, originally printed 1904), p. 1.

     Silvestro Fiore, Voices From The Clay (Norman: Oklahoma University Press, 1965), pp. 3–43

2.   Neufeld, p. 94.

3.   Neufeld, p. 70.

4.   Neufeld, p. 78.

5.   Neufeld, p. 10.

6.   Neufeld, p. 151.

7.   Neufeld, p. 151.

8.   Ruggero Stefanini, personal correspondence to Paul D. Hardman (Berkeley: September 9, 1983), pp. 1–2; Enclosure, Le Leggi Ittite, (Rome: Steneo, 1964), pp. 218–219.

9.   Neufeld, p. 101.

10. John Boswell, Christianity, Social Tolerance and Homosexuality (Chicago: University of Chicago Press, 1980), p. 21.

11. Stefanini, pp. 1–2.

12. Stefanini, p. 1.

13. Stefanini, p. 2.

14. Stefanini, p. 2.
     The Italian translation provided by Fiorello Imparati, quoted by Stefanini from Le Leggi Ittite (Roma: Ateneo, 1964) p. 55, is: "Se un servo per un giovane libero il prezzo della sposa paga e lui come genero (maritato nella sua casa) prende, allora lui (da questa matrimonio) nessuno fa uscire." A more complete discussion of the different interpretations may be found in Imparati's book on pages 218–220, in Italian.
     For a discussion of homosexuality in ancient Mesopotamia see: Erich Ebeling and Bruno Meissner, Reallexikon der Assyriologi und Vorderasiatischen Archaeologie (Berlin: Walter de Gruyter, 1972–1975) Vol. 4, pp. 160–169. The article on homosexuality is credited to J. Botter and H. Petschow.

15. Pierre Grimal, The Civilization of Rome, trans. Professor W. S. Maguinness (New York: Simon and Schuster, 1963), pp. 121–122.

There were two types of marriages in the early period of the Roman Republic: "confarreatio," which was unique to patricians and essentially a religious ceremony, and "coemptio," which was the plebeian form of marriage. "Coemptio" represented the mutual purchase of one another by the married pair. A third form of marriage developed later in Rome derived from "coemptio" which resulted when a woman lived in a man's house for a year: marriage "per usum."

16. Neufeld, pp. 9–10, 147.

17. Neufeld, p. 53.

18. Neufeld, p. 54.

19. Neufeld, p. 188.

20. Neufeld, p. 54.

21. Neufeld, p. 56.

22. Neufeld, p. 56.

23. Neufeld, pp. 110–111.

24. James H. Breasted, Dawn of Conscience (New York: Charles Scribner's Sons, 1935), p. 336.

25. Breasted, p. 337.

26. Breasted, p. 337.

27. Breasted, p. 337.

28. Breasted, p. 338.

29. Breasted, p. 348.

30. Breasted, p. 349.

31. Edwards, p. 111.

32. Jack Finegan, Light From The Ancient Past (Princeton: Princeton University Press, 1959), pp. 68–70, 111.

     Finegan gives an explanation of the word "Hebrew" and its possible origins and its Biblical usage.

33. Breasted, p. 349.

34. Breasted, p. 250.

35. Encyclopedia Judaica (Jerusalem: Keter Publishing House, Ltd., 1971), Vol. 15, p. 70.

36. New American Catholic Edition, The Holy Bible (New York): Benziger Bros., Inc., 1961).

37. Encyclopedia Judaica, Vol. 15, p. 70.

Other references to inhospitality as the cause of the destruction of Sodom are: Amos 4:11; Edom (Jer. 49:18); Babylon (Jer. 50:40); Jer. 23:14; Ezek. 16:49 and Moab (Zeph. 2:9).

38. Encyclopedia Judaica, Vol. 15, p. 70.

The geological phenomenon known as the "Jordan Rift" now beneath the southern end of the Dead Sea was formed by tectonic action.

39. Encyclopedia Judaica, Vol. 15, pp. 70–71.

The law dealing with taking only a trifle (less than a perutah) is given as Job 28:6 and Sanh. 1092.

40. Encyclopedia Judaica, Vol. 15, p. 71.

The four judges are listed as: 1. Shakrai ("Liar"); 2. Shakurai ("Awful Liar"); 3. Zayyafi ("Forger"); 4. Mazle Dina ("Perverter of Justice").

41. Boswell, pp. 98–99.

42. Boswell, p. 93.

43. John J. McNeill, S.J., The Church and the Homosexual (Kansas City: Sheed, Andrews and McMeel, Inc., 1976), pp. 68–75.

McNeill points out that the Book of Jubilees was a product of the second century B.C., written at the time of the Palestinian apocrypha. Until that time, he notes, the sin of Sodom was never interpreted as being primarily sexual and certainly not homosexual. He cites Jubilees XVI, 5–6 to make his point: "they were wicked and sinners exceedingly, and that they defiled themselves and committed fornication in their flesh, and worked uncleanness on the earth." It was in a Pharisaic work of the same time known as the "Testament of the Twelve Patriarchs" that the sin of Sodom was made homosexual in nature with a warning that the people should "... become not as Sodom, which changed the order of nature." Reference was made to those who "changed the order of nature" at the time of the flood and were punished for it. The reference here is to the possible homosexual conduct of the son of Noah, Ham, who is presumed to have done more than look at his father's nakedness; he presumably did something to him. McNeill equates the story of Noah (Gen. 9:18–27) with an episode in the ancient

Egyptian epic entitled "The Contending of Horus and Seth" in which Horus is sodomized by Seth in the Egyptian tradition, which meant the domination and subjection of Horus. By dominating Horus, Seth could claim the kingdom of Horus. For details see McNeill, pp. 58–59.

44. McNeill, p. 71.

45. Boswell, pp. 100–101.

Boswell points out that the Hebrew word *toevah* is translated "abomination," but it is also translated as "uncleanness" especially as related to the practices of pagans; in some cases the word can be translated to mean "idol." He cites examples where the word is used to mean "idol" in connection with homosexual acts associated with idol worship. With such acts in mind, Boswell contends, Leviticus 18 specifically distinguishes Jews from the pagans among whom they live or might live. The rejection of their dominant neighbors' practices and customs are made clear: "After the doings of the land of Egypt, wherein ye dwelt, shall ye not do: and after the doings of the land of Canaan, whither I shall bring you, shall ye not do: neither shall you walk in their ordinances (3, KJV)."

46. Addison G. Wright, Midrash (Staten Island, N.Y.: Society of St. Paul, 1967), pp. 44–45.

Wright compares the *Midrash* with the *Aggadah* which is either an interpretation of or free of scriptures. Oral tradition, he notes, includes both Midrash and *Aggadah*. The term *Midrash* is used in modern Hebrew to identify a technical literary form, but there does not seem to be much agreement among the experts on the precise meaning. It is a form of exegesis derived from Rabbinical usage and oral Jewish tradition. It is not synonymous with the Talmud, for there is exegesis in the Talmud, and it is not called *Midrash* and study of the Bible is not called *Midrash*, although it contains oral tradition. The *Encyclopedia Judaica*, Vol. 15, pp. vi–v discusses the word "Midrash" with reference to Aggadah and indicates that the term Aggadah is used to encompass sections of the Talmud and the *Midrash* which includes homiletic expositions of the Bible. The Talmud, as distinct from other writings and teachings, is comprised of *Mishnah* and the *Gemara*, with the word Talmud having the connotation "learning." It is the collected ancient Rabbinic writings which constitute the basis of religious authority for traditional Judaism. The *Gemara* is but the second half of the Talmud which consists primarily of interpretations of the *Mishnah*. Thus the *Midrash* provides a method of interpreting scripture to elucidate legal points, while the *Mishnah* is the earliest codification of Jewish oral law. For more details see: Henry Malter, *The Treatise 'TA'ANIT of the Babylon Talmud* (Philadelphia: Jewish Publication Society of America, 1967). The term "Torah" is applied to that particular scroll which contains the Pentateuch, or five books of the Hebrew Bible, used in a synagogue during services. For more details on the *Mishnah,* also see: Herbert Danby, *The Mishnah* (London: Oxford University Press, 1933).

47. Herbert Danby, The Mishnah (London: Oxford University Press, 1933), p. 329.

   Danby cites Kiddushin 4:14 wherein Rabbi Judah is quoted. He notes that Rabbi Judah also asserted that "a man should not teach his son a craft that is practiced by women."

48. Encyclopedia Judaica, Vol. 10, p. 334.

   By way of accusation a story is told about Rabbi Judah that when his sister died, a leading scholar of Palestine, Mana, refused to attend the funeral.

49. Danby, pp. 382–400.

CHAPTER III

GREEK AMBIVALENCE

As we approach the Greeks and their influence on law and their attitude regarding homosexuality, it is essential to recognize the ambivalence they projected. On the one hand the ancient Greeks are depicted as the epitome of erotic homosexuality, and at the same time they are the source of its antithesis, "Platonic" love, which ideally transcended sexual desire. We must understand this dichotomy in order to comprehend later Christian attitudes which are reflected in their laws and subsequent religious dogma.

Like their Eastern neighbors, the early Greeks were active merchants who probed the islands and shores of the Mediterranean Sea for markets. Again like their Eastern neighbors, it seems to have been the practical merchants and farmers who controlled local governments, having displaced priests and kings. The priests and kings had used fear of gods to rule; they encouraged superstition. The merchants were more impressed by logic and common sense. To them it was the individual living in a real world who dominated Greek thought, especially as Greece approached its golden age. Homosexuality in the context of their logic was a normal and expected phenomenon.

Developing at the same time was a trend toward mysticism, the antithesis of logic. The personification of mysticism was Pythagoras, a native of Samos who thrived in 532 B.C.[1] Most people, especially those who studied algebra, will identify Pythagoras as the mathematician who perfected the "Pythagorean Theorem," used to find the length of the hypotenuse of a right-angled triangle. He was more than a mathematician; he was a philosopher who was also a mystic. He hoped to escape the vicissitudes of life by transcending birth through the belief in the transmigration of the soul.[2]

Despite his mysticism, he was one of the great mathematicians of all time. He became fascinated by the mathematics of music and speculated on the harmony of physical phenomena in general. The notion that everything could be reduced to numbers, especially ratios, was developed. However, when he discovered that certain mathematical equations produced "irrational" numbers, he responded by concealing the information. He hid the truth.[3] Pythagorean preoccupation with mathematics inspired the theory of ideas or universals which we find later in the writings of Plato. Mysticism strongly influenced Plato, who in turn strongly influenced Christian attitudes.

Plato's *Laws*, which he wrote late in life, seem to be the earliest extant writings on legal theory; while his laws were never codified or actually used by any government, they are important in any study dealing with homoerotic behavior. Plato's attitude regarding homosexuality is clearly reflected in his earlier work, *Symposium*. The apparent change in that earlier attitude shown in the late work the *Laws* needs to be understood.

His *Laws* may seem to be serious, yet they are so tinged with facetiousness that it leads to the conclusion that Plato was not expecting anyone actually to believe everything he had written. Statements in his *Laws* regarding homosexuality are inconsistent with his own writings elsewhere.

To demonstrate this point, let us consider the speech of Aristophanes found in Plato's *Symposium* in which he expresses the theory that the human race began as having three sexes, male, female, and combined. According to Aristophanes' explanation, the original progenitors of the human race were globular in shape with four arms and four legs, and a head with a face on one side and one on the other; four ears and two sets of sexual organs completed the picture. In a battle with the gods they committed the sin of "hubris" (overbearing arrogance), and Zeus punished them by cutting them in two! Apollo rearranged the parts but Zeus took pity and repositioned their genitals. After that each part sought its twin.[4] Aristophanes explains:

> Each of us then is the mere broken tally of a man, the result of a bisection which has reduced us to a condition like that of flat fish, and each of us is perpetually in search of his corresponding tally. Those men who are halves of a being of the common sex, which was called, as I told you, hermaphrodite, are lovers of women, and most adulterers come from this class, as also do women who are mad about men and sexually promiscuous. Women who are halves of a female whole direct their affections towards women and pay little attention to men; lesbians belong to this category. But those who are halves of a male whole pursue males, and being slices, so to speak, of the male, love men throughout their boyhood, and take pleasure in physical contact

with men. Such boys and lads are the best of their generation, because they are the most manly. Some people say that they are shameless, but they are wrong. It is not shamelessness which inspires their behavior, but high spirit and manliness and virility, which lead them to welcome the society of their own kind. A striking proof of this is that such boys alone, when they reach maturity, engage in public life. When they grow to be men, they become lovers of boys, and it requires the compulsion of convention to overcome their natural disinclination to marriage and procreation; they are quite content to live with one another unwed. In a word, such persons are devoted to lovers in boyhood and themselves lovers of boys in manhood, because they always cleave to what is akin to themselves.

Whenever the lover of boys – or any other person for that matter – has the good fortune to encounter his own actual other half, affection and kinship and love combined inspire in him an emotion which is quite overwhelming, and such a pair practically refuse to be separated even for a moment. It is people like these who form lifelong partnerships, although they would find it difficult to say what they hope to gain from one another's society. No one can suppose that it is mere physical enjoyment which causes the one to take such intense delight in the company of the other. It is clear that the soul of each has some other longing which it cannot express, but can only surmise and obscurely hint at. Suppose Hephaestus with his tools were to visit them as they lie together, and stand over them and ask: 'What is it, mortals, that you hope to gain from one another?' Suppose too that when they could not answer he repeated his question in these terms:

Is the object of your desire to be always together as much as possible, and never to be separated from one another day or night? If that is what you want, I am ready to melt and weld you together, so that, instead of two, you shall be one flesh; as long as you live you shall live a common life, and when you die, you shall suffer a common death, and be still one, not two, even in the next world. Would such a fate as this content you, and satisfy your longings?' We know what their answer would be; no one would refuse the offer; it would be plain that this is what everybody wants, and everybody would regard it as the precise expression of the desire which he had long felt but had been unable to formulate, that he should melt into his beloved, and that henceforth they should be one instead of two.[5]

Plato includes a conversation in the *Symposium* between Socrates and a wise woman, Diotima, who explains love and its relationship to physical beauty. First she points out that love is male and half god: "He is a great spirit, Socrates; everything that is of the nature of a spirit is half–god and half–man." [6] The maleness of love is important to notice, as is the obvious mysticism. "God does not deal directly with man; it is by means of spirits that all the intercourse and communication of gods with men... is carried on," Diotima states.

Love, says Diotima, was born with "an innate passion for the beautiful"; his father was Contrivance and his mother Poverty.

> He is always poor, and far from being sensitive and beautiful, as most people imagine, he is hard and weather–beaten, shoeless and homeless, always sleeping out for want of a bed, on the ground, on doorsteps, and in the street... He schemes to get for himself whatever is beautiful and good; he is bold and forward and strenuous, always devising tricks like a cunning huntsman; he yearns after knowledge and is full of resource and is a lover of wisdom all his life, a skillful magician, an alchemist, a true sophist.[8]

What we see here is love of young men by men, seemingly described by someone who knew the experience and had enjoyed the good with the bad. This is not a description of extramarital affairs nor even romantic seduction as a prelude to procreation. It is simply a description of homoerotic love between males, a "prescribed devotion to boyish beauties." [9]

Procreation, according to Diotima, "...is the nearest thing to perpetuity and immortality that a mortal being can attain." [10] This is the kind of love whose end is immortality through procreation. However, the thrust of Plato's arguments in the *Symposium* is to extoll the virtues and the joy of loving "comely boys or lads."

> The man who would pursue the right way to his goal must begin when he is young, by applying himself to the contemplation of physical beauty, and, if he is properly directed by his guide, he will first fall in love with one particular beautiful person and

beget noble sentiments in partnership with him.

Plato goes on to advise a lessening of passion for one particular person once experience and knowledge are obtained.[11] "He may no longer be the slave of a base and mean–spirited devotion to an individual example of beauty, whether the object of his love be a boy or a man."

Love of women is not a part of the basic theme of Plato's work. He puts it bluntly in *Symposium* when he declares:

> When a man, starting from this sensible world and making his way upward by a right use of his feeling of love for boys, begins to catch sight of the beauty, he is very near his goal. This is the right way of approaching or being initiated into the mysteries of love.

Plato has "the woman from Mantinea" comment on:

> The beauty of boys and young men, the sight of whom... throws you and many people like you into such an ecstasy that provided that you could always enjoy the sight of your darlings, you would be content to go without food or drink, and to pass your whole time with them in the contemplation of their beauty.[12]

This, one may conclude, is a more accurate description of what Plato and his contemporaries really believed. What he writes later in *Laws* is too fraught with facetiousness and contradictions to be taken seriously.

Plato's discussion of marriage in Book Six of his *Laws* would seem to refute what he practiced and believed as reflected in his earlier writings. This suggests that what we read in *Laws* is a description of the perfect ideal to which reality may be compared but never achieved.[13]

The purpose of marriage, according to the Athenian speaker, is to find "a suitable partner for the procreation of children, he should get married, and in any case before he reaches thirty."[14] This statement still follows Plato's earlier ideas, and the custom of the Greeks which allows young men to enjoy a long, unencumbered youth.[15]

The Athenian goes on to assert, "You must make a marriage that will be approved by sensible folk..." [16] As he goes on in this vein, it becomes obvious that love has nothing to do with marriage: "One general rule should apply to marriage: we should seek to contract the alliance that will benefit the state, not one that we personally find alluring...." [17]

When the speaker suggests that "no rich man (is) to marry into a powerful house..." Plato is being facetious. It is this facetiousness which suggests that Plato was toying with his readers. He was being facetious when he set down the rules for procreation. He allows that it may be proper to become inebriated during a feast of the god of wine, but it would be wrong to drink at one's own wedding because "any child they may have, should have parents who were sober when they conceived them." [18]

Since it is illogical and inconsistent with human behavior, we can hardly believe the Plato is serious when he has the Athenian recommend that marriage inspectors see to it that people approach the act of procreation in an approved manner:

> They should be supervised by a woman whom we have chosen.... The officials should appoint the number they think right, at times within their discretion. These women (the supervisors) must assemble daily... for not more than a third of a day, and when they have convened each must report to her colleagues any wife or husband of childbearing age... who is concerned with anything but the duties imposed... If children come in suitable numbers, the period of supervised procreation should be ten years and no longer. But if a couple remain childless... (it is the responsibility of the female officials) to help them decide the terms of divorce.[19]

The Athenian even states that: "The female officials must enter the homes of the young people and by a combination of admonitions and threats, try to make them give up their ignorant and sinful ways." [20] Among the punishments to be meted out for not fornicating in a prescribed manner is to be "deprived of the privilege of attending weddings and parties celebrating the birth of children."

If we took Plato seriously on the question of homosexuality as expressed in *Laws*, then same–sex friendships would be "Platonic" and would lack passion and sexual relations: homosexuality would play no part in Greek life. This was hardly the case. Cleinias, the Cretan speaker in the *Laws*, cites the perfect rejoinder: "I dare say. But a lot of these proposals, sir, are incompatible with the average state's social structure..." This reply written by Plato into the book is convincing; he was not being serious, he was writing satire.

Although Plato shows that he is a poor source for the understanding of legal attitudes regarding homosexuality among the Greeks, he is important in order to comprehend subsequent misconceptions.

The parallel between the homoerotic sentiments found in Plato's *Symposium* and the Gilgamesh epic as analyzed by George F. Held was discussed in Chapter I. What is also apparent is the greater emphasis on homoaffectionate aspects of the male bonding which are the essential elements of both the epic and the *Symposium*. The same striving for love between males dominates the themes, not erotic gratification alone, but something more important. Held argues that the explanation of love in the Symposium as stated by Diotima makes the point quite simply. It is the desire for the beautiful, that is the possession of the beautiful, which is the object of love. Since the possession of what is beautiful is good, possessing what is good will make a person happy. Plato was convinced that wanting what is beautiful is good and will provide happiness. That is all that is necessary for Plato: "The answer is already final." No other reason ought to be expected to understand the desire to possess that which is beautiful. The beautiful being considered by Plato is the beautiful young man between puberty and the development of a beard, who is well proportioned and cultured.[21] The relationship being recommended is homoaffectionate.

In the *Laws*, Plato writes about problems of sexual conduct and included "pederasty" among the sexual urges, which he considers "affairs of the heart." The Athenian admits that Crete and Sparta do not support his argument, but he maintains that "one may have sexual intercourse with a woman but not with men or boys." As evidence he points to the animal world where "the males do not have sexual relations with each other, *because such a thing is unnatural*".[23]

"Such a thing is unnatural" – these are the particular words in Plato's *Laws* which attract the later Christians as they attempt to rationalize their homophobia. These are the words of later bigots as found in laws promulgated against homosexuals in the Western world. It is interesting to observe that in citing examples of homosexuality (pederasty), Plato uses Crete and Sparta as examples of places where homosexuality is a common phenomenon. He does not mention Athenian pederasty, where it seems to have been endemic. "Everyone will censure the weakling who yields to temptation and condemn his all–too–effeminate partner who plays the role of the woman," declares the Athenian as he sets out to define "the friendship... we call love."

The idea of "Platonic love," free of carnal lust, emerges in the *Laws*:

> He is confused and torn between two opposing instincts: one tells him to enjoy his beloved, the other forbids him. The lover of the body, hungry for his partner who is ripe to be enjoyed, like a luscious fruit, tells himself to have his fill, without showing any consideration for his beloved's character and disposition. But in another case physical desire will count for very little and the lover will be content to gaze upon his beloved without lusting for him, a mature and genuine closeness of soul for soul.[24]

To preclude lust and enjoyment of homoerotic passion from Plato's description of the "two opposing" instincts is to indulge in self–delusion. None but an experienced participant could dwell so earnestly on a "beloved," whose body was "ripe to be enjoyed, like a luscious fruit." While the words of Plato's recommendation are meant to suggest restraint from homoerotic behavior, the rhetoric is that of a passionate admirer of men and boys: the rhetoric of a pederast.

Again, in the *Laws*, Plato is being deliberately facetious and obviously out of character, compared to his other writings. The *Symposium*, for example, is one of the most famous and most influential rationalizations of homoaffectional conduct. In it Plato wrote, "Love will make men dare to die for the beloved–love alone." Pausanias, another speaker in the *Symposium*, identifies Aphrodite as the goddess of "heavenly love." Aphrodite, whom the myths say was born only of the male, rules the love of youths:

> There is no wantonness in her.... Those who are inspired by this love turn only to make and delight in him who is the more valiant and intelligent nature; anyone may recognize the pure

enthusiasts in the very character of their attainments. For they love not boys but intelligent beings whose reason is beginning to be developed, much about the time at which their beards begin to grow. And in choosing young men to be their companions, they mean to be faithful to them and pass their whole life in company with them, not to take them in their inexperience and deceive them, and play the fool with them, or run away from one to another. But the love of young boys should be forbidden by law... much noble enthusiasm may be thrown away upon them....

Pausanias, then, is advising against sexual relations with boys below puberty. His admonition is two–fold; the second part warned the would–be lover that he might be wasting "much noble enthusiasm" on someone too young to appreciate it!

It is interesting to notice that the speaker would require that "the coarser sort of lovers ought to be restrained by force as we restrain or attempt to restrain them from fixing their affections on women of free birth." He goes on, "these are persons who bring a reproach on love, and some have been led to deny the lawfulness of such attachments because they see the impropriety and evil of them; for surely nothing that is so decorously and lawfully done can justly be censured." These last words by Plato would make a contradiction of his *Laws*, if we were to consider *Laws* to be anything but facetious.

The thoughts expressed in *Laws* reflect the mood of an aging man, half serious, half in jest and facetious. Plato's real sentiments were more accurately expressed in *Phaedrus* and *Symposium*. Those are the sentiments of a younger, sexually–active, homoaffectional Athenian aristocrat. To him, like others of his class in his level of society, homosexual love was perfectly normal. Homoaffectional bonding among men was not only common, it was consistent with the low opinion manifested by the early Greek men toward women.[25]

Misogyny may be one extreme manifestation of male homoaffectionalism. The expression of that phenomenon is found in both heterosexual and homosexual men. In ancient Greece, where homoaffectionalism was particularly strong, the lesser status of women may be regarded as evidence of misogyny particularly in its milder forms. Arno Karlen alludes to the point in his book *Sexuality and Homosexuality*, wherein he quotes Plato's *Republic*:

50

"The gifts of nature are alike diffused in both men and women; all the pursuits of men are the pursuits of women also, but in all of them a woman is inferior to a man." [26]

Homoaffectionalism and concomitant lesser regard for women among ancient Greek men may be observed in their concepts of physical beauty as depicted in their art. The ideal human body was that equated with male pubescence: the young boyish figure was the criterion. Sir Kenneth J. Dover made an exhaustive study of that aspect of Greek culture as found in vase painting, particularly that produced in the fifth century B.C.[27] Supporting these data, H. A. Shapiro published an analysis of men courting youths on Attic black and red–figure vases of the period of c. 560–475 B.C. Both researchers noted the depiction of females with narrow hips and slender buttocks. The popularity of Attic tastes for boyish figures is evidenced by its widespread acceptance and imitation throughout Greece.[28]

If we take a closer look at Attic vase painting and its imitators of the sixth and fifth centuries B.C., it becomes obvious that women are depicted in awkward and subjugated sexual positions: women are seen orally copulating with men, but not the reverse; women are shown almost standing on their heads to accommodate their male sexual partners. Male courting scenes, where the partner is a boy, do not show oral copulation or demeaning positions taken by the boy. When male oral copulation with males is depicted, it is by Satyrs or other comic male characters. Even the overly large penis is avoided except in comic or gross depictions of Satyrs.[29]

As might be expected, the lesser role assigned to women by the male–dominated ancient Greek religions follows the social pattern. The formalization of marriage as a religious institution was primarily an attempt by the male to seek protection of his children by the gods. The birth of a child was ritualistically unclean. This uncleanliness extended beyond the mother, and encompassed the nurses and other women who attended her. A purification ceremony was required to render the women acceptable again. The announcement of a birth was also used to mark the distinctions between male and female children. If a boy were born, the honor would be announced by affixing an olive wreath on the front door of the family home. The olive wreath signified the potential honor the child would bring to both the family and the state. If a girl were born, her limitations were announced by affixing a few fillets of wool. The wool represented domestic life and weaving.[30]

Of course, there were brilliant women like Diotima who made their opinions felt. She is depicted with considerable respect in *Symposium*, and represented the intellectual influence of women in a hedonistic world dominated by men. There can be no doubt that women made substantial contributions; just as there can be no doubt that the male–dominated society gave them little credit. Indeed, the one–sided image of the Greek world must certainly reflect a strong historical bias which relegated women to the background.

However, the picture presented by the Greeks through their art and literature is a picture of homoaffectionalism culminating in erotic homosexual conduct. The ideal of the perfect love enjoyed by perfect lovers was then, as now, but a philosophical ideal more fanciful than real. Men like Plato could intellectualize about the qualities of an ideal lover. But the ideal beloved and the ideal lover are nothing more than mystical concepts of an elusive desire against which the real world may be yearningly compared.

There was a real world in Athens. It was in life's ordinary functions that those who enjoyed or suffered the events shaped reality. Homoaffectionalism was a part of their lives. To understand how they felt about homoerotic sex and its role in the lives of people, we should analyze the trial of an Athenian politician named Timarkhos who was prosecuted in Athens in 346 B.C.[31] It was the law that defined the boundaries of homosexual conduct.

The trial was heard before a jury of hundreds of ordinary citizens of Athens. Timarkhos was politically active in Athens and had been one of the men who was sent to placate King Philip of Macedon after the military defeat of Athenian forces. The peace which he helped negotiate was apparently necessary, yet there was a strong faction in Athens which resented having to make peace. They attacked Timarkhos simply because he was one of the peace negotiators.

They knew there was an Athenian law which prohibited any man who had sex with another man for money from holding public office. By discrediting Timarkhos they hoped to discredit the treaty of peace he helped to frame. What we learn from the trial is significant and reflective of the true Athenian attitude toward homoaffectionalism, as well as homoerotic behavior, including male prostitution.

Athenian legal custom did not allow for a judge, or even a parliamentarian, to give legal advice to the participants. The participants themselves had to persuade hundreds of jurors to favor their view. A convincing style was more important than the facts. Relevancy of the presented material was not questioned. It was the effect of the delivery on the jury that really mattered.[32]

The sentiments expressed in the trial were obviously the sentiments believed to be best to expose before a jury. K. J. Dover in his book *Greek Homosexuality* notes that only those sentiments which would be "prudent to profess in public" would be expressed by the defendant. All those things which would shock or offend the jury would be asserted by the accusors.[33] If the jury were shocked or offended, they could have deprived Timarkhos of his life. Dover warns us not to equate the sentiments of the *Symposium* written a hundred years before the trial of Timarkhos with those depicted by Aiskhines in 346 B.C.

At issue was not the question of Timarkhos' homosexual activity, but whether or not he sold his favors as a prostitute. The use of certain words, especially *kalos*, was noted by Dover, as it was applied to young men meaning "beautiful," "handsome," "attractive" and even "pretty." [34] As Dover noted, the Greeks did not refer to a person as "beautiful" "by virtue of that person's morals, intelligence, ability or temperament, but solely by virtue of shape, colour, texture and movement...." [35]

After studying courtship scenes in Attic vase painting, Shapiro concluded that there was a reaction against the homoerotic morals of the aristocratic class that was noticeable after 480 B.C. This would suggest that there was a less tolerant public attitude by 346 B.C., the year of Timarkhos' trial. The point to note here is that there was perhaps less tolerance, but not intolerance.

From the record of the trial we learn that homoerotic activity was not unusual. The language suggests that the kinds of relationships which were most acceptable were those between a mature male and a younger male. Sexual activity between same–aged men seems to be precluded. The standard acceptable relationship would be between the active, older and aggressive lover and the younger, passive beloved, who had reached maturity.

The Greeks were not dealing with relations with children, but were dealing with youths who were sexually capable. The youthful beloved would be referred to as *eromenos*, the "loved one;" the senior partner would be called *erastes*, the "lover." The word *Paidika* was used to describe an acceptable kind of love. What was unacceptable was called *pornia*, prostitution. The word *pornia* was apparently applied broadly, and used as a word to attack persons not liked by the one using the term.[36] The word *aiskhropoiein* would be used to describe an action which was "ugly, disgraceful, shameful." [37]

The trial exonerated Timarkhos. He had engaged in honorable, acceptable homoaffectional and homoerotic behavior and was thus in conformity with Athenian standards. He had been beloved, as *eromenos*, and he had had lovers, *erastes*. He had not been a prostitute, *pornia*, who had charged men a price to have sex with him. He had accepted gifts from his lovers, but not payment.[38]

What we learn from the persecution of Timarkhos is the fact that homoerotic behavior was a factor in the homoaffectional relationships of ancient Athens; we learn that there was honor and integrity encompassed by the relationship. More importantly we learn that male bonding and homoerotic behavior were acceptable if the relationship was not *pornia*, this is, not involving prostitution.

Prostitution of or by citizens was what offended the ancient Greeks, not homosexuality. Even prostitution was acceptable just so long as the male prostitute had paid his fee to the state to engage in the business of prostitution. No second thought would be given to a non–citizen engaging in prostitution. Male citizens of Athens were expected to have a higher regard for their virtue and their bodies; as a consequence, no one who had engaged in prostitution was permitted to participate in politics or government service.

One of the most significant influences manifested by the growing awareness of homoerotic conduct among the ancient Greeks is its use as a means of discussing the subject. This was particularly true during the nineteenth century. Under the rubric "Greek love," scholars were able to discuss a subject which would ordinarily be avoided. As a consequence, pederasty became an acceptable subject when tied in with ancient Greek studies. This phenomenon enabled a host of writers to expound on the subject; the public could hardly avoid the issue. This intellectualizing of homosexual conduct undoubtedly helped balance the moralizing directed against it, and led to greater understanding and acceptance.

The use of the Greek ethos to mitigate legal and religious intolerance toward homosexual expression is exemplified by many nineteenth century and early twentieth century writers, among whom are Karl Friedrich Ulrichs, Richard Burton, Edward Carpenter, John Addington Symonds, and André Gide, to name but a few.[39]

They created the literary genre which permitted the subject to be included in the study of history, anthropology and law. Thus the example of the ancient Greeks has become one of the most important factors in effecting change. Classical studies became the catalyst which induced changes in the religiously–based homophobic laws which are found in Western culture.

Even if it were argued that the ideal among the ancient Greeks was "Platonic" love, devoid of erotic expression, a case is still made for homoaffectionalism.

NOTES

1. Bertrand Russell, Wisdom Of The West (Garden City, N.Y.: Doubleday & Co., Inc., 1959), p. 20.

2. Bertrand Russell, p. 21.

3. Bertrand Russell, p. 23.

4. Alistair Sutherland and Patrick Anderson, Eros (New York: The Citadel Press, 1963), p. 60.

    Plato, The Symposium, trans. Walter Hamilton (Middlesex, England: Penguin Books, Ltd., 1982), pp. 59–62.

5. Symposium, pp. 62–64.

6. Symposium, p. 81.

7. Symposium, p. 82.

8. Symposium, p. 82.

9. Sutherland, p. 62.

10. Symposium, p. 87.

11. Symposium, p. 92.

12. Symposium, pp. 94, 95.

13. Plato, The Laws, trans. Trevor J. Saunders (Middlesex: Penguin Books, Ltd., 1980), p. 251.

14. The Laws, p. 252.

15. The Laws, p. 255.

16. The Laws, p. 251.

17. The Laws, p. 252.

18. The Laws, p. 255.

19. The Laws, p. 266.

20. The Laws, p. 268.

21. George F. Held, "The Parallel Between the Gilgamesh Epic and Plato's Symposium," Journal Of Near East Studies (Chicago: University of Chicago Press, 1983), 42, No. 2, pp. 133–141.

22. The Laws, p. 333.

23. The Laws, p. 244.

24. The Laws, p. 335

25. Kenneth J. Dover, Greek Homosexuality (London: Duckworth Co., Ltd., 1978), pp. 10–15.

   Robert Flacelière, trans. James Cleugh, Love In Ancient Greece (New York: Crown Publishers, Inc., 1962), p. 9.

26. Arno Karlen, Sexuality and Homosexuality (New York: W. W. Norton & Co., 1917), p. 29.

27. Dover, pp. 91–124.

28. H. A. Shapiro, "Courtship Scenes in Attic Vase–Painting," American Journal of Anthropology (New York: Archeological Institute of America, 1981), Vol. 85, No. 2, pp. 132–158.

29. Dover, pp. 100–109.

30. Arthur Fairbanks, Handbook of Greek Religion (New York: American Book Co., 1910), pp. 35, 122.

31. Dover, pp. 13–14.

32. Dover, p. 13.

33. Dover, p. 14.

34. Dover, p. 15.

35. Dover, pp. 15–16.

   A more detailed explanation of this phenomenon will be found in H. A. Shapiro's "Courtship Scenes in Attic Vase–Painting," American Journal of Archaeology (New York: Archaeological Institute of America, 1981), Vol. 85, No. 2, April 1981, pp. 133–143. This article deals with Davies' treatment of the subject with support being provided by analyses of scenes of men courting youths depicted on vases produced in Greece between the years 560 to 475 B.C., especially those collected by J. D. Beazly, "Some Attic Vases in The Cyprus Museum," Proc. Brit. Ac. 33 (1947) pp. 3–31. The decline of male erotic scenes after 480 B.C. is noted to suggest a decline in interest.

36. Dover, pp. 16, 17.

37. Dover, p. 17.

38. Dover, pp. 20–109.

   A complete analysis of the trial of Timarkhos is covered by Dover in great detail.

39. Karl Friedrich Ulrichs, trans. Michael A. Lombardi, Vindex: Social–Juridicial Studies on the Sexual Love Between Men (Los Angeles: Urania Manuscripts, 1978, orig. pub. by Max Spohr Publications, 1898).

Richard Burton, "Sotadic Zone," The Vice (Atlanta: M. G. Thevis, 1967), pp. 15–53.

Edward Carpenter, Ioläus (London: George Allen & Unwin, Ltd., 1902), pp. 67–93.

John Addington Symonds, Studies In Sexual Inversion (Privately printed, 1931), pp. 9–97.

Andre Gidè, Corydon (New York: Farrar, Straus & Co., 1950)

This book is an example of the genre in the sense that a classical name, "Corydon," was given to a book which was not itself concerned with the ancient world or its culture.

Other authors who used the classical reference are: Derrick Sherwin Bailey, *Homosexuality and the Western Christian Tradition* (London: Archon Books, 1975); Robert Flacelière, trans. James Cleugh, *Love in Ancient Greece* (New York: Crown Publishers, Inc., 1962); Arno Karlen, *Sexuality and Homosexuality* (New York: W. W. Norton & Co., 1971); Kenneth J. Dover, *Greek Homosexuality* (New York: Vintage Books, 1980).

This is but a small selection of the material available.

CHAPTER IV

ROME — A SENSE OF GUILT

"Roman, remember, these shall be your arts: to rule the empire of the world, to impose the custom of peace, to spare the defeated and to crush the proud." With these words from Book VI of *The Aeneid*, the poet Virgil defined the Roman images of their destiny as they saw it. Romans were inculcated with myths of their noble, moral, rustic progenitors. Their noble ancestors, they believed, were the epitome of virtue against which they judged themselves.

Virgil's attitudes expressed in writing during the first century A.D. reflect the spirit of Roman expansionism beginning with Julius Caesar. These attitudes endured for at least the next five hundred years. It is this period of Roman law and custom which we shall now investigate to discern Roman attitudes toward homoaffectionalism and homoerotic behavior.

As we have seen in studying the Greeks, Babylonians, and Hittites before the Romans, the laws of governments reflect the idealized norms demanded as minimum standards of behavior expected to maintain the family unit and the social order. Personal behavior not affecting the family or the state was left unregulated. The concern of law was directed toward conduct which affected inheritance and property rights. Paternity, not sexuality, was of interest to the state. Consequently, as we shall see, the heterosexual conduct of women was of great interest to authorities, but not the sexual pleasure of men, nor lesbianism.

Homosexuality may have been subject to peer pressure in Roman culture and not as overtly endorsed as among the Greeks, but it was not officially proscribed by Roman law. Its practice was widespread, and though subject to disdain by some, it was obviously practiced by many. As in Greece, it was endemic; unlike the Greeks, the Romans seemed to have allowed themselves to feel guilty about it.

To understand this sense of guilt or "naughtiness" about sexual behavior, we must look to the myths Romans learned in their childhood and passed on to their children in turn. The Romans tended to glorify their humble, rustic origins as farmers who would set aside the plow to go off to war and victory and then return humbly to the plow when virtue and justice triumphed over their enemies. Roman literature abounds with examples of this particular characteristic. A favorite tale was that of Lucius Quinctius Cincinnatus, who was chosen Consul in 460 B.C. Two years later, when Rome was under attack, he was asked to be dictator. When the people went to tell him that he had been selected to take control, he was busy plowing his fields. He laid aside his plow to lead the fight against the enemy. Once he had defeated them, sixteen days after his appointment as dictator, he gave up dictatorial power and returned to his plowing.

At the time of Augustus, the historian Livy could honestly assert:

> If any nation can have the right to hallow its own origin and to attribute its foundation to gods, the Romans are so renowned in war that when they call the war god Mars the father of their founder and their people, the world accepts the Roman boast as contentedly as it accepts the Roman empire.[1]

Cornelius Tacitus, a contemporary of Livy, was also a historian who appealed to the noble myths of Rome's origins by comparing Rome with the noble rustics in Germany, lately conquered by Julius Caesar and others. He evoked the image of noble rustics close to the soil, and the family hearth, to chide the Romans of his day for slipping away from their own noble rustic heritage.[2]

It is an important aspect of the Roman character that they believed their heroic myths as religiously as a modern Christian believes the myths of the Bible. To that extent they were "fundamentalists," and like their modern Christian counterparts, they based their moral premises on mythical ideals which had never existed. Their "fundamentalism" served as the criterion by which morality was judged and from which they surely departed. It was this Roman "fundamentalism" which engendered feelings of guilt and perhaps led to their later dissatisfaction with their gods. Philosophy rather than religion played the major role in ethical thought and as the basis of lifestyle.

Romans justified their lifestyles and beliefs by their use of philosophy. Epicureanism, for example, allowed for a pleasant degree of moderate hedonism, which could be rationalized as basically good. Indeed the prime good was pleasure, pleasure of the mind and of the body. However, for Epicurus, the virtuous man was to be circumspect and somewhat aloof and detached from responsibility.[3] Obviously this would rationalize indifference.

Seemingly, it was a way to escape harsh realities.

Romans took their philosophies seriously, as some today view religion. Hostility was not uncommon between advocates. To illustrate this, note an entry in the works of Cicero when he learned that a friend had returned from the wars of Caesar in Gaul: "Pansa informed me that you were turned Epicurean. O rare camp!" [4] What makes this comment significant was the fact, according to Conyers Middleton in his *Life of Cicero*, that Cicero was an ardent foe of Epicureanism. He thought it "destructive of morality, and pernicious to society." [5]

Stoicism seems to have had a stronger influence on the Romans; its rather austere precepts suited their rather dour character. It held sway for about five centuries until the advent of Christianity. It had its beginning with a Phoenician Cypriot called Zeno during the second half of the fourth century B.C. Stoicism had its appeal in ethical principles which fostered courage in the face of danger and suffering, and taught indifference to material circumstances. [6] Essentially it glorified cold indifference and fatalism. It was certainly more in keeping with the Roman temperament and required less intellectualizing than the teachings of either Plato or Aristotle. It is doubtful if Roman Stoics were as concerned with Zeno's other theoretical views on natural laws and the role of fire as a prime element as they were with his rationale for aloof indifference.

Indifference to matters not affecting the state and the family may be the clue to Roman acceptance of nonreproductive sexual pleasures, including homosexuality. Even marriage, which does affect the family and the state, was not an exalted institution. The Roman emphasis seems to be on producing legitimate children to carry on duties to the state and family. Sexuality was encouraged for its own sake, for men to enjoy; prostitution of various types was always a part of the Roman scheme of things. Their attitude was nicely expressed by Horace in one of his *Satires*: "If you are aroused and a slave girl or slave boy that you crave in the heat of the moment is standing by, why would you choose to remain dissatisfied? I wouldn't. I like a love that is cheap and available." (I,2)

Sexual gratification was more important than the sex object; they seemed indifferent to the source of their pleasure. Again, it is acceptance which characterizes their attitude toward homoeroticism.

From the very beginning, Roman law was indifferent to the sexual behavior of men and countenanced extramarital relationships. The foundation of Roman social life was the monogamous marriage dominated by the husband. The *Patria Potestas*, the authority of the father, governed the domestic life of family members; however, "free love" and prostitution were coexistent with marriage, at least for the husband.[8]

Morality to the Romans seldom concerned itself with man's sex habits unless they infringed on the rights of a father and husband. Official censors concerned themselves with the conduct of senators, knights, and important people, yet that concern was more often directed toward bribe–taking and maintenance of financial status than with sexual conduct. Financial standing determined one's standing in Rome. As Cicero noted, the censors "had the power to punish vice and immorality, by some mark of infamy, in all ranks of men, from the highest to the lowest."[9] It is significant to notice that when Cicero writes that "They expelled above sixty-four from the senate for notorious immoralities," the censors were not dealing here with sex scandals, they were dealing with bribery![10]

Romans maintained a rather indiscriminate attitude toward marriage and sexual intercourse. They found glory in the legend of the rape of the Sabine women and continued to be proud of that conduct all through their later development. They retold the story to edify each generation of Roman men.

While the early Romans may have gone through a period of matriarchy, by the time of its rise to prominence, Roman society was male dominated. Husbands dominated their wives and families. Undoubtedly this male power over wife and family lent the impetus to supreme political power. Cicero was aware of the state of early Roman sex habits and the Roman male's sexual freedom: "No one knew of lawful marriage, no one had seen legitimate children of his own."[11]

As Rome developed, the right to marry also developed. The laws which dealt with regular marriage (*iustum matrimonium*) made a sharp distinction between marriage which put the woman "into the hands" (*in manum*) of her husband and a marriage which did not put her in her husband's control (*sine in manium conventione*). In the later case she technically remained under the control of her father or his assigned agent. The husband had three ways to acquire control (*manus*) over his wife: one was by marriage *confarreatio*; the second by marriage *coemptio*, and the third by marriage *usus*.[12]

Confarreatio was the oldest form. It was religiously instituted and celebrated before a domestic altar and restricted to Patricians. Plebeians utilized the *coemptio* form, which was similar but took the form of mutual purchase of each other by the couple. The third form, *usus*, developed from the Plebeian form and resulted when a couple lived together for a year with no separations for more than three successive days. After the continuous cohabitation the couple were deemed to be married.[13]

As social changes occurred and the submission of women to legal servitude became more repugnant to them, the form of marriage changed to one without submission (*sine manu*) to the husband.[14] During the early days of the Republic it was a simple matter for a Plebeian husband to divorce his wife; he merely had to demand the house keys in the presence of witnesses and then tell the wife to take her things from the home. However, custom did mitigate the harshness of this system and established strict rules of procedure.[15] Women had no such rights. Although the marriage between Patricians was essentially indissoluble by custom, even these marriages could be negated by legal ceremony.[16] By the second century B.C., divorce became more common.[17] As women gained more rights and greater control over their personal wealth, more women divorced their husbands than husbands divorced their wives.[18] Marriage was not a romantic enterprise; the overriding purpose for marriage in Rome was to enable a man to have progeny. The birth of a child ensured the material permanence of the family and of Rome itself.[19] Marriage was a self–sacrificing duty; it was part of the self–discipline expected of all citizens and the Patricians in particular.[20]

In the very early days of Rome, only the Patricians were expected to get married, and they were not permitted to marry Plebeians. The right of Patricians to marry was a matter of custom and not codified until the appearance of the Twelve Tablets circa 445 B.C. The social stigma felt by Plebeians who were denied the right to marry into Patrician families caused the law to be changed by the Tribune Canuleius at the same time that he introduced the Canuleian Marriage Laws. This not only allowed Plebeians to marry with Patricians, it enabled the declining population of Patricians to introduce new blood into their system, and provided a needed source of new wealth for them by marrying wealthy Plebeian daughters.[21] Thus both groups benefited.

In the regular marriage (*coemptio*) and the most sacred form of marriage (*confarreatio*), the Romans indulged in a mock siezure of the bride from her family, symbolizing the more primitive, forcible nature of marriage. Regardless of the form of marriage, the use of phallic symbols and ribald songs was a part of the ceremonies. Sex was hardly a private matter either; originally custom allowed the husband's friends to have intercourse with the bride first. They apparently believed that marital chastity was an affront to nature, and had to be earned by a period of free prostitution on the wedding night. Bachofen writes that "She purchases the chastity of marriage by preliminary unchastity." [22] Seneca was considered accurate when he said: "Immodesty was not a vice but a monstrosity." [23] All of this sets a tone for the attitude demonstrated by Romans toward sex, women, and homosexuality in particular.

Although women were dominated by their husbands, in compensation the Roman matron was given great respect in the form of ritual and polite manners. She was addressed as *domina,* mistress; she was approached with politeness and accorded such dignities as allowing her to pass with deference in a public place. People were required to speak modestly in front of her and no man would dare to touch or molest her. She could attend the theater, law courts, and religious functions with the consent of her husband and with an escort. However, she was absolutely forbidden to drink wine upon pain of death.[24]

Plutarch sarcastically noted that "Cato married a wife with more nobility than wealth; he thought that both nobly–born and rich women were proud and arrogant, but noble women had more shame of base conduct." [25]

In their inferior, ascribed place women were not usually educated. As a result, Roman men, like the Greeks, sought out and enjoyed the company of other men. Rome was a state run for men. Even when it came to divorce, which had been impossible in the earlier years, only a man could obtain one. However, a husband had to prove adultery, the drinking of wine, perverse and disgusting conduct, poisoning her children, or counterfeiting his keys![26] The law also allowed that: "If you take your wife in adultery, you may freely kill her without trial." [27] Interestingly, early Christians appealed to women in Rome by asserting: "Among us, what is forbidden to women is equally forbidden to men." [28]

Enforceable adultery charges against men did not appear until the moral codes of Augustus in the first century A.D. Yet even he realized that there were problems: "Banish prostitutes from society and you reduce society to chaos from unsatisfied lust."[29] Augustus' penalties allowed corporal punishment only for the lower class. Years later the penalties were increased. Under Constantius, adultery could be punished by burning alive or drowning in a sack. In the sixth century A.D., Justinian compelled adulterous women to be shut up in convents.[30]

In 131 B.C., Livy noted the Censor Matellus as declaring, "If we could live without wives we should not have all this trouble. Since nature has brought it about that we can neither live with them in peace nor without them at all, we must ensure eternal benefit rather than temporary pleasure."[31] As the Empire aged, divorce became easier.

The flight from marriage by Romans caused Augustus to enact legislation. He enacted *Juliae rogationes*, which included the *lex sumptuaria*, the *lex Julia de adulteriis et de pudicitia*, the *lex Julia de maritandis ordinibus* and the *lex Papia Poppaea*. Enacted between the years 18 B.C. and A.D. 9, they imposed property disqualifications on those men who remained "celibate," unmarried men between the ages of 20 and 50, and on childless men over 25 and childless women over 20. Benefit would accrue to families with three or more children.[32]

The official preference for larger families is seen in an action taken by Julius Caesar, even before Augustus' laws. When he was consul, he divided up certain public lands around Rome, "without casting lots, among 20,000 citizens who could show three children or more."[33] It is difficult to know how effective these laws were. Petronius wrote in the *Satyricon*, at the time of Nero: "What use are laws where money is king... There's no justice at law, it's the bidding that counts and the job of the judges is to fix the amounts."[34]

However, there was nothing to indicate an anti–homosexual attitude. The Romans did not perceive sexual behavior as neatly divided into two separate categories based on the sex of the partners. What we can discern in the development of the Roman ethos is a strong anti–pleasure bias. In their myths and legends the Romans stressed the self–sacrificing hardships expected of citizens. They looked upon their success in war and conquest as a direct result of their self–sacrifice and endurance of suffering. Loyalty to one's family reflected the same concepts which required self–sacrifice for the good of the clan. Stoicism suited their preconceived notions of the world. Yielding to pleasure, even sexual pleasure, put them in conflict with the ideal, and thus engendered a sense of guilt. It is this developing sense of guilt which became the precursor of Christian morality, as we shall see.

The same Julius Caesar who so politically favored the families of Rome also enjoyed homoerotic sex. If we are to believe Edward Gibbon in his famous *Decline and Fall of the Roman Empire*, the only Roman emperor who was completely heterosexual in his preference was the reputedly dim–witted Claudius.[35]

According to Suetonius, it was during Caesar's first tour of duty in Asia that he earned his reputation as being homosexual in preference. He was dispatched by the praetor Marcus Thermus, in whose domestic retinue the youthful Caesar was serving, to go to Bithynia and commandeer a fleet of ships from King Nicomedes. Caesar lingered there and "made his abode with King Nicomedes, not without foul rumor raised that he prostituted his body to be abused by the king."[36] "His good name for continency and clear life nothing verily blemished, save only the abode and inward familiarity with Nicomedes; but a foul stain that was, which followed with shame forever; yea, and ministered taunting and reproachful matter unto everyman. I omit the notorious verses of Calvus Licinius: Look what it was that Bithyne land had ever more or less;/ And he that Caesar did abuse, in filthy wantonness," Suetonius continued.

Suetonius then goes on to list insults said of Caesar regarding his homosexuality: "The King's concubine in the Queen's bedroom"; "Nicomedes' filth and harlot"; "The Bithynian Queen"; "after he (Octavius) called Pompey king, (he) saluted Caesar by the name of Queen"; "Gaius Memmes likewise laid it in Caesar's dish that he stood with the rest of the stale catamites as cup–bearer, to serve Nicomedes."[37] One of the more colorful stories told about Caesar is credited by Suetonius to Cicero: "...the pensioners of the said king (Nicomedes) being conveyed into the king's bedchamber, Caesar lay down upon a bed of gold, arranged in purple; and so the maidenhead of him who descended from Venus became defiled in Bithynia...."[38]

Caesar was selected as one of many examples of Roman men who indulged in and enjoyed homoerotic relationships. Being well known and a central figure, he evoked both the best and the worst comments of his countrymen. Although they may have mocked him after his death, nevertheless they respected him. Those mocking him had to be cautious; there was always the danger of provoking the wrath of a powerful descendant or beneficiary, which may have tempered some contemporary remarks. Of major interest was the fact that Caesar's homoerotic behavior did not diminish overall respect for him. His sexual conduct may have titillated Romans, but it certainly did not surprise or shock them. Obviously the phenomenon was common enough. Even Suetonius, who was writing to amuse and poke fun at the greats as much as he was writing to instruct in history, relaxes and records some of Caesar's more tender moments:

> In affectionate love and faithful protection of dependents, he was not wanting in his youth. Upon a time he defended Masiatha, a noble young gentleman... and also kept him close a long time in his own lodging... When he went into Spain, he took the young gentleman away in his own litter.[39]

There seems to have been a custom at the time which encouraged young men to pluck the hairs on their buttocks, undoubtedly to maintain a more youthful appearance: "...his hair plucked, insomuch as some cast it in his teeth and twitted him therewith," [40] they said of Caesar. Caesar was also criticized for the provocative way he dressed and deported himself: "He also wore a girdle over it, and that very slack and loose; whereupon arose for certain that saying of Sulla who admonishes the nobles often–times, to beware of the boy that went girdled so dissolutely." What we see here is a description of body–language enhanced by style affectations intended to broadcast sexual preference. "He was exceedingly addicted to neatness in his house, and sumptuous fare at his table." Again, these remarks seem inferential of the type intended to evoke titillation rather than condemnation.

The jests at Caesar's expense should be compared with harsh reality. He was also a strict moralist by Roman standards. Caesar was seemingly praised when it was told that "a freedman of his own... he put to death for dishonoring by adultery a Roman Knight's wife." [41] The moral offense in this case threatened both the state and the family structure. Who could abide the audacity of having a man of lower social class seducing the wife of a knight and perhaps impregnating her with a false heir? Morality, we see, is a matter of rights and honor being violated, not sexual conduct *per se*. The crime here is all the more outrageous since Rome permitted a wide choice of sexual outlets including prostitutes of either gender. While jaded courtiers like Petronius and sophisticated writers like Suetonius and Livy may be callous regarding homosexuality, the poets of Rome understood and wrote of homoaffectionalism.

John Dryden's translation of Virgil, for example, shows homoaffectionalism. Dryden published the first edition at age 70 in 1697, during the ribald period of the "restoration" in England which allowed a more honest rendering of his original. It is the bane of researchers to suffer the censorship imposed on later translators of ancient works. The following is a compressed series of excerpts from Virgil's *Second Pastoral*, which traces an impassioned encounter of Corydon, a mature man, and a lovely young shepherd boy, Alexis:

Ah, Corydon! ah, poor unhappy swain!
Alexis will thy homely gifts disdain:
Nor, shouldst thou offer all thy little store,
Will rich Iolas yield, but offer more...

Come to my longing arms, my lovely care!
And take the presents which the nymphs prepare...

Love has no bounds in pleasure, or in pain...
Quench, Corydon, thy long unanswered fire...
And find an easier love, though not so fair.[42]

Perhaps it is because Virgil was Celtic that he was better able to depict Roman homoaffectionalism in his poetry. In any case, it is important to consider the implications of these observations regarding Roman attitude devoid of Celtic sentimentalism before continuing our study of Roman law beyond Augustus.

Attitude reflects the influence of ingrained beliefs and devised values. For example, it is hardly surprising to find Roman men insensitive to rape and sadism when we observe that they believed that their noble progenitors raped the Sabine women. That act of sexual aggression was thought to have been a manifestation of Roman manhood and prowess. Power and manhood were valued as synonymous; they believed the rape occurred and was noble; their attitude had to be one of noble indifference to sexual aggression. The same factors would tend to glorify the sex drives of men, who were considered to be superior, and to deprecate the role and feelings of women who were seen as inferior. With these attitudes we should expect more homoeroticism than the more benign manifestation of homoaffectionalism, and certainly a good deal of homoeroticism coupled with sadism.

Before people knew how babies developed in the womb, naiveté and ignorance encouraged men to believe that it was they who planted their seed in a woman and their seed grew there to become a baby. By this view the baby was the man's. The woman was a mere receptacle in which the seed developed. The myths of Rome, like those of Greece, perpetuated the belief that the gods, at least, produced offspring without the need for women or a womb. All of this was designed to negate the female role in reproduction.

These strange beliefs produced legends about super–babies, *wunderkinder*, like Dionysus who sprung forth from the thigh of Zeus. The adoration of divine babies was often depicted in Roman art, but "surprisingly few" super–babies occur in the myths, as Edwin R. Goodenough noted in his definitive volumes *Jewish Symbols In The Greco–Roman Period*.[43] Those which did occur were depicted over and over. Perhaps the subsequent depiction of the Christ–child is but another manifestation of the Greco–Roman *wunderkinder*, at least in the form of adulation it was accorded.

For our study, these myths are recalled to explain Roman attitudes: attitudes toward women, sex, and ultimately homosexuality. They are important to understand the lesser role assigned to women, even in the act of procreation. They also explain the diminished role marriage played in ancient Rome. The baby Dionysus often appeared in the "likon," the cultic cradle–basket,[44] essentially the crib, as reflected in the Christian story of Christ's infancy. The similarities between the ancient *wunderkinder* and the Christian myth are striking, especially the "born again" aspects: double births, resulting in the glorified baby, were depicted in Jewish art of the Roman world.[45]

It is significant to find that the *wunderkinder* are associated with the god Priapus, which is the deification of the male erection.[46] The erected phallus was not immoral. The Romans tended to equate immorality with the emancipation of women. Ironically, it was the acquisition of empire which they saw as the turning point. Appian noted that Rome ceased to be a state of yeoman farmers and recorded the "ominous changes" about the time of the second Punic war: "As the Romans gradually conquered Italy, they took portions of conquered territories and built cities on them, or sent their own citizens to colonize previously existing cities." [47]

It was as if they lost their simple virtues, as the bucolic life competed with the newly growing city life. Slaves, acquired by conquest, provided a free labor force and afforded Romans more leisure time. As the older order passed and luxury flooded into Rome, new standards of conduct pushed the old moral code to the background. Velleius Paterculus could write: "Private luxury followed hard on public ostentation." He was commenting on the beautification of public buildings at the time.[48]

Velleius also noted the increase in cruelty as wealth and power grew: "A new horror appeared in later times. Greed was a reason for cruelty, and a man's guilt was measured by his possessions; anyone who was rich was a criminal, and paid the price of his own life and safety; nothing was dishonourable if it was profitable." The power of the family was breaking up, the *patria potestas* (power of the father) no longer governed the family, and it no longer guaranteed a standard for morals.[49]

Not only were women being criticized for "immorality, extravagance, debauchery"; men, according to Sallust, for example, "gave themselves to unnatural vice." It was a time of developing guilt.[50] The growing sense of guilt in response to natural sexual instincts seems to be particularly Roman. It was their sense of guilt which was left as a legacy to subsequent Christians. Seneca wrote a letter (Epistle 97), "If you think that our age is peculiar for luxury, dessave ertion of moral standards... these are the faults of mankind, not of any age. No time in history has been free from guilt."[51] The whole of Tacitus, and his "Germany" in particular,[52] is geared toward engendering guilt particularly by his comparison of the "undegenerate [sic] morality of the Germans to the debauchery of Rome." He reinforces the myth that original virtue resided in their ancestors: "May we in Rome long strive to rival our ancestors in virtue."[53]

What can be seen in this and similar tales of lost virtue is the incessant inculcation of the myth of lost virtue, which was left in a Roman garden of Eden. It is as fundamental a belief as that deeply rooted in the tales of the Christian Bible of later times. If we agree that attitudes, particularly attitudes toward sexual variation, are dependent on beliefs and concepts of virtue and acquired values, then their fundamental beliefs and values must be understood if the Roman attitude toward homosexuality is to be comprehended.

As noted previously, in the early days of Rome the ruling aristocratic families were the only ones to have had formal marriages. Originally, they alone were required to marry for life, without divorce, with the woman *in manum*, which meant she was totally dominated by her husband. As the empire grew, all that began to change. So–called "free marriages" developed; the wife could keep her own property, though not her dowry, after her husband died. Women became more independent of men. They were growing so strong financially that in the year 169 B.C. the *lex Veronia* was enforced to prohibit women from receiving legacies. It is doubtful that the law had much effect, but it is an example of reactionary attitude.[54]

It is certain that Roman women had no political rights. As Gellius put it: "Women are debarred from taking part in the citizen–assembly." Yet with all, the Roman women had greater freedom and power than their sisters in ancient Greece. Regardless, women remained sex objects; the institution of prostitution was an integral part of their culture. As Seneca the Elder wrote: "He has done no wrong; he loves a prostitute, a usual thing; wait, he will improve, and marry a wife."[55] Once again, we discern an attitude which encouraged Roman men to be promiscuous: "They would have considered continence by young men to be gross and absurd."[56]

Promiscuity was an accepted part of Roman culture, and this must be recognized in studying sexual expression, including homosexual expression. Cruelty was another prominent characteristic of the Romans. These characteristics could be consistent with endemic homoerotic behavior, but not very conducive to the benign homoaffectionalism idealized by the Greeks. Homoerotic lust devoid of affection could find expression in the use of males by heterosexual men to satisfy sexual appetite. Of course, homosexual men could also engage in homoerotic lust.

Whether the Romans "learned" their taste for cruelty from their earlier Etruscan neighbors has been discussed by some historians. Indeed, it may well be true that the funeral statues of Etruscans pouring libations to the gods are depicting the deceased pouring blood. Even gladiatorial games are traced to the Etruscans.

71

Nevertheless, the Romans perfected and embellished sadism to a fine art. They were exceedingly cruel. Ritualistic blood ceremonies were common. It is hardly surprising to find the blood sacrifice as part of later Christian symbolism as developed in Rome.[57] Cruelty and the will to dominate are two sides of the same coin; this is true whether expressed in the behavior of nations or of individuals. There is ample evidence to indicate that flogging was a frequent practice, especially in the Roman schools. Leather thongs on a stick were used to chastise *ad nates* (on the buttocks).[58]

Cruelty flourished with the expansion of power. Gladiatorial games increased. Julius Caesar bought up large numbers of well–trained gladiators: "Such sort of fencers from all parts out of every school, and putting his adversaries, of other factions, in great affright thereby, he gave occasion unto the state to provide a special act in that behalf, for a certain set number of swordplayers, above which no man might retain any at Rome...."[59] Thus we notice that Rome had to limit the number of armed bullies any private citizen could keep in the city.

While Roman law did inflict the death penalty, death alone did not always satisfy the law. For slaves, cruel, slow death was the rule, and this was manifest. Executions were begun with mistreatment and torture of the victim. Flogging preceded decapitation, for example. Victims were often bound like sacrificial animals when slaughtered. Flogging and crucifixion were favorite Roman forms of capital punishment. Suetonius quotes Caligula, who ordered an executioner to "strike so that he feels he is dying."[60] Death alone was too easy a punishment for the Romans; again, it reflected their attitude toward, and their penchant for, cruelty.

What is apparent, then, is the fact that sexuality in Rome, including homosexuality, flourished in a ruthless, sadistic society fraught with a self–imposed sense of guilt which engendered a sense of shame in the act of loving. This tendency adversely affected subsequent religious attitudes as they developed in Rome. Guilt in sex, guilt in pleasure, coupled with sadism expressed in self–flagellation, became the foundation for Christianity and the laws developed by Christians. Despite the guilt, the Romans made flagrant use of sexual symbolism in their worship.

Whether associated with the god Priapus or as the *facinum*, the male erection was worshipped by phallic cults in Rome. They believed in the power of male fertility. The erect phallus was called the *facinum* which, not incidentally, is the somewhat remote origin of the word "fascination." The facinum was worn about the neck of children, placed above doors of shops, and on the chariot of a general. As *deus*, the phallus was worshipped by the Vestal Virgins in Rome.[61] The god Priapus, as worshipped in Rome, was nothing more than a depiction of a giant phallus, associated with a face. Statues of Priapus adorned the gardens of Rome, serving also to scare birds away. Kiefer suggests in his book *Sexual Life In Ancient Rome* that the phallus was made into an instrument of punishment used to chastise "through gross sexual acts"; again, this evidences sadism.

The Bacchanalia are closely associated with the fertility gods and sex orgies. The outrageous nature of the nocturnal orgies associated with the Bacchanalia cannot be known with certainty. They were reaching their peak at a time when Rome was becoming over-whelmed by its sense of guilt regarding sex. A copy of an edict, cast in bronze and ordered by the Senate of Rome to be posted in 186 B.C., condemned the Bacchanalia and prohibited its celebration in Italy. Although the Senate of Rome apparently considered the rites to be a danger to the state, religious orgies continued to occur in Rome. The worship of Bacchus reappears in the worship of Isis, Mithras and the Magna Mater.[62]

The worship of Magna Mater, like the others, involved sex. Like the other female fertility goddesses, Magna Mater had a male "lover," Attis. Attis, however, castrates himself (thus denouncing sex), dies, and then rises again from the dead.[63]

Isis may have been another sex goddess; she too is associated with a male fertility god. She appears as a holy mother image, a precursor to the image of the holy virgin of Christianity. The writer Juvenal would have us believe that the priestesses of Isis were little more than "bawds."[64] However, some authorities do not identify Isis with sexuality at all; she may have reflected the sexual guilt feelings manifested in Rome during the Imperial Period.

More to the point would be the worship of Antinous, the boy–favorite of Hadrian. The boy, who was the catamite of Hadrian, met his death while he and the Emperor were in Egypt. Hadrian's grief led to the creation of numerous statues of Antinous all over the empire and the creation of a cult to worship his lost love. Antinous is the nearest "deity" to a homosexual god in Rome. Unlike Greece, there was no deification of homosexuality in Rome. There was no Eros in the Roman pantheon to represent homosexuality. Obviously, we can conclude that the Romans did not idealize homosexuality, even if they did engage in it. They were too austere; too stoic; too guilt–ridden to recognize pleasure without shame. They were ripe for Christianity with its fatalistic morbidity. Horace could write of the Roman: "If the universe broke and fell, he would stand undismayed as its ruins struck him." [65]

The impact of the relationship between Hadrian and Antinous must be considered in the context of the morals and ethics of the time in which it occurred. Close male bonding was common in Rome at the time of Hadrian and homosexual liaisons were acceptable. However, there were standards of acceptable conduct. Dio gives a clear indication of those standards when praising one of Hadrian's appointments: Turbo, he wrote, "displayed neither effeminacy nor haughtiness in anything that he did." [66] Thus a clear distinction is made between deportment and sexual conduct. On another occasion Dio writes about Seneca and criticizes him because "he delighted in boys past their prime." [67] Here we note that sexual conduct with boys who have not passed their prime would have been acceptable and that sexual conduct with mature men was not. As we have observed with the Greeks, it was the sexually maturing boy who was the ideal and acceptable object of homosexual expression.

The relationship between Hadrian and Antinous is a tantalizing historical marker, appearing as it does at the advent of Christianity as a social force. Rome was at the apex of its power and its new Emperor Hadrian was seeking world peace.[68] He had adopted the policy set down by the founder of the empire, Augustus, who sought to confine the imperial boundaries to their natural locations: the Rhine, Danube, and Euphrates Rivers.[69]

Much has been written about the "scandal of the centuries." [70] However, factual data are scarce. The modern historian Royston Lambert has conducted extensive research on the subject to sort out fact from fiction.[71] While these facts are important, they are not crucial to the comprehension of the impact the affair had on the contemporary public. As Lambert found while analyzing contemporary sources, "Hadrian's private sexual life has been generally ignored or treated laconically or wrapped up in sanitary euphemisms." [72]

The facts establish that Antinous was a "Greek from Bithynia."[73] From the hordes of statues and coins still extant, we know that he was strikingly handsome and athletic in his appearance. While there is "not a scrap of evidence," Lambert conjectures with assurance that there are sufficient data, both textual and archaeological, to establish the date of Antinous' year of birth as between 110 and 112 A.D.[74] There are sufficient data to assert that he was the beloved of Hadrian. Greek texts refer to Antinous as *meirakon* and sometimes *ephebe*, which are terms for boys in late adolescence.[75] The Christian polemicist Tertullian of Carthage wrote in 197 A.D., in less subtle terms, that Antinous was an "odious catamite–cum–god."[76] Hadrian caused an obelisk to be erected to honor his deceased lover and speaks of his lover as having been "taken away" from his home as a youth, thus conjuring up images of Zeus abducting Ganymede from Mount Ida. Dio states very simply that Hadrian regarded Antinous as "his love." [77] The author of *Scriptores Historiae Augustae* comments that Hadrian "lost Antinous, his favorite, and for this youth he wept like a woman" and that the Greeks "at Hadrian's request" deified him.[78]

Antinous died by drowning in the Nile in the year 130 A.D.[79] The sources are not clear on just what occurred and how it happened. The legends suggest that the young man sacrificed himself for Hadrian out of some mystical belief that Hadrian would benefit by his death. Others, like Dio, infer that Antinous was induced to make the sacrifice.[80] The impact and the drama comes from what the public believed. Judging from their acceptance of the new cult of Antinous which developed, they were impressed by the apparent self–sacrifice.

Hadrian himself declared that "a star had really come into being from the spirit of Antinous" at the time of his deification.[81] This and other imagery, especially those associated with the Eleusinian Mysteries, suggest a Christ–like status for Antinous.[82] Antinous appears in history as a precursor to Christ as a cult figure. Ironically, Antinous' cult glorified sexual tolerance; that of Christ was intolerant. By the end of the second century A.D., Emperor Marcus Aurelius refused to list Antinous among the friends of his predecessor, no doubt because he had learned from his father "to suppress all passion for young men." [83]

The Stoic creed suited the personality of the Romans and it flourished. "Cosmopolitanism" replaced the concept of national boundaries; and thus we have the precursor to "Christian brother-hood." [84] The same beliefs that supported the empire were used to justify domination by the church later on. The general malaise evoked by the stoic philosophy developed into a general sense of ascetism which militates against all pleasure, including sexual pleasures. Homosexuality continues, of course, but it is now only tolerated, and not enthusiastically espoused as it was among the Greeks.

Neoplatonism, as developed by the mystic Plotinus (c. A.D. 250), began to have its impact on Rome at this time. He considered the best life to be the life of contemplation, free from the requirements of the body; the *vita contemplativa*: "To lapse into carnal love is a sin." [85] Obviously, homosexuality would be "a sin" using Plotinus' reasoning. This marked the emerging reasoning of the Christian era.

The belief that self–denial and ascetism would lead to inner peace seems to be a natural consequence of stoic sadism. Self–flagellation replaced overt cruelty to others as Christianity emerged with its new morality. New attitudes developed for a gloomier world. Homosexuality retreated from center stage. Eros had gone, and the great god Pan was dead.

Before proceeding to analyze the changing attitudes regarding same–sex conduct as Christianity began to influence the Roman world, we should be aware of the state of the law in the empire up to that point.

The case of C. Scantinius Capitolinus was put before the Roman Senate in about the year 226 B.C., according to Valerius Maximus. As he recorded the scandal, Capitolinus propositioned the son of a Patrician, M. Claudius Marcellus. Capitolinus was reportedly a tribune of the Plebs; however, Plutarch described him as a *co-aedile* with Marcellus. He was found guilty and heavily fined. As a consequence of this case, the *Lex Scantinia* is supposed to have been enacted, and that law has been interpreted to be an anti–homosexual law.[86] John Boswell also analyzed the case, which he concluded involved a free–born youth who was defiled by someone who "had tried to corrupt the virtue of someone for whom he should have been setting an example." [87] Boswell reviewed a number of similar cases which occurred in that period. Six involved homosexual conduct and the others involved heterosexual conduct. In each case, Boswell noted, the victim was the minor child of a Roman citizen or a subordinate to an official. The cases were not brought because of homosexual conduct; the conduct was offensive regardless of gender.[88]

Derrick S. Bailey also reviewed Roman criminal cases and noted that the "Lex Scantinia" was applied in 50 B.C. in accusations brought by Pola Servius against M. Caelius Rufus, who in turn filed the same charges under that law against his accuser. Bailey contends the motive for the suits was political and the outcome was not known, suggesting that the case was of small importance.[89] To further refute the anti–homosexual intent of the *Lex Scantinia*, Boswell finds it unbelievable to have a law named after an accused.[90] Boswell also calls attention to the celebrated case which involved a young soldier in the army of Gaius Marius who killed a tribune who attempted to seduce him. When brought to trial, the soldier had to prove that he had not accepted favors from the tribune, nor had he accepted the advances of fellow soldiers: he had to prove he was virtuous and would have been defiled.[91] This reinforces the idea that it was undefiled virtue that was being protected, and not an effort to prohibit homosexual conduct. We certainly know that male and female prostitution was being taxed by the government, at least until the emperor Philip outlawed mercenary catamites in 249 A.D.[92] If the facts convince some writers that there were laws in Rome against homosexuality prior to the Christian era, then we can contend they were not enforced. The change, however, will soon begin, as we shall see.[93]

NOTES

1. Otto Kiefer, Sexual Life In Ancient Rome (New York: Barnes & Noble, 1956), p. 13.

2. Cornelius Tacitus, Complete Works, trans. A. J. Church and Wm. J. Brodribb (New York: Random House, 1942), pp. 709–732.

3. Bertrand Russell, Wistom Of The West (Garden City: Doubleday & Co., Inc., 1959), p. 108.

4. Conyers Middleton, The Life Of Marcus Tullius Cicero (London: J. Wright, 1804), Vol. I, p. 188.
   The statement appears in a letter written to Trebatius by Cicero.

5. Middleton, p. 188.

6. Russell, p. 110.

7. Kiefer, p. 5.

8. Middleton, p. 124.

9. Middleton, p. 124.

10. Middleton, p. 124.

11. Kiefer, p. 9.

12. Pierre Grimal, trans. W. S. Maguinness, The Civilization Of Rome (New York: Simon & Schuster, 1963), pp. 119–123.
    Kiefer, pp. 10–17.
    Kiefer uses the term *iustae nuptiae* for regular marriage as contracted between Patricians, as codified in 445 B.C.

13. Grimal, p. 122.

14. Grimal, p. 123.

15. Grimal, p. 123.

16. Grimal, p. 124.

17. Grimal, pp. 124–125.

18. Grimal, p. 124.

19. Grimal, p. 125.

20. Grimal, p. 125.

21. Arthur E. R. Boak, A History Of Rome To 565 A.D. (New York: The

Macmillan Co., 1947), p. 80.

22. Kiefer, p. 21.

23. Kiefer, p. 22.

24. Kiefer, p. 23.

25. Kiefer, p. 23.

26. Kiefer, p. 30.

27. Kiefer, p. 32.

28. Kiefer, p. 32.

29. Kiefer, p. 32.

30. Kiefer, p. 33.

31. Kiefer, p. 34.

32. Kiefer, p. 36.

33. Gaius Suetonius Tranquillus, trans. Philemon Holland, The Lives of the Twelve Caesars, Emperors Of Rome (New York: Heritage Press, 1965), pp. 14–15

34. Titus Petronius, The Satyricon (New York: Penguin Books, Ltd., 1983), p. 36.

35. Edward Gibbon, The Decline And Fall of the Roman Empire (London: J. F. Dove, 1825), 8 Vols.

     John Boswell, Christianity, Social Tolerance and Homosexuality (Chicago: University of Chicago Press, 1980), p. 61.

36. Suetonius, p. 4.

37. Suetonius, pp. 35–36.

38. Suetonius, p. 36.

     Suetonius quotes Julius Caesar on p. 6 as follows: "My aunt Julia... by her mother is lineally descended from kings, and her father united with the race of the immortal gods; for from Aeneas Marcius are derived the Marcii surnamed Reges (kings), which name my mother was styled with; and from Venus the Julii draw their origin."

39. Suetonius, p. 50.

40. Suetonius, p. 34.

41. Suetonius, p. 35.

42. Virgil (Publius Vergilius Maro), trans. John Dryden, 1697, The Works of Virgil (London: James Swan, 1806), pp. 10–11. One of the greatest of the Latin poets, he was born in 70 B.C. in a Celtic community near Mantua, in Cisalpine Gaul. His name, Vergilius, is Celtic.

43. Erwin R. Goodenough, Jewish Symbols in the Greco–Roman Period (New York: Bollinger Foundation, 1964), Vol. IX, p. 212.

44. Goodenough, p. 213.

45. Goodenough, p. 214.

46. Goodenough, p. 214.

47. Kiefer, p. 38.

48. Kiefer, p. 42.

49. Kiefer, p. 43.

50. Kiefer, p. 45.

51. Kiefer, p. 47.

52. Tacitus, Germany 17–19, pp. 717–718.

53. Kiefer, p. 47.

54. Kiefer, p. 50.

55. Kiefer, p. 55.

56. Kiefer, p. 57.

57. Kiefer, p. 65.

58. Kiefer, p. 72.

59. Suetonius, p. 8.

60. Kiefer, p. 80.

61. Kiefer, p. 115.

62. Boak, p. 80.
    The author was shown a replica of the plaque at Columbia University by Prof. Walter Lynn Westerman in 1949.

63. Kiefer, p. 126.

64. Kiefer, p. 129.

65. Kiefer, p. 134.

66.   Cassius Dio Cocceinanus, trans. Ernest Cary, Dio's Roman History (Cambridge: Harvard University Press, 1961), p. 457.

The historian Royston Lambert, in his book Beloved And God (New York: Viking, 1984), p. 57, discusses Dio as the principal source of information about Hadrian. He points out that Dio had a bias against the emperor since Dio was of the senatorial class which was traditionally hostile to the emperors. There is also a problem with the works themselves. The originals were lost and what we have are only the epitome of the books written by Xiphilinus of Trapezus.

67.   Cassius Dio Cocceinanus, p. 457.

68.   Aelius Spartianus, trans. David Magie et al., "Hadrian," The Scriptores Historiae (Cambridge: Harvard University Press, 1967), Hadrian IV.10–V.4, pp. 14–15.

Magie calls attention to ancient texts which show that Hadrian's predecessor Trajan had conquered the Moors, Sarmatians and the Britons, and that they were among others who were in revolt when Hadrian came to power. Hadrian chose to consolidate the empire for the sake of peace. It should be noted that the name of the author, Aelius Spartianus, is considered to be a pen name. The work was credited to six different authors writing at different times between 290 and 320 A.D. According to Lambert (see Note 66, above) recent research indicates that there was only one author, and that this contention is supported by computer analysis. Another view was offered by the historian Sir Ronald Syme in 1971, who called the work "a fraud." Lambert maintains that the first portion of the work is based on valid sources, including that dealing with Hadrian, and can be used. See Lambert, p. 57.

69.   Tacitus, Annals 1.10–11, pp. 10–12.

"All these details Augustus had written with his own hand, and had added a counsel that the empire should be confined to its present limits."

70.   Lambert, pp. 1–14.

71.   Lambert, pp. 1–14.

72.   Lambert, p. xviii.

73.   Cassius Dio Cocceinanus, p. 445.

74.   Lambert, p. 19.

75.   Lambert, p. 19.

81

76. Lambert, p. 60.

77. Cassius Dio Cocceinanus, p. 447.

78. Aelius Spartianus, "Hadrian," XIV.7–8, p. 45.

79. Aelius Spartianus, "Hadrian," XIV.6, p. 45.

80. Cassius Dio Cocceinanus, p. 447.

81. Cassius Dio Cocceinanus, p. 447.

82. Cassius Dio Cocceinanus, p. 445.

    Lambert, p. 39.

83. Boswell, p. 121.

84. Kiefer, p. 138.

85. Kiefer, p. 141.

86. Boswell, p. 63.

    Derrick S. Bailey, Homosexuality And The Western Christian Tradition (Hamden: Archon Books, 1975), p. 64.

87. Boswell, p. 63.

88. Boswell, p. 63.

89. Bailey, p. 65.

90. Boswell, p. 63.

91. Boswell, p. 64.

92. Bailey, p. 67.

    Boswell, p. 64.

93. Bert C. Verstraete, "Homosexuality in Ancient Greek and Roman Civilization: A Critical Bibliography," Journal Of Homosexuality, Vol. 3 (1), Fall 1977, pp. 79–89.

    This is an excellent reference for both Greek and Roman homosexuality, for those who might want to read further.

CHAPTER V

CHRISTIANITY: THE DECLINE

As Western Civilization approached the Christian era, law began to play a larger role in the lives of people. Before this time public peace and the orderly conduct of commerce were the primary objectives of the Roman imperial legal system. The *Pax Romana*, enforced first to assure control and next to ensure peaceful commerce, was a blessing for all citizens. Rome flourished and grew rich. Homosexuality, like other forms of sexuality, was outside the purview of the state and its laws. *Patria potestas*, the authority of the father over his family, regulated personal conduct and sexual matters where the conduct did not interfere with state interests.

Formal Roman family law was not to be an important factor in Europe as would be other aspects of Roman law. Undoubtedly this was due to the rather limited control which Rome actually exerted over the northeastern peoples of Europe, and to the emotionally charged issues involved. People tended to keep more rigidly to their own local customs regarding sex and marriage despite political and economic conquest and subjugation. It was the burgeoning Christian influence which appears to have had the greater impact on Europe in family matters, in part because of the weak legal basis for family law developed by Rome.

While it is noticeable that some Christian ideas regarding sexual conduct penetrated the body of Roman law (*Corpus Juris*), it penetrated only to a limited extent. The very lack of strong Roman legal expression in the area left room for the development of church canon law which did concern itself with marriage and sexual conduct.

As previously noted, the Roman institution of marriage was not particularly well developed. As H. F. Jolowicz stated in his book *Roman Foundations Of Modern Law*, "The question of whether two people were married or not was as much one of fact as it was of law." [1] If a woman "remained married" (*nupta preseverabat*) to a man for a year, she came under her husband's control (*manum*). The point in time when she actually became "married" is an unanswerable question which was eventually perfected after one year of "marriage." [2] The importance of this becomes apparent if we observe that the authority of the father over the children of the union was also perfected, and he became the unquestioned authority after one year of married cohabitation. Thus it was the principle of *patria potestas* which was perfected by the father over his heirs and wife.

The consideration of this phenomenon as male–centered, reflecting male dominance over the female, is the essential element in the understanding of the nature of the relationship. The married woman was legally and totally in the hands of the spouse; she was *in manum*. Cicero commented, facetiously, about the early Romans: "No one knew of legal marriage, no one had seen legitimate children of his own." [3] He was aware of the fact that as relatively late as 445 B.C. there was still no regular marriage, even among the Patrician ruling class.[4] Regular marriage developed later and was known as *justae nuptiae*.

The laws did not concern themselves with the sexual pleasures of men; they were concerned with the fidelity of women to their husbands. This was the guarantee of legally identifiable heirs of a husband, which was at the root of Roman family law. Law, like everything else Roman, was dominated by men, for the benefit of men. Once the legitimacy of their heirs was assured, they were free to philander with either available women or other men. Homosexuality was not a concern of the Romans at the opening of the Christian era.

In the early days of Rome even adultery was solely within the purview of the family, the *patria potestas*. It was as late as the time of Augustus, at the opening years of the Christian era, that adultery became a "civil crime." [5] While there was no punishment for male adultery, Roman custom allowed that a man could kill his wife if she were taken in the act of adultery. Augustus reduced the penalty to denying subsequent marriage.[6]

The *Lex Julia de Adulteriis*, which criminalized a woman's adultery, included a precursor to later church canon law. It contained the principle that marriage was "the joining of a man and woman, a partnership in the whole of life, sharing of human and divine rights." Though Rome gave up the idea of permanent marriage, the Christian church reinstated the principle. "Divine rights," also an important element contained in the adultery laws, was an element which played an important role in later Western history and the church. These early indicia of the absorption of civil law by the Christian church are significant in tracing the gradual

84

restrictions placed on human sexual expression as manifested by later church divines. Marriage arrangements seldom concerned themselves with affection. The *maritalis affectio*, marriage for love, was apparently a secondary consideration.[7] Express intention to wed was a requisite, affection was not!

With marriage relegated to a civil status legitimizing heirs, the man could then exercise his authority under *patria potestas* and be free to indulge in any form of sexual liaison he might wish, including homosexual behavior.

Except for the Patrician class, the dissolution of a marriage was as easy as getting married. At first, the Patricians had to marry for life. But, as the empire grew, divorce became easier. Although the male had to agree, either party could end a marriage. Thus there was no obligation for a husband to support his wife![8] The husband did have to return a wife's dowry upon the divorce; that economic loss would often be sufficient to make the husband do right by his wife, but he still had the last word. It is important to realize that only citizens could marry citizens.[9] While this had only a limited impact on sexual attitudes, it certainly explains the rapid extension of Roman citizenship as the empire expanded.

Eventually, Roman laws and customs came into direct conflict with the rise of the Christian church. Even when Christianity became the state religion, the issues were not easily resolved. As late as the fourth century A.D., the Christian church had little influence on marriage, which was still a civil matter. Only with the collapse of the empire did the church find an opportunity to regulate marriage and profit from the revenues it produced. Then as the church developed, it devised a new principle which regarded an engaged couple as being bound by oath to rigid rules of conduct. Being betrothed then subjected the parties to charges of adultery under the new canon law. This bit of "moral" philosophy obviously developed in the eastern part of the empire; it reflected the attitudes of the Jews and eastern Christians who derived their beliefs from Judaism.[10]

Thus we see the gradual intrusion of Judeo–Christian moral concepts into Western culture. The transition may be exemplified by comparing the first century A.D. *Lex Julia* of Augustus, which barred an adultress from further marriage, to the laws of Justinian in the sixth century A.D., which punished adultery with lifelong imprisonment in a convent. We will see that the reign of the

Emperor Justinian in the sixth century A.D. marked a new era for many questions of sexuality.

By the beginning of the sixth century, the Western Roman Empire had collapsed, leaving the Eastern Roman Empire centered at Constantinople, at the Golden Horn where the Sea of Mamara joined the Aegean Sea to the Black Sea. Strongly influenced by Greek values, it had become the Byzantine Empire, or so later historians called it. However, those who lived in Constantinople at the time considered themselves Romans.

While Rome itself was subject to barbaric invasions with Goths occupying the once imperial throne, the Eastern Empire flourished at Constantinople. With ransom, it bought off the hordes who pressed in on its borders. Thus despite its great wealth, the need for more and more money became essential for survival. To make matters even more difficult, plagues and earthquakes put an added drain on resources.

This was the age of Justinian and his empress Theodora. It was also a time when the civil authorities sought to condemn homosexuality. Just why Justinian sought to attack individuals because of their sexual orientations can only be understood in the context of the time and with some insight into the personality of the Emperor himself. Although Byzantine civilization was to endure for a thousand years, it was born at a time when the world seemed to be facing destruction. Indeed, the early Christians were preaching that the end of the world was nigh. The fall of the Western Roman Empire, the spread of the Vandals to North Africa, and the incursions by Persia into new areas gave reality to the belief.

Doomsayers produced apocalyptic literature to underscore this general flight from reality. Icons began to proliferate, especially images of the tortured divinity. The sorrowful, suffering Madonna haunted the conscience of superstitious men who in turn demanded suffering to match the suffering being evidenced by the heavenly hosts of angels, saints, and minor deities, as well as the godhead. Aside from the heavenly multitudes, they developed an extensive group of demons apparently inspired by paganism, especially Eastern paganism. Desperation inspired by religion, coupled with the reality of barbaric invasion, fostered imperial Christianity. Constantine I, the Roman emperor who adopted Christianity and moved his capital to Byzantium in the fourth century, had faced and solved some of the problems.

There were no fewer than six Roman emperors at one time. In the course of events Constantine, otherwise known as Flavius Valerius Aurelius Constantinus, made himself the sole emperor of a newly reunited Roman empire. Just before a crucial battle at the Milvian Bridge near Rome in 312 A.D., Constantine claimed he envisaged a flaming cross inscribed "In this sign, you will conquer." Being victorious, if not sincere, he became a Christian.[12] Jointly with Licinius, an imperial contender, Constantine issued the Edict of Milan and gave civil rights and toleration to Christians throughout the empire. By 323 A.D., Constantine the Christian defeated Licinius and killed him, and became sole Emperor. Christianity became the state religion a year later in 324 A.D.

In 330 A.D., he chose the small Greek city of Byzantium as the site of his new imperial capital; he named it Constantinople, the City of Constantine. Despite his public stand on Christianity, he did not permit himself to be baptized until a few years before his death on 22 May, 337 A.D.[13] Butchery and bloodshed marked Constantine's latter life. The historical scandal surrounding his baptism by Pope Sylvester was uncovered years later, when it proved that the *Donation of Constantine,* by which the Papacy claimed temporal power, was fake and entirely fraudulent.[14]

Despite Christianity's becoming imperial, the plight of people who enjoyed homoaffectionalism was not yet affected. Romans may have been made to feel shameful for their erotic expression, but not to the extent of prohibition. Thus far in history, homosexuality continued to flourish. Young men and women were still available as prostitutes as they freely offered themselves in the market. It was only in 249 A.D. that the Emperor Philip abolished the *exsoleti,* mercenary catamites; they were taxed like any business operators before that. The Emperor Philip was also known as Philip the Arab. Some Christian historians would like to claim him as the first Christian emperor of Rome; however, while his wife was Christian, he certainly was not.

The Romans, if not the Greeks, may have been made to feel shameful for their erotic expression, but not to the extent of prohibition. Thus far in history, homosexuality continued to flourish. Despite the restrictions enacted against male prostitutes, there is no indication of widespread enforcement. The prohibition seems to have been aimed at the upper class and not at the population in general.

87

Similar restrictions seem to be found in some rabbinical opinions, especially for males who assumed a passive role; both were condemned.[15] Yet the Halakah seems to exonerate males who were passive minors under the age of nine, or under the age of three in more severe opinions. While death is seemingly recommended, there is no evidence that such severe punishment was actually practiced. The threat seems to have been mainly theoretical, according to Derrick S. Bailey after he analyzed the data.[16]

One of the arguments used to sell Christianity to women was the contention that both men and women should be treated equally by the marriage and sex laws. By the third century, the *Lex Julia de Adulteriis* was being reinterpreted to cover male sexual activities, too.[17] In 390 A.D. the Theodosian Code (IX vii.6) declared: "All persons who have the shameful custom of condemning a man's body, acting the part of a woman's to the sufferance of an alien sex (for they appear not to be different from women), shall expiate a crime of this kind in avenging flames in the sight of the people." Once again, we see the words of condemnation, but find no evidence of enforcement.[18] It is both amusing and significant to note that John Chrysostom spoke out against those men who attended church merely to look lustfully at the handsome youths who also attended. Surely the practice must have been common to have him make such a public fuss over it.[19]

Saul of Tarsus, known as St. Paul, is credited with writing Romans 1:24 *et seq.*: "Therefore God has given them up in the lustful desires of their heart to uncleanliness, so that they dishonor their own bodies among themselves — they who exchanged the truth of God for a lie and worshiped and served the creature rather than the creator who is blessed forever." This statement is the prelude to St. Paul's seeming condemnation of homosexual conduct which follows. In fact, it is under that section of Romans which deals with "punishment of idolators." Presumably referring to temple prostitution, he wrote:

> For this cause, God has given them up to shameful lusts; for their women have exchanged the natural use for that which is against nature, and in like manner the men also having abandoned the natural use of women, have burned in their lusts one towards another. Men with men doing shameless things and receiving in themselves the fitting recompense of their perversi-

ty... They have not understood that those who practice such things are deserving of death.[20]

Paul is also credited with writing I Corinthians 6:9–10, which deals with "Lawsuits before pagans: Do not err; neither fornicators, nor idolators, nor adulterers, nor effeminates, nor sodomites, nor thieves... etc... will possess the kingdom of God."[21] The active words here are "effeminates" (*malakoi* in Greek, or according to the Latin Vulgate version, *molles*), and "abusers of themselves with men" (*arsenokoitai* in Greek, and in the Latin of the Vulgate, *masculorum concubitiones*). *Malakoi*, like *molles*, does seem to have the meaning of being soft or effeminate in the sense that it is a description of a person's innate quality, a natural quality that is basic to the personality. *Arsenokoitai* is the other word used in Greek, and it, according to John Boswell, is a word normally applied to prostitution. In fact, Boswell notes the Latin equivalent *masculorum concubitores* as applying to male prostitutes. Even *malakoi*, as used in Corinthians, Boswell contends, is incorrectly equated with homosexuality.[22] *Arsenokoitai*, in its most literal English translation: *arseno* means "male," and *koitai* means "fucker."[23] However, as Boswell notes, the word is ambiguous; it is not clear whether "male" is the object or the gender of the active party.

Homosexual activity was endemic at the time of Justinian and was commonly and openly practiced as a well–established custom, especially in the Greek world. But religious zealots wanted to curb all human pleasure, including human sexual pleasures. An astute monarch might well capitalize on this minority sentiment to accomplish other objectives. With the reconquest of North Africa and the need to consolidate the laws to manage the empire, Justinian saw an opportunity to use the homosexual issue for both political and economic gain.

Procopius is one of the best sources from which to judge the homophobia of Justinian. The vicious attacks he made on the Emperor Justinian and Empress Theodora cannot be ignored. In his *Secret History* (6.21) Procopius notes, "He is not interested in preserving established institutions, but always wanted to innovate in everything." To Procopius, Justinian was a malevolent force.

We can best judge any ruler by the laws he first implements upon the acquisition of power. His first enactments must be closest to his point of view. This should be especially true of a ruler like

89

Justinian who was already sharing power with his uncle, Emperor Justin, long before the Emperor died. On Justin's death, Justinian vigorously prosecuted and persecuted those he opposed. The targets of his laws were heretics, pagans, and male homosexuals. As previously noted, there were some laws which were already antagonistic to homosexuals, but they were not vigorously enforced.

At the beginning of his purge, Justinian made an overt display of his intolerance toward homosexuals by publicly castrating two bishops accused and convicted of sodomy. However, what becomes more and more apparent as the facts are studied is that Justinian was more interested in leveling the charges against the upper classes who could be extorted to have the charges dropped. Greed, not morality, seems to have been the motive. Of course, religious superstition aided this thinking. The establishment of imperial Christianity as an adjunct to the *Imperium Romanum* by the emperor Constantine was a crucial factor in tracing the sources of homophobia in Western law and religious attitudes today. It is necessary to explain carefully the facts and analyze the character of people who ultimately created the climate which incubated Western religious homophobia and injected it into Western laws. This analysis shows that two grossly amoral people, the Emperor Justinian and his Empress, with their religious minions, left a legacy of hate and persecution of homosexuals which has lasted for centuries.

In the beginning, Christianity was but reformed Judaism. It proliferated in the Roman provinces, absorbing localized religious cults in the process. The Christianity of Egypt, Syria and Asia Minor were all distinct from Latin Christianity. It was the city of Byzantium which provided the melting pot out of which modern Christianity emerged. Obviously, Byzantine Christians were strongly influenced by Oriental religious myths from beyond the borders of the empire, from Persia in particular.

It is important to study the growth and development of Byzantine civilization and its dominance to understand imperial homophobia and how it became the impetus for Christian homophobia later in the history of Western culture. Like the so–called "fall" of Rome itself, the process which induced Constantine to establish his New Rome, Constantinople, follows a very logical progression. Selecting the small Greek town of Byzantium on the Golden Horn, at the gateway of the Black Sea by the Sea of Mamara, was not a happenstance of fate, nor was it an expression of personal vanity by Constantine to name the capital of the empire after himself.

There were two key factors in the selection, and they were the same factors which accounted for the "Decline and Fall of Rome" as Gibbon called the phenomenon. The defense of the empire was the first consideration; economic security was the second factor. Logistical facts affecting trade mandated a change. The later Christian complaint that debauchery and moral degeneration brought about the decline of Roman power in the West is simply not supported by facts. Indeed, a better argument was made by Gibbon in his classic history of the decline and fall by relating the rise of Christianity to the troubles of the period. To the extent that Christianity was not logical, and was mystical rather than reasoned and factual, Gibbon correctly concluded that it ran counter to the need for a realistic approach to trade and commerce as well as defense.[24] However, Constantine had very real problems to solve. Ironically, he pragmatically used Christianity to gain very real and earthly objectives. Religiosity and deep faith had less to do with his reasoning than economic considerations.

Rome had for centuries dominated world trade and manufacturing. Rome conquered its competitors and seized their markets because monopolizing world commerce was its objective. However, as Rome proliferated and citizenship of the city of Rome was expanded to include its far flung extremities, Roman citizens were everywhere. They quickly realized that it was commercially advantageous to develop local manufacturing facilities near to markets rather than import from Italy itself. Enterprising Romans including soldiers who had served their time obtained farm lands in the provinces. They planted grape vines, olive trees and other produce once available only from Italy. Wine could be made locally and sold at a greater profit than the imported wine. Natural competition soon relegated the homeland to a minor status, and Rome and Italy began to decline as a significant commercial provider in world trade.

Furthermore, as the availability of large numbers of slaves diminished with pacification, the cheap labor force which helped build the economy was disappearing. Italy had become dependent on the outside world to feed itself.[25] Not only was the Roman population expanding, so was the population of those outside the empire. The pressures being exerted by the barbaric hordes on each other encouraged them to press in on the Roman empire. Like an endless tide, the Goths and others penetrated the extensive borders. The movement of troops and military supplies became a major problem for the central government.

Obviously the city of Rome could no longer provide sufficient manpower or talent to control the worsening situation. The emperors themselves had long since ceased being actual Romans; they were Greek, Spanish, Slavic and other ethnic and racial mixtures. By the fourth century A.D., one of the greatest threats perceived by those running the empire was the potential access of the barbarian tribes to the Mediterranean Sea by way of the Black Sea. They could easily come from the Black Sea through the Bosphorus and the Sea of Mamara on the way to the Mediterranean. It was to block this threat that Constantine built his New Rome, Constantinople, on the Golden Horn.[26] Besides that, iron ore needed for the manufacturing of military weapons was also more accessible in the East, especially from Greece. Thus trade routes and military considerations gave rise to New Rome.

To avoid the obvious vacuum in the West, with the excessive weakening of Rome itself, the concept of co–emperors was developed to maintain an imperial presence there. However, the efforts failed and Rome degenerated to a barbaric Christian state. As the authority of the once–imperial government waned, the Papacy assumed more and more authority. The Christian church leaders later concocted a fake "Donation of Constantine" to provide "proof" of their temporal authority over Rome itself. Thus they laid down a fraudulent foundation which generated centuries of bloodshed, predicated on deceit.

Against this background we should direct attention to the personalities who shaped Roman and "Neo–Roman" laws relating to homosexual conduct. The one Byzantine figure which stands out from the rest is Justinian; he was certainly homophobic. Technically he was a "barbarian," born at Tauresium in a district of Illyricum, probably on May 11, 483 A.D. He was either Teutonic or Slavic. His original name, Upravde, is Slavic and is derived from the old Slavic word *pravda*, which is translated as *Jus* or *Justitia*. According to one authority, *pravda* is a "breathing" prefix attached to Slavic names.[27] He took the name Justinianus when he was adopted by his uncle, the emperor Justin I. As a Roman, he took the official name Flavius Anicius Justinianus.[28]

Apparently he went to Constantinople as a youth and was well educated, especially in Latin. As fate and Roman politics would have it, his uncle Justin was proclaimed Emperor as a solution to civil strife. In 521 A.D. Justinian was named consul, and then in 527 A.D. his uncle proclaimed him to be his colleague in running the empire. However, Procopius, who worked in the royal palace at the time, indicates that Justin relied on Justinian much earlier than 527 A.D. "His nephew Justinian, though still quite young, used to manage all the affairs of state...." [29] Thus Justinian was very experienced when he finally came to the imperial throne in 528 A.D.

Justinian had an almost equally famous wife, Theodora. Neither of them was too highly regarded by contemporary historians, at least on moral and humanitarian issues. Procopius' *The Secret History* was almost exclusively dedicated to exposing the evils of their reign.[30] As vitriolic and critical as his book may be, there is apparently sufficient corroboration from other sources to confirm the general impression he conveyed.[31]

From Procopius it is possible to confirm that Justinian's reign was devastated by plagues, earthquakes, and famine on an unprecedented scale. He also confirms the role Theodora played in resisting their overthrow during the Nika rebellion of 532 A.D. and the gratitude evidenced by Justinian for his wife's support. Even Procopius had no specific criticism of Theodora's sex life after she married Justinian. This lends more credence to his contention that prior to the marriage she was a common whore.[32]

Apparently Theodora had a great influence on her husband and ruled jointly with him, exercising her will over every aspect of government. Thus she was a factor in the pattern of imperial homophobia reflected in Justinian's laws. Procopius contended that "She destroyed the Roman state root and branch."[33] Her father was a "keeper of circus animals" called Acacius. He was a member of a circus faction and had the title of Bearward, which was associated with a larger group known as the Greens. The Green and Blue factions of Constantinople were potent political forces among the people of the city. Her father died when she was still a child. This left Theodora's mother with the task of raising her children without the protection of her late husband's official status as Bearward of the Greens. The mother was rejected, even though she married again and offered a bribe to have her new husband get the job and the prestige of being the caretaker of the circus animals for the Greens.[34]

Undaunted, according to Procopius, the mother put Theodora and her two sisters on the stage as dancing girls. As they became mature enough, both girls became harlots.[35] The eldest, Comito, soon became one of the most popular harlots in the city. Theodora was next to go into the profession; she was described as "very attractive." As a slave girl, she appeared in the required dress, a little tunic and long sleeves.

While she was still too small to have intercourse like a woman, "She acted as a sort of male prostitute engaging in anal intercourse to satisfy customers of the lowest type, and slaves who seized the opportunity when accompanying owners were at the theater (in this revolting manner); and for some considerable time she remained in a brothel, given up to this unnatural bodily commerce." Procopius went on in this vein and noted that when Theodora was old enough she became a "courtesan of the type our ancestors called the dregs of the army... putting her whole body at their disposal."[36]

Having no musical talent nor the ability to dance, she became a comedienne and served as the foil or butt of ribald jokes and gestures on the stage. Even Procopius admits she displayed a clever wit, especially "by cracking dirty jokes and wiggling her lips suggestively (inviting) all who came her way, especially if they were still in their teens." [37]

"Often she would go to a bring–your–own–food dinner party with ten young men or more, all at the peak of their physical powers and with fornication as their chief object in life, and would lie with her fellow diners in turn the whole night long. When she reduced them all to a state of exhaustion, she would go to their menials, as many as 30 on occasions, and copulate with every one of them, but not even so (many) could satisfy her lust." [38]

Procopius makes it clear that she orally copulated with men. "(She) brought three openings into service, she often found fault with nature, grumbling because nature had not made the openings in her nipples wider than normal, so that she could devise another variety of intercourse in the region." [39] Some of the tales told about her conjure up outrageous, bawdy, ribald images: "... she would spread herself out and lie face upwards on the floor. Servants on whom this task had been imposed would sprinkle barley grains over her private parts, and geese trained for the purpose used to pick them off one by one with their bills... for she was not only shameless herself, but did more than anyone else to encourage shamelessness." [40]

When Procopius writes of her as "making her body the tool of her lawless trade," he suggests that prostitution was illegal while at the same time flourishing.[41] This is very important to notice, for it is one thing to have laws, but it is quite another to enforce them.

Theodora was a popular entertainer and was hired for private parties by the wealthy men of Byzantium. History does not record the meeting of Theodora and Justinian. Whatever her past may have been, Justinian wanted her. He wanted her so badly that he had the law changed to permit Patricians to marry their concubines. Otherwise she would have been forbidden to him. Once married to him, even her enemies had to agree she behaved herself.

As for Justinian himself, he is described as being "both prone to evil–doing and easily led — both knave and fool, to use a common phrase: he never spoke the truth himself to those he happened to be with, but in everything that he said or did there was always a dishonest purpose; yet to anyone who wanted to deceive him he was easy meat. He was by nature an extraordinary mixture of folly and wickedness inseparably blended." [42] Undoubtedly this is a biased description by someone who detested him; nevertheless, it must be considered.

Justinian was no fool, and he obviously knew how to pick subordinates with ability, including Theodora. Duplicity served him well as Emperor, and if survival is a criterion, he was an expert. Even the laws originating during his reign attest to his ability to get a project done effectively, regardless of what we may think about the individual laws or their impact on homophobia. His enemies may have hated him; he was no less capable as an Emperor.

The depth of the hatred of Justinian felt by Procopius may be gleaned from the following quotation: "In addition to everything else he was far too ready to listen to false accusations, and quick to inflict punishment. For he never ferreted out the facts before passing judgment, but on hearing the accusations immediately had his verdict announced. Without hesitation he issued orders for the seizure of towns, the burning of cities, and the enslavement of entire nations, for no reason at all. So that if one chose to add up all the calamities which have befallen the Romans from the beginning and to weigh them against those which Justinian was responsible for, I feel sure that he would find that a greater slaughter of human beings was brought about by this one man than took place in all the preceding centuries." [43]

Procopius may be a harsh critic, and his stories may be vitriolic; nevertheless he was in a position to know. He was born in Palestine, at Caesaria, in the year 499 A.D. and died during the reign of Justinian in 565 A.D. Identified as a student of law, his fame derives from his association with Belizarius. Belizarius was one of the greatest and most successful generals in history. It was he who won Justinian's victories and who protected the empire. Procopius accompanied Belizarius on his campaigns and shared his favors at the Imperial Palace. Close personal association with all the personalities of note, including the Emperor and Empress, provided the opportunity for scrutiny, and he did observe them. [44] Obviously, Justinian had high regard for Procopius' ability, even appointing him prefect of Constantinople in 562 A.D. Procopius provides necessary context with insights into the life and times of Justinian and may be used to understand the pressures which caused Justinian and Theodora to act the way they did toward homosexuality. Whether Justinian's responses were based on genuine religious beliefs or simply on superstitious fear, he did use religious pretexts for his actions. However, while he may have found religious superstitions convincing as arguments to support his attacks on homosexuals, he did not fail to profit financially by his policies. Greed seems to have provided the added element that made his homophobia practical.

NOTES

1. H. F. Jolowicz, Roman Foundations Of Modern Law (Oxford: Clarendon Press, 1957), p. 141.

2. Jolowicz, p. 142.

3. Otto Kiefer, Sexual Life In Ancient Rome (New York: Barnes & Noble, 1956), p. 9.

4. Kiefer, p. 10.

5. Jolowicz, p. 143.

    (Lex Julia de Adulteriis)

6. Kiefer, p. 32.

7. Jolowicz, p. 143.

8. Jolowicz, p. 145.

9. Jolowicz, p. 146.

10. Jolowicz, p. 150.

11. Jolowicz, p. 151.

12. David Patrick, Chambers Biographical Dictionary (London: W. F. R. Chambers, Ltd., 1902), p. 242.

    Arthur E. R. Boak, A History Of Rome To 565 A.D. (New York: Macmillan Co., 1947), p. 419.

13. Patrick, p. 242.

    Boak, p. 431.

14. Norman F. Cantor, The Medieval World 300–1300 (London: Collier–Macmillan, Ltd.), p. 131.

15. Leviticus 2:13, New American Catholic Edition, The Holy Bible (New York): Benziger Bros., Inc., 1961).

16. Derrick S. Bailey, Homosexuality And The Western Christian Tradition (Hamden: Archon Books, 1975), p. 63.

17. Alistair Sutherland, Eros (New York: The Citadel Press, 1963), p. 104.

18. Sutherland, p. 104.

19. Sutherland, p. 104.

20. Romans 1:24 et seq.

21. I Corinthians 5:9–10.

22. John Boswell, Christianity, Social Tolerance, and Homosexuality (Chicago: University of Chicago Press, 1980), pp. 340–345.

23. Boswell, p. 342.

24. Edward Gibbon, The History of the Decline And Fall of the Roman Empire (London: G. Cowie & Co. et alia, 1825), Vols. I to VIII.

25. H. W. Haussig, A History of Byzantine Civilization, trans. from the German by J. M. Hussey (New York: Praeger Publishers, 1971), pp. 31–34.

26. Haussig, p. 33.

27. Cantor, p. 131.

Encyclopedia Britannica, 9th Ed. (Edinburgh: Adams & Charles Black, 1881), p. 792.

28. Patrick, p. 545.

29. Procopius, The Secret History, trans. G. A. Williamson (Middlesex: Penguin Books, Ltd., 1966), p. 70 (6.16).

30. Procopius, pp. 94–129.

31. Boswell, pp. 173–174.

Boswell analyzed several sources including the writings of Joannes Malalas, Valesius, and Evagrius in the original Greek and finds corroboration. He finds Procopius "credible in spite of his hostility to the emperor."

32. Procopius, pp. 82–83 (9.1–9.15).

33. Procopius, p. 82 (9.1).

34. Procopius, p. 82 (9.1).

35. Procopius, p. 83 (9.15).

Since Procopius is the only source for these allegations against Theodora, fairness dictates that we notice that other contemporary writers like Evagrius or Zonaras do not say a word about her profligacy. Indeed, her reputation remained unsullied in history until Procopius was translated in 1623. See David Patrick, p. 910.

36. Procopius, p. 83 (9.15).

37. Procopius, p. 84 (9.15).

38.   Procopius, p. 84 (9.15).

39.   Procopius, p. 84 (9.15).

40.   Procopius, p. 85 (9.27).

41.   Procopius, p. 86 (9.27).

42.   Procopius, p. 80 (8.22).

43.   Procopius, p. 81 (9.1).

44.   Patrick, p. 764.

CHAPTER VI

CODE OF JUSTINIAN

Although there is a wealth of material which has survived from the period of Justinian and the years preceding his reign, some of it is unique and from one source. The writings of Procopius, especially his Secret History, are the principal source of criticism of Justinian's personal habits and the scandalous reports regarding his wife, the empress Theodora. Nevertheless, the sources are rich with details which do enable us to gain insights.

Histories flourished as a literary form, and were widely read at the time. Despite some nationalistic movements and uprisings, like those of the Jews during the first few centuries of the Christian era, the empire created a common feeling of being Roman. Thus Roman history comes from Greek, Egyptian, Slavic, and other varied racial and linguistic groups, each contributing to the details and flavor of the story. Not only are there vivid secular sources, but there is an abundance of ecclesiastical sources as well as archaeological data from which to draw. Biographies were also written in abundance at that time.[1]

For the study of the origins of homophobia, we are fortunate in having the legal codes. The code of Theodosius, for example, provides an account of imperial legislation covering the enactments of the emperors from Constantine in 312 A.D. through the year 437 A.D.[2] Not all the documentation is complete, of course; however, about eighty *novellae* (new laws) survive from the period after 437 A.D. issued by Theodosius II and Valentinian III plus a few from other emperors. The code of Justinian, which was the principal source for the growing imperial homophobia, ironically also contains those laws of the homoaffectional Emperor Hadrian, which were still in force in 531 A.D. Over 180 *novellae* of Justinian have survived along with a very few from his successors.[3]

We also have Justinian's guide to the study of his laws, the so-called "Institutes of Justinian." They form the preface, or *Prooemium*, as he called it. It is evident from these laws that religion had penetrated deeply into the secular law. The *Prooemium* begins "In the name of Our Lord Jesus Christ,"[4] and, though brief, provides the best insight into the attitude of Justinian regarding himself, his approach to law, and his rationale:

In the name of Our Lord Jesus Christ.

The Emperor Caesar Flavius Justinian, conqueror of the Alamanni, the Goths, the Franks, the Germans, the Antes, the Alani, the Vandals, the Africans, pious, prosperous, renowned, victorious, and triumphant, ever august.

To the youth desirous of studying the law:

The imperial majesty should be armed with laws as well as glorified with arms, that there may be good government in times both of war and of peace, and the ruler of Rome may not only be victorious over his enemies, but may show himself as scrupulously regardful of justice as triumphant over his conquered foes.

With deepest application and forethought, and by the blessing of God, we have attained both of these objects. The barbarian nations which we have subjugated know our valour, Africa and other provinces without number being once more, after so long an interval, reduced beneath the sway of Rome by victories granted by Heaven, and themselves bearing witness to our dominion. All peoples too are ruled by laws which we have either enacted or arranged. Having removed every inconsistency from the sacred constitutions, hitherto inharmonious and confused, we extended our care to the immense volumes of the older jurisprudence; and, like sailors crossing the mid–ocean, by the favour of Heaven have now completed a work of which we once despaired. When this, with God's blessing, had been done, we called together that distinguished man Tribonian, master and exquaestor of our sacred palace, and the illustrious Theophilus and Dorothus, professors of law, of whose ability, legal knowledge, and trusty observance of our orders we have received many and genuine proofs, and specially commissioned them to compose by our authority and advice a book of Institutes, whereby you may be enabled to learn your first lessons in law no longer from ancient fables, but to grasp them by the brilliant light of imperial learning, and that your ears and minds may receive nothing useless or incorrect, but only what holds good in actual fact.

You, who have been so honoured and fortunate as to receive both the beginning and the end of your legal teaching from the mouth of the Emperor, can now enter on the study of them without delay...

When you have compassed the whole field of law you may have ability to govern such portion of the state as may be entrusted to you.[3]

There is no pretense regarding the majesty of Justinian's imperium. Unlike the earlier emperors who ruled at Rome itself, the delusion of the Republic has been eliminated. The "Senate and the People of Rome" are not the source of authority. Justinian, Father of his country, the ever august, is simply identified as "ruler of Rome."

With all the verbiage recognizing the "blessing of God" laced through the declaration, the heavy and pragmatic hand of Justinian is reflected. The juxtaposition of God and the Emperor as the combined source demonstrates the cleverness of the propaganda used by Justinian to reinforce his claims of divine rights. He was essentially self–beatified. Such wording as "the sacred constitutions" used to describe the laws of old Rome are obviously calculated to impress the people with a sense of religious awe for laws enacted by the pagan emperors and leaders of the past.

The document also identifies the distinguished and learned jurists who were actually involved in the wording of the new compilation. It was really not a new code; it was legal house cleaning augmented by *novellae*, that is "new laws." Tribonian was the great master and legal mind behind the actual rewriting of the code. He worded Justinian's laws and defined official imperial homophobia. He was a great and gifted legal writer; indeed, it is just that skill which makes those laws so damaging to homosexuals.[4] Unlike earlier Roman legal proscriptions against sodomy and the actions of senatorial censors, Justinian's *novellae* were implemented sufficiently to influence Western law.

Justinian's compilation of laws and the definition of "justice and law" were so ably written that they must engender respect. Book 1, Title 1, "Of Justice and Law," reads as follows:[5]

Justice is the set and constant purpose which gives to every man his due. Jurisprudence is the knowledge of things divine and human, the science of the just and the unjust.

The precepts of the law are these: to live honestly, to injure no one, and to give every man his due. The study of law consists of two branches, law public, and law private. The former relates to the welfare of the Roman State; the latter to the advantage of the individual citizen. Of private law then we may say that it is of threefold origin, being collected from the precepts of nature, from those of the law of nations, or from those of the civil law of Rome.

TITLE II of The Law of Nature, The Law of Nations, and the Civil Law: The law of nature is that which she has taught all animals; a law not peculiar to the human race, but shared by all living creatures, whether denizens of the air, the dry land, or the sea. Hence comes the union of male and female, which we call marriage; hence the procreation and rearing of children, for this is a law by the knowledge of which we see even the lower animals are distinguished. The civil law of Rome, and the law of all nations, differ from each other thus. The laws of every people governed by statutes and customs are partly peculiar to itself, partly common to all mankind. Those rules which a state enacts for its own members are peculiar to itself, and are called civil law: those rules prescribed by natural reason for all men are observed by all peoples alike and are called the law of nations.[6]

Both the Prooemium and the definition of "Justice and Law" in *The Institutes* clearly show the introduction of God, divine law, and natural law into secular matters. They also declare Justinian, as emperor of Rome, to be "father of his country, ever august." [7] Obviously implied by this accolade is the assumption of absolute power over the country, as a father exercised over the early Roman family under the ancient tradition of *patria potestas*.[8]

The subtlety of the use of the title "father of his country" is particularly interesting since Book I, Title IX of *The Institutes* reflects the weakening of the power of the father as found in the Code of Justinian VIII, xi vii. *The Institutes* confirm the paternal power of a father over his children, their wives, and over grandchildren, except that according to Justinian the offspring of a daughter is no longer in her father's power but in the power of the child's own father.[9]

There were many changes taking place in the sixth century. Byzantine laws, economy, and diplomacy had their impact on the countries surrounding the empire, from the tribes of Germany to the merchants of India. The silk trade from China was important to Byzantium. Trade with the East was the dominant consideration behind the diplomacy and military ventures in the Caucasus. Countering Persian ambition was a major factor. The conflict between the two powers was the backdrop for the legal and social changes which were rapidly engulfing each; the endless struggle gradually assumed the nature of all-out warfare.

The laws promulgated by Justinian against homosexuals also attacked Jews. The spark which set off open hostility with Persia was the cancellation of the autonomy of a small Jewish community on the island of Jotabe, at the mouth of the Gulf of Akaba. In 527 A.D., Justinian had decreed a revocation of the rights enjoyed by the community. What is significant to our study of official homophobia is the emerging pattern of persecution which will repeat itself throughout subsequent history: as homosexuals are singled out for persecution, so Jews are concomitantly persecuted.[10]

In response to Justinian's discrimination against the Jews, sanctions against Roman merchants were imposed by the Arab king of Southern Arabia, who was of the Jewish faith. This was roughly in the area known today as Yemen. The caravan routes to Gaza, in Palestine, were closed. This affected the principal trade routes from ports on the Indian Ocean by way of Mecca. The Persians assisted the Arab king who was obviously responding to the persecution of Jews in Palestine and Syria, which gained momentum with the enforcement of Justinian's newly vitalized code and his *novellae*.[11] The oppressive features of this new code instigated anti-Christian excesses in Southern Arabia. This in turn inflamed exaggerated responses in Syria, Palestine, and Egypt, fanned by Roman propaganda.[12]

Thus we can trace the root sources of open conflict in the region, which laid the basis for the eruption of Islam a generation later. The open conflict strained the resources of both the Persian and Byzantine empires and left them both vulnerable to later attacks by Muslims. Mohammed could employ the military equipment and knowledge learned from both empires to challenge the power of both.

Again, what we see here is a historical pattern of interconnecting phenomena: homophobia, discrimination, and prejudices leading to major social upheavals. There is a special lesson for fundamentalists who are Jewish: discrimination against homosexuals is fashioned by the same mentalities who have organized persecution of Jews. The pattern is consistent down through the holocaust of Hitler's Germany.

The Roman law had generally spared the private lives of citizens and concerned itself more with the activities of citizens which related to the administration of government and mercantile relationships. That which concerned blood relationship, sexual conduct, and the family was left to the family itself. However, as the *patria potestas* weakened and religious institutions were imposed upon the public, the state, aided by the church, reduced personal freedom. Individuals became bound to the state and servile to the church. As the secular power expanded its jurisdiction, the church also expanded its control over otherwise personal family matters.

Earlier Hellenic civilization had championed and respected individual rights as well as sexual and family privacy. It had respected freedom and personal privacy. But those were pagan sentiments, inconsistent with the dictates of imperial Christianity.

To be sure, Justinian's laws were in many cases an improvement over earlier codes, especially where sex with slaves was involved. The prostitution of a female slave was forbidden and she was granted immediate freedom as a consequence. The code improved the lot of slaves and made manumission easier. If an unmarried man kept one of his slaves as a concubine and died intestate, she and her children became free.[13] On the other hand, the laws regulating serfs became more rigid as they were bound tightly to the soil.[14]

The influence of Christianity was in direct contradiction to the tendencies of the early empire. Augustus had found it necessary to promulgate laws designed to encourage people to marry and have children; he imposed penalties on celibacy. Penalties were inflicted on the childless and bachelors. However, under Justinian, celibate Christians and ascetics were encouraged. Second marriages were ranked almost as a crime comparable to the crime of heresy.[15]

The reorganizing of the law was one of the first projects of Justinian's reign. He issued an edict to launch judicial reforms on February 13, 528 A.D. The code was compiled with remarkable speed and was ready by April 8, 529 A.D. and put into effect seven days later. The genius of the code was Tribonian. His plan for the "Digest" (which followed the code) reduced the essential pronouncements of jurisprudential law from 2,000 volumes to 50 books. The official "Digest" of the new code was available to the world by December 16, 533 A.D. Justinian forbade any commentaries on the new "Digest" which he rendered in Latin. Only he was to be the arbiter of the meaning of the new laws.[16]

One of the important elements included in Justinian's code was the principle of "natural law." The "Law of Nature" justified "the union of male and female, which we call marriage; hence the procreation and rearing of children."[17]

The antithesis of natural, of course, is unnatural, or *innaturale*. This became the means to exclude homosexual conduct from the protection of the law by seeing it was excluded from the law of nature. We know now, of course, that this view was a misunderstanding, and that homosexual behavior exists among many species.[18]

As John Boswell pointed out in his *Christianity, Social Tolerance and Homosexuality*, Christian society equates "good" with what was "common."[19] The concept of "sins against nature" was discussed by John Chrysostom in response to the Manichean antipathy to pleasure, and his sympathy for pagan stoicism.[20]

"The passions in fact are all dishonorable," he wrote as part of *In Epistolam ad Romanos*. Ironically the argument he used was based on the concept that pleasure is not to be pursued, while at the same time asserting that homosexual activity was not pleasurable. "Sins against nature... are more difficult and less rewarding, so much so that they cannot even claim to be a pleasure, since real pleasure is only in accordance with nature."[21] St. Cyprian also objected to homosexual activities because they "could not be pleasing to those who commit them."[22] St. Paul concluded that it was excess desire that gave rise to homosexual acts, in addition to heterosexual acts.[23]

Chrysostom, never understanding why many people limited themselves to one sex or the other, merely concluded that God had abandoned them. "Whatever sin you mention, you will not name one which is the equal to this... There is nothing, absolutely nothing more demented or noxious than this wickedness." Yet he declares elsewhere "there are ten thousand sins equal to or worse than this one."[24]

What we see in Chrysostom's vitriolic attacks on homosexual conduct is the foundation for the proscriptions of Justinian's code. "If those who suffer it really perceived what was being done to them, they would rather die a thousand deaths than undergo this... For I maintain that not only are you made into a woman (by it), but you also cease to be a man; yet neither are you changed by nature, nor do you retain the one you had," wrote Chrysostom.

Then we have Augustine, himself once an ardent Manichean, who loved another man, a friend who died. In contemplating his lost lover he wrote:

"I lived in misery, like every man whose soul is tethered by the love of things that cannot last and then is agonized to lose them... I wept bitter tears and found my only consolation in their very bitterness..." The story goes that Orestes and Pylades were ready to die together for each other's sake, because each would rather die than live without the other:

> ... I doubt whether I should have been willing... to give my life for my friend... I was sick and tired of living and yet afraid to die. I suppose the great love I had for my friend made me hate and fear death all the more, as though it were the most terrible of enemies, because it snatched him away from me... I wondered that other men should live when he was dead, for I had loved him as though he would never die. Still more that he should die and I remain alive, for I was his second self. How well the poet put it when he called his friend the half of his soul. I felt that our two souls had been as one, living in two bodies, and life to me was fearful because I did not want to live with only half a soul. Perhaps this, too, is why I shrank from death, for fear that one whom I had loved so well might then be wholly dead... What madness, to love a man as something more than human![25]

He obviously changed his way of life and decided it was sinful to allow the body of a man to be used "as that of a woman... the body of a man is superior to that of a woman as the soul is to body." It was the nonsense of just such reasoning which led to strange reactions exemplified by Cassian who related the tale of terrible suffering of a young monk who "burned in an intolerable passion with the desire to submit rather than commit an unnatural act,"[26] that is, to act the passive role and be penetrated.

Despite the saintly protestations of Chrysostom and the others, most Christians seem to have recognized homosexual attraction as perfectly natural. Saint Basil, for example, while specifying techniques for avoiding homosexual arousal, wrote:

> It is frequently the case with young men that even when rigorous self-restraint is exercised, the glowing complexion of youth still blossoms forth and becomes a source of desire to those around them. If, therefore, anyone is youthful and physically beautiful, let him keep his attractiveness hidden until his appearance reaches a suitable state.
>
> Sit in a chair far from such a youth; in sleep do not allow your clothing to touch his, but rather have an old man between you. When he is speaking to you or singing opposite you, look down as you respond to him, so that you do not by gazing at his face take the seed of desire from the enemy sower and bring forth harvests of corruption and loss. Do not be found with him either indoors or where no one can see what you do, either for studying the prophecies of Holy Scripture or any other purpose, no matter how necessary.[27]

Despite his concern for temptation, Basil did not consider erotic attractions between males unnatural.[28] There was ambivalence in the late Roman empire regarding homosexuality, with only a few people strongly moved one way or the other. Justinian, however, was in a position to enforce his personal will regardless of motivation. His *Novellae* #77 and #141 set into law his homophobia regardless of any rationale other than that it was his will to do so. The religiously righteous tone of the *novellae* is significant. It gives credence to fallacy and dignifies myths as part of the law. *Novellae* #77 reads as follows:

> Since certain men, seized by diabolical incitement, practise among themselves the most disgraceful lusts, and act contrary to nature: we enjoin them to take to heart the fear of God and the judgment to come, and to abstain from suchlike diabolical and unlawful lusts, so that they may not be visited by the just wrath of God on account of these impious acts, with the result that cities perish with all their inhabitants. For we are taught by the Holy Scriptures that because of like impious conduct cities have indeed perished, together with the men in them.
>
> ... For because of such crimes there are famines, earthquakes,

and pestilence; wherefore we admonish men to abstain from the aforesaid unlawful acts, that they may not lose their souls. But if, after this our admonition, they are found persisting in such offenses, first, they render themselves unworthy of the mercy of God, and then they are subjected to the punishment enjoined by the law.

Section 2. For we order the most illustrious prefect of the Capitol to arrest those who persist in the aforesaid lawless and impious acts after they have been warned by us, and to inflict on them extreme punishments, so that the city and the state may not come to harm by reason of such wicked deeds. And if, after this our warning, any be found who have concealed their crime, they shall likewise be condemned by the Lord God. And if the most illustrious prefect find any who have committed any such offense, and shall omit to punish them according to our laws, first, he will be liable to the judgment of God, and he will also incur our indignation.[29]

Six years later this was followed by a second edict, *Novellae* #141, dated 15 March, 544 A.D., and directed solely against homosexual practices:

Preamble: Though we stand always in need of the kindness and goodness of God, yet is this especially the case at this time, when in various ways we have provoked him to anger on account of the multitude of our sins. And although he has warned us, and has shown us clearly what we deserve because of our offenses, yet he has acted mercifully towards us and, awaiting our penitence, has reserved his wrath for other times — for he has 'no pleasure in the death of the wicked; but that the wicked turn from his way and live.' Wherefore it is not right that we should all despise God's abundant goodness, forbearance, and longsuffering kindness and, hardening our hearts and turning away from penitence, should heap upon ourselves wrath in the day of wrath. Rather, we ought to abstain from all base concerns and acts — and especially does this apply to such as have gone to decay through that abominable and impious conduct deservedly hated by God. We speak of the defilement of males [*de stupro masculorum*] which some men sacrilegiously and impiously dare to attempt, perpetrating vile acts with other men.

Section 1. For, instructed by the Holy Scriptures, we know that God brought a just judgment upon those who lived in Sodom, on account of this very madness of intercourse, so that to this very day that land burns with inextinguishable fire. By this God teaches us, in order that by means of legislation we may avert such an untoward fate. Again, we know what the blessed apostle says about such things, and what laws our state enacts. Wherefore it behooves all who desire to fear God to abstain from conduct so base and criminal that we do not find it committed even by brute beasts. Let those who have not taken part in such doings continue to refrain in the future. But as for those who have been consumed by this kind of disease, let them not only cease to sin in the future, but let them also duly do penance and fall down before God and renounce their plague (in confession) to the blessed Patriarch; let them understand the reason for this charge and, as it is written, bring forth the fruits of repentence. So may God the merciful, in the abundance of his pity, deem us worthy of his blessing, that we may all give thanks to him for the salvations of the penitents, whom we have now bidden (to submit themselves) in order that the magistrates too may follow up our action, (thus) reconciling to themselves God who is justly angry with us. And we also, wisely and prudently having in reverence the sacred season, entreat God the merciful that those who have been contaminated by the filth of this impious conduct may strive for penitence, that we may not have to prosecute this crime on another occasion. Next, we proclaim to all who are conscious that they have committed any such sin, that unless they desist and, renouncing it (in confession) before the blessed Patriarch, take care for their salvation, placating God during the holy season for such impious acts, they will bring upon themselves severer penalties....[30]

It is important to notice that the text of the *Novellae* refers to homosexual conduct as a "disease" and a "plague" indicating that the concept of homosexuality as an illness is not new to modern psychology.

D. S. Bailey correctly calls attention to the "sententious and hortatory tone characteristic of their author." He also notices that no new crimes were created by the *Novellae* and concludes that the *Lex Julia* was extended to punish male as well as female adulterers, and the code of Theodosius, IX, vii, 3 and 6 defined the crimes.[31]

Justinian's use of the myth of Sodom and Gomorrah undoubtedly solidified the idea that homosexuality was the theme of that Biblical story, a conclusion not accepted before then. His *Novellae* also reflect his concern for the salvation of homosexuals and do not mandate harsh punishment. Justinian's concern regarding earthquake and famine was justified in that his reign was reportedly plagued by both. Whether he actually believed in the nexus between homosexual conduct and the destruction caused by natural phenomena hardly matters. He must have felt that he had to do something to quell the fears of the populace. Aside from the castration of two bishops and the use of the law against political enemies, it is difficult to find evidence of wide enforcement of the *novellae* against homosexuals on any grand scale. The enforcement of any such laws would be difficult at best and almost impossible over the vast empire.

The importance of the *Novellae* lies in the fact that they served as a point of reference and precedence for later bigots and oppressors of homosexuals and homoaffectionalism.

The *Novellae* were neglected compared to the rest of the *corpus juris civilis*. They were the highly personalized edicts of the Emperor himself and therefore given limited use after his death. Thus the immediate effect on Western law was minimized. Their maximal impact came much later in history.

NOTES

1. A. H. M. Jones, The Decline of the Ancient World (London: Longmans, Green & Co., Ltd., 1966), p. 3.

2. Jones, pp. 4–5.

3. J. B. Moyle, The Institutes of Justinian (Oxford: Clarendon Press, 1923), pp. 1–2.

4. Procopius, The Secret History, trans. G. A. Williamson (Middlesex: Penguin Books, Ltd., 1966), p. 142.

5. Jones, p. 5.

6. Moyle, p. 1.

7. Moyle, p. 2.

8. W. M. Gordon Holmes, The Age of Justinian and Theodora (London: G. Bell & Sons, Ltd., 1912), two Vols., Vol. 2, p. 713.

   "The despotic power exercised by a Roman father over his family, dispensed by patria potestas, was almost peculiar to that nation... By this convention wife and children were subjected to the male parent almost as completely as if they had been his slaves...."

9. Moyle, p. 12.

10. H. W. Haussig, A History of Byzantine Civilization (New York: Praeger Publishers, 1971), p. 105.

11. Haussig, pp. 105–106.

12. Haussig, p. 105.

13. Holmes, pp. 709–710.

   Quoting Seneca, De Clementia i.24, "No badge of servitude was contemplated to avoid letting slaves realize how numerous they were." See Code VII, vi; 2nd Code VII, xv, 3, for right of female slaves not to be prostituted.

14. Holmes, p. 711.

   "Any serf migrating to another locality forfeited any chance of emancipation," Code XI, xvii, 23, etc.

   W. M. Buckland, Textbook of Roman Law (Cambridge: University Press, 1932), p. 595.

15. Holmes, p. 719.

16. Robert Browning, Justinian and Theodora (London: Weidenfeld & Nicolson, 1971), p. 104.

17. Moyle, pp. 3–4.

18. R. H. Denniston, "Ambisexuality in Animals," in Homosexuality: A Modern Reappraisal, ed. Judd Marmor (New York: Basic Books, Inc., 1980) p. 29–30.

19. John Boswell, Christianity, Social Tolerance and Homosexuality (Chicago: University of Chicago Press, 1980), pp. 312–313.

20. Boswell, p. 156.

21. Boswell, p. 156.

22. Boswell, p. 157.

23. Boswell, p. 157.

24. Boswell, p. 157.

25. St. Augustine, trans. R. S. Pine–Coffin, Confessions (Middlesex: Penguin Books, 1961), pp. 75–87.

26. Boswell, p. 157.

27. Boswell, p. 160.

28. Boswell, p. 160.

29. D. S. Bailey, Homosexuality and the Western Tradition (London: Longman, Green & Co., Ltd., 1975), p. 33.

30. Bailey, p. 73–75.

31. Bailey, pp. 73–75.

CHAPTER VII

Section 1

EUROPE AFTER THE FALL

As we approach the end of the ancient era dominated by the peoples of the Mediterranean, we should take stock of the subtle changes that occurred during the centuries of transition which presage the Christian epoch. Attitutes toward homoaffectionalism and homosexuality in particular began to respond to morbid mystical beliefs about the nature and meaning of life. While the *novellae* of Justinian appear as a dramatic change in the official civil attitude toward homosexuality, their enactment reflects the results of a gradual phenomenon. As the Western Roman Empire slipped into despair and the population abandoned logic for mysticism, blind faith devoid of reason controlled the minds of the masses. Many factors and individuals prepared the way for what Justinian did in 528 A.D.

We have previously noted that the Romans demonstrated a predisposition for a fundamentalism based on their belief in their ancestors' reputations for hard work and disdain for frivolous pleasures. They developed a morality which glorified the rape of the Sabine women and exalted self–sacrifice, including suicide for the sake of honor and family image. Pain and suffering had to be stoically endured to preserve family status. In all this adaptive behavior we can detect the precursors of Christian teachings which valued the spirit, or soul, over the flesh, or body. While this put a high value on the spiritual, it rationalized cruelty and minimized empathy for the suffering of others. As the mystics gained influence, sexual pleasures including homosexual activity became morally suspect.

As the personification of sexual pleasure, women began to lose the substantial social gains they had achieved under the Roman Republic and during the early imperial period. The rights of women were eroded as Christian influence grew. Christians could boast that women and men were to be treated equally under Christian standards when it came to punishment for sexual transgressions. But the boast was shallow; it merely oppressed women more and extended that oppression to men. This was particularly true, as we shall see, with the enforcement of adultery laws. The lower status

114

of women among the invading hordes which overran the empire only exacerbated the situation.

The early Patristic struggle to preclude or discourage sexual activity clashed with the natural urge to procreate: celibacy was extolled and coition was only minimally tolerated.[1] The new emphasis on celibacy was in direct opposition to the earlier official policies of the government, particularly those policies of Augustus at the beginning of the Christian era. He struck out at the unwed and childless by enacting punitive legislation.[2]

As we have seen, it was the family which regulated personal behavior including homosexual behavior, if it were regulated at all. Some historians have made much of the celebrated scandal involving C. Stantinius Capitolinus and the son of M. Claudius Marcellus, circa 226 B.C., to focus on opposition to condemned homosexual conduct. Careful examination of the facts in that early case reveals that it was not the homosexual activity, *per se*, which was the cause of the outrage, but rather the abuse of a minor, regardless of gender.[3] The case is supposed to have brought about the enactment of the *Lex Scantinia*, but there is insufficient evidence to support that contention with any degree of certainty.[4] The shadowy references to proscriptions against homosexual conduct in pre–Christian Rome do not support the contention that there was any serious homophobia before the Christian era. However, there were early signs of things to come. The case of Lucius Quintius Flaminius in 184 B.C., for example, implied that sodomy was one of the crimes charged against him by Cato which brought about his expulsion from the Roman Senate. Yet the more likely cause of outrage in that case was not the homosexual implication, but rather the fact that Quintius murdered a man to please his catamite.[5] The Roman government was still enjoying the revenues from taxing mercenary catamites as late as the third century when the emperor Philip began to legislate against the professional catamites.[6] By that time the *Lex Julia de Adulteriis*, which had only been applied against females who committed adultery, began to be applied against males as well.[7] The word "stuprum" as associated with the crime proscribed by the *Lex Julia* had a meaning that was vague: until 213 A.D. it was defined as a sexual offense committed against a virgin or a widow, to thus differentiate the offense from that committed with a married woman, which was adultery. It was about that same time that the word "stuprum" was expanded by the jurist Herennius Modestinus to include homoerotic sexual acts with boys.[8] Other subtle changes occurred simultaneously. Julius Paulus declared that "stuprum" with a boy under the age of seventeen was a capital crime, if the crime were perfected.[9] It should be noted here that a capital crime at that time meant a crime which merited the loss of life, liberty or citizenship, but not necessarily death in all cases. With the expansion of the *Lex Julia* and the addition of the concept of "stuprum," we should not be surprised to find the change reflected in the later Code of Justinian. It is found in the title of relevant sexual proscriptions in the Code as in "ad legem Juliam de adulteriis et stupro."[10] The death penalty was suddenly stressed in the year 533 A.D. for sexual offenses.

Christian influences can be clearly discerned in the changing legal attitudes. The enactments of the Emperor Theodosius in the fourth century presage the Justinian Code:

"COD. Theod. IX. vii. 6: All persons who have the shameful custom of condemning a man's body, acting the part of a woman's to the sufferance of an alien sex (for they appear not to be different from women), shall expiate a crime of this kind in avenging flames in the sight of people."[11] How effective this law was may be judged by noting that mercenary catamites continued to flourish.[12] For all their efforts, the Christians ironically got caught in their own web in the early years: the ascetic view of celibacy which they espoused sometimes led to accusations of immorality against Christian women who were brought before Roman judges, who would impose the penalties for "stupatio" against them.[13] Women who refused husbands and marriage were considered suspect. This was the climate of sexual conduct at the end of the ancient period of the Roman world. The stage had thus been set for the medieval response to human sexuality, homoaffectionalism and homosexuality in particular.

The medieval response to homosexuality, like the medieval response to almost everything, was devoid of any remarkable intellectualizing. Nevertheless, the transitional period was extremely important to the comprehension of subsequent legalized homophobia. After the collapse of Roman authority in Italy and Europe, the region was left to be governed by primitive tribal leaders. While it would be wrong to conclude that the Teutonic tribes, the Burgundians, Lombards, Franks, Goths, Visigoths, and others were savages, they were certainly unsophisticated, living under very rudimentary conditions with simple political and economic customs.

Laws and customs develop from the exigencies of the people who fashion them. The tribes which moved in on the Roman world in the West had adequate laws and customs for their particular needs. However, once they assumed the overlordship of Roman provincials in conquered territory, important adjustments had to be made. As with all conquests, the vast and diverse peoples snared in the net of military conquest continued to live their lives and conduct their affairs as they were used to doing. Customary methods of farming, landholding, trading, and mating persisted.

Tribal harmony was the rationale for tribal laws and customs. General principles were laid down to avoid socially disruptive retaliation and blood feuds. The European tribes developed a system of value payments to compensate for wrongs done. The *wergeld* or value placed on a man was the measure of the penalty paid for a transgression by that particular man. The more important the man was in the social order, the higher was his worth, or *wergeld*. He had to pay more if he transgressed, and his kinsmen were entitled to receive more if he was slain or injured, for example.[14]

While Rome and the Hellenized world had the need to perfect a highly sophisticated legal structure, the need was not present for tribal Europeans. Nevertheless the invading tribes were aware of the need for Roman provincials to have their own laws. Indeed, it was the custom among the various tribes to judge a man by the laws and customs of his own tribe. Essentially, different men, in the same situation, committing the same act, were judged separately, according to the rules or customs of each individual's tribe, not because he had individual rights, but because he was bound to the customs of the tribe with which he was identified. He had tribal rights, not individual rights. The so–called "barbarians" who invaded Roman territory extended tribal rights to the Roman provincials and judged them by Roman legal standards as best they could.[15]

Rome itself had a similar custom in its early Republican days. They had the *jus gentium*, law of people. These laws were made applicable to the many strangers who came to Rome who could not be held to or protected by the *jus civile*, designed for Romans. The *jus gentium* were simple principles which were believed to be basic rules of personal and economic conduct common to all human beings.[16] Undoubtedly the merchants who came to Rome from all about the Mediterranean brought their commercial customs with them. These were customs based on the concept of *ratio naturalis*, or natural reason believed to be common to all peoples.[17]

In the course of time, the *jus gentium* and *jus naturale* became a combined concept. What we see here is the development of equity. But more importantly for our study of legal homophobia are the semantics of the idea of *jus naturale* or natural law. It was through the expanded concept of natural law that churchmen intruded their religious precepts into Western law. The fiction of natural law became associated in legal thinking with *aequitas* or equity as a supposed phenomenon of nature which eventually was equated with "god–given" law.

By the time we approach the Middle Ages, these subtle legal principles become blurred into a more pragmatic form. Roman law was reduced to epitomes of law. All the fine intellectual distinctions were stripped down to blunt rules. The art of jurisprudence, which developed to a high state in the Roman world, depended on a body of intellectually capable legal scholars who interpreted the laws of legislators as well as the edicts of the emperors.

The new Visigoth and Lombard rulers of Europe gleaned what they found useful in Roman law and adapted the laws to their simpler requirements. When the new conquerors of the Western world found a need to adjudicate legal problems among the former Roman provincials, they simply applied Roman law as they understood it. If there were homosexual elements in the Roman law, then those elements were applied.

One of the problems created by this continued application of Roman law was the problem of deciding which law to enforce for what reason. As it happened, a degree of homophobia was fashionable in the fifth century at the time of Emperor Theodosius II and Valentinian. Laws promulgated by them had been religiously–inspired Christian ideas, which were incorporated as intolerant of homosexuality. While little enforcement seems to have accompanied these laws against homosexual conduct, they did serve as a model for Visigothic laws to be applied to former Roman provincials.

Thus, while homosexual conduct may or may not have been of any real concern to the "barbarians," they by their own custom applied Roman law to Roman people in their territory. It seems that the earlier homophobic laws of the newly–Christianized Roman emperors had a greater impact on the emerging laws of pagan

Europe than the law of Justinian. Justinian's *Novellae* were reserved as reference to be used at a later stage of development in Western law as promulgated by the church.

The study of Roman law, including the efforts of Justinian, was reduced to a study of summaries of his code. Justinian's *novellae*, which make specific adverse reference to homosexual conduct, were known to Europeans through condensed versions. The *Epitome of Junianus*, prepared by a Byzantine scholar toward the end of Justinian's reign, was the condensation most widely used.[18]

As noted, it was the earlier Theodosian code and certain other legal works of jurists which had the principal impact on developing European law. Goth and Burgundian kings, for example, relied on these sources when codes were drawn for Roman and Gallo–Roman subjects in their territory.[19] As a consequence, homophobic legal concepts begin to appear during the formation of European law. A body of law called the *Papianus* was prepared about 502 A.D. for Gandebaud, king of the Burgundians, by a skilled Roman jurist. It was more in the form of a textbook than a code.[20] This compilation seems to be substantially the same as that used by the Visigoths in the collection of laws known as the *Breviarium*, which eventually superseded the *Papianus*, even in Burgundy.[21] The *Breviarium* was promulgated about 506 A.D. by King Alaric II for the Roman provincials of southern Gaul. It was also known as the *Lex Romana Visigothorum*.[22]

There were *Interpretatio* or interpretations accompanying the texts of the *Breviarium* itself. These interpretations soon came to be used without the texts themselves. This process continued the degeneration of jurisprudence to rules and formulas devoid of intellectual constraints. Roman law as it passed into modern European law was thus in the form of summaries, epitomes and interpretations.[23]

By the very scarcity of information dealing specifically with sodomy from original sources of the time, we must depend on more general data gleaned from the few sources we have from the early Middle Ages. To this end, let us take a closer look at the Visigoths, for whom we seem to have more information than we have on others who moved into Roman provincial areas as conquerors. Their appearance as invaders in the fourth century and their subsequent impact on the Roman empire is known in much greater detail than the records of the Alamanni, the Vandals, the Ostrogoths, or others.

Before they migrated to Spain, the Visigoths were driven from the Black Sea region to what is now Romania, south of the Danube, about 376 A.D. They were the first of the major barbarian peoples to be accommodated by the empire as a group, and given land. By 395 A.D., they began to press westward, even capturing Rome itself in 410 A.D. Finally, they migrated through southern France into Spain.

What is significant for our study is the fact that they had adopted some homophobic laws. That phenomenon becomes more understandable if we notice they were Christianized after their incursion into the former Roman province of Dacia. They even produced a Gothic Bible and were the first of the German tribes to become Christian; Arian Christians, however, rather than Catholic. Thus, since it was customary for the invaders to apply Roman law to conquered Roman provincials, the Visigoths absorbed the negative sex attitudes of Christians found in Roman territory and included negative sex ideas in its laws when applied to conquered territory.

Law for the Teutonic tribes was something to preserve the security of the tribe itself, and not to provide personal freedom. However, the overriding need to protect the larger group did leave the individual free from excess policing by the state. Essentially, sex habits were of small concern to the state. There were both real and imaginary dangers plaguing the people of Europe. Just maintaining peace and security was enough for the state and the king to worry about. The king had a duty to keep peace within the tribe, within a band of warriors. He was believed to be ordained by God with a divine right to keep the peace. Security was subsequently apportioned among groups, as among clans or families. Individuals could claim protection through the family head or the clan leader.

Warriors could choose to follow a leader of a war band and rely on him for protection and security. Concern with sodomy was of little or no interest. If we look at the *Lex Salica*, codified by Clovis about 500 A.D., more attention is paid to specific things or objects stolen, or specific injuries inflicted on persons for which specific payments were exacted as compensation for the specific wrong identified. *Wergeld*, which is a man's "price," was used as the measure of compensation. Failure to pay resulted in expulsion from protection: a person was outlawed and left to be the prey of any who might choose to harm him.[24]

With each group of unique peoples enjoying the right to their own laws, it soon became obvious that some coordination of legal customs was required. As time passed, towns, regions, and districts, rather than an individual's tribe, established the criteria used to select which law governed a particular legal question.

The relative indifference manifested by tribal leaders to the personal sex habits of their subjects was of concern to the early church. Indeed, the refusal of the early kings to interfere in basic family matters inspired the church to develop canon law. Thus it comes about that canon law concerns itself with family matters and with sexual and marriage conduct. Canon law was also influenced by Roman law, and it is through canon law that the oppressive homophobic features of later Roman law surface.

Roman law in the hands of clerics did not rise above acceptance: the approach was uncritical and certainly nonintellectual. The long period from the 7th to the 12th century is marked by a dearth of legal enlightenment. Canon law did not derive from the imperial power of secular rulers; the source was God. Clerics asserted that the canonical books of the Bible were of irrefutable validity. They tied canon law to *jus naturale,* or natural law, and by this prestidigitation transformed the authority for church law to Christ himself.

Augustine embellishes this argument by declaring, "By its authority the *jus naturale* prevails over customs and constitution." Constitution here means edicts of an emperor or other ruler. Augustine goes on to assert:

> Since therefore nothing is commanded by natural law other than what God wills to be and nothing is forbidden except what God prohibits, and since nothing may be found in the canonical scripture except what is in the divine laws, the laws will rest divinely in nature. It is evident that whatever is proved to be contrary to the divine will or scripture or the divine laws, over that ought the *jus naturale* to prevail. Therefore whatever ecclesiastical or secular constitutions are contrary to natural law are to be shut out.[25]

In studying early church law regarding homosexuality or other issues, there is the problem of false and forged documentation, which was accepted at various periods as authentic. Arguments based on forgery may be noted in the ninth century after the death of Charlemagne. Most noteworthy, and widely accepted, was a collection of false "capitularies" or ordinances attributed to Charlemagne and Louis the Pious, but actually forged by a certain deacon named Benedictus Levito of the church of Mainz. Even more infamous was the *False Decretals*, probably forged at Rheims to imitate the works of Isidore of Seville. Included were some forged letters ascribed to earlier popes, among which was the epistle or *Donation of Constantine* by which the Papacy exerted false temporal power in Italy.[26]

By the tenth century, critical methods were employed in scrutinizing earlier documents. The twelfth century saw the development of a more intellectual approach, especially at Bologna and by a monk named Gratianus at the monastery of St. Felix. This, however, did not deter homophobes from generating other rationales, especially as they began to link homosexual conduct with witchcraft. As the church gained more temporal power, or as temporal powers were able to use the church more for their own ends, new and more vicious manifestations of homophobia developed. The Christianizing of pagan Europe foisted religious homophobia on a people who do not otherwise appear to have been concerned about the personal sex habits of others.[27]

It was the Visigoth Ulfila who proselytized among his people, particularly in the mid fourth century; he preached Arian Christianity. Ulfila was created a bishop, but he was not always successful and was forced to flee when a Gothic chieftain, Auxentius, decided to persecute Christians.

He was present in Constantinople as early as 360 A.D., after the conversion of Constantine to Christianity. He must have been influenced by the recently developing homophobic trends in Roman laws. While there appears to have been little enforcement of the homophobic laws of Emperor Theodosius, the atmosphere was becoming negative toward homosexuals.

With the official attitude toward sexual conduct changing in Constantinople, and with Ulfila an eager convert himself, it becomes more significant that Ulfila translated the Bible into Gothic. This required him to invent the alphabet or utilize the newly–created Gothic alphabet. Whether he invented the new Gothic alphabet or not is not as significant as the fact that he used the new alphabet to convert the Germans. Within a few years, the so–called *codex argenteus* was to appear in the Ostrogothic kingdom in Italy, written in Ulfila's alphabet.[28] His influence seems to have been felt, even if very few Visigoths were literate.

Writing, whether runic or the newly–developed Gothic, had a great significance in the years to come. Writing was equated with magic as well as religion. In the superstitious ages which comprise medieval time, superstition, magic, and religion were to play an important role in homophobia. Vern L. Bullough is critical of the writings of Edward Westermark, who suggested that only a painful death by burning could atone for homosexual acts in the Middle Ages. Westermark gave no evidence for his conclusion. He seems to have assumed that the Justinian code was the applicable law, and that the early church fathers actually enforced it.[29]

Bullough contends that only the texts of the Visigoth law had any reference to what might be regarded as homoerotic sex. This suggests that despite Roman references in their law, the Germanic tribes did not take much interest in men's sexual practices, especially if it were private conduct not violative of any other man's property rights. The right to a woman, as we have noted, was in the nature of a property right.[30]

The only sex crime that seems to have bothered the old German tribes was the adultery of a wife! It was left to the Christian church to assume authority over other types of sexual activity, not on the theory of a property right, but as crimes against God and nature. This is the underlying rationale which was to plague people over the centuries to the present. However, Tacitus, in his *Germania*, notes:

> In their councils an accusation may be preferred or a capital crime prosecuted. Penalties are distinguished according to the offense. Traitors and deserters were hanged on trees, the coward, the unwarlike, the man stained with abominable vices, is plunged into the mire of the morass with a hurdle put over him. This distinction in punishment means that crime, they think, ought, in being punished, to be exposed, while infamy ought to be buried out of sight.

This statement indicates that "abominable vices" were capital crimes, but does not define them. They may have been included by Tacitus as a lesson to Romans, rather than as information regarding Germans.

When dealing with "infamy," its origin and use as a word are of interest. The word in Latin comes from the root word *infama*, which as an adjective, *infamis*, means disgraceful, disreputable, causing an evil report. When used as *infamis digitus*, for example, it refers to the middle finger when displayed as an accusation or an insult. Tacitus may or may not have been referring to homosexual conduct when he used the word, as above. Even if he were, we must keep in mind that he was writing to moralize, and was not above exaggeration to teach his fellow men a lesson. The significance of this item in Tacitus is that it evidences changing attitudes toward private conduct at the beginning of the Christian era.[31]

Section 2

THE MIDDLE AGES AND RENAISSANCE

Negative Christian attitudes toward sexuality and homosexuality in particular did not have as much impact on ordinary people as might be thought. Superstition at the popular level did captivate the attention of the masses and influence them to believe in a variety of strange ideas. Ignorance and fear had replaced scholar-ship and logic after the collapse of the Roman world, especially in the West.

Despite the prevalent use of the term "barbarian" to describe the early peoples who lived beyond the Hellenic–Roman boundaries, the term is meaningful only to the extent that they were "foreign." The Celtic and Germanic tribes had not reached the level of social complexity and sophistication attained by peoples of the Mediterra-nean basin; nevertheless, they had a well developed and complex culture. Like all human beings, they had sexual customs and attitudes.

Boswell writes that many commentators, among them Aristotle, Strabo, and Diodorus Siculus, described the cult of homosexuality among Celts. He adds: Germanic literature suggests very strongly that homosexuality was familiar and accepted, possibly even institutionalized.[32]

The attitude of people in southern France and Spain, in the Pyrenees, may also be indicative of general European attitudes during the Middle Ages. This region is of particular interest because it may have preserved attitudes introduced by the Visigoths in the fifth and sixth centuries after they were exposed to Christianity during their migratory sojourn in the region below the Danube.

Significantly the Visigoths became Arian Christians and did not espouse Orthodox or Catholic Christianity. Thus, the development of heresies in that part of Europe must have its roots in early Visigothic beliefs. Typical of the Germanic tribes, as we have noted, the Visigoths permitted all ethnic groups which they conquered to be judged by their own laws and customs. So it was with Roman provincials in Gaul and Spain, who were judged by epitomized "Roman Law," which had begun to include anti–sodomy statutes.

Emmanueal Le Roy Ladurie scrutinized a small village in the south of France and called his book *Montaillou* after that village. Isolated as the village was, it preserved ancient beliefs among the peasants. This provides insight into much older customs. Social and sexual intimacy was characteristic of the peasants of Mantaillou. Mutual grooming was practiced by women. Delousing implied kinship or close alliance "always carried out by a woman." This was not considered demeaning.[33]

Delousing was also performed by a mistress for her lover, the lover's mother and future mother–in–law. The future mother–in–law would also delouse the prospective son–in–law. However, people did not bathe.[34] Cleanliness was confined to the face, mouth, and hands when used for eating. Sexual organs and the anus were not included in a sanitary regimen. They accepted dirtiness as a social norm, with body odor being considered a sign of virility in men.[35]

Obscene gestures and speech were also common enough. Striking the fist against the other hand was typical of such gestures. A villager is recorded as saying: "'Do you know how God was made?', I asked Raymond de l'Aire of Tignac. 'God was made fucking and shitting', answered Raymond de l'Aire, and he struck one hand against another. 'You ought to be killed for saying such things' was the response."[36] The gesture and the reference to defecation as part of the birthing process clearly implies anal intercourse, that is, sodomy.

There were just over two hundred people in the village of Montaillou at the beginning of the 14th century. Almost all were arrested and questioned by the Inquisitors. The detailed records revealed a good deal of sexual promiscuity. Homosexuality seems to have been but one phase of general sexual activity, particularly among the young sons of the "good families" who were sent to town schools where homosexual networks developed. These were in urban developments rather than rural. Of course, it may have been less noticeable in rural areas, rather than less prevalent.[37]

The testimony of Arnold de Verniolles is revealing:

> I was between ten and twelve years old. It was about twenty years ago. My father sent me to learn grammar with Master Pons de Massabucu, a school teacher who later became a Dominican friar. I shared a bedroom with Master Pons and his other pupils, Pierre de l'Isle (of Montaigne), Bernard Balessa (of Palmiers), and Arnaud Auriol, the son of Pierre Auriol, the knight. Arnaud was from La Bastide-Serow; he had already started to shave, and now he is a priest. My brother Bernard de Verniolles was also

there, and others whose names I have forgotten.

In the bedroom shared by master and pupils, I slept for a good six weeks in the same bed with Arnaud Auriol... On the fourth or fifth night, he began to embrace me and put himself between my thighs... and moved about there as if I were a woman. And we went on sinning thus every night. I was still no more than a child, and I did not like it. But I was so ashamed I did not dare tell anyone of this sin.[38]

Testimony was obviously self–serving. After it was given, subsequent Verniolles' records show that he had other male bed partners. To rationalize his homosexuality, he related how in the city of Toulouse he gave up women:

At the time when they were burning the lepers, I was living in Toulouse; one day I 'did it' with a prostitute. And after I had perpetrated this sin, my face began to swell. I was terrified and thought I had caught leprosy; I thereupon swore that in the future I would never sleep with a woman again, in order to keep this oath, I began to abuse little boys.[39]

He seems to have been quite active, even aggressive, as a pederast. His conquests included adolescents of 16 to 18 years of age. One was Guillaume Ros, and another was Guillaume Bernard who had come to the city from the countryside. Arnaud apparently laid his young conquests on a dung heap. On other occasions he took lads to a little cabin in the country. "Arnaud threatened me with a knife, twisted my arm, dragged me by force despite my struggles, thew [sic] me down, and made love to me, kissing me and ejecting his sperm between my legs," Guillaume Fos testified.

Arnaud denied any force or violence, but did admit he performed acts of sodomy in various positions, including from behind. He described the foreplay as including dancing and wrestling and dressing in tunics. Sometimes he and his "lover" would undress one another and swear on the Bible not to ever tell. Arnaud gave little presents.[40]

Masturbation was part of the activity:

I told Guillaume Ros, in perfectly good faith, that the sin of sodomy and those of fornication and deliberate masturbation

127

were, in point of gravity, just the same. I even thought, in the simplicity of my heart, that sodomy and ordinary fornication were indeed mortal sins, but less serious than deflowering virgins, adultery or incest.[41]

The Inquisitors' records reveal a wide circle of distinguished people in the group who engaged in homosexual conduct with Arnaud. Their records show a good deal of activities in the rural areas among those who had no knowledge of urban life. The schoolboys courted by Arnaud were generally rural boys of good families, from the gentry and the bourgeoisie, who attended school in town. Arnaud declared that there were over a thousand males whom he knew were practicing sodomy. Recruiting was done among schoolboys and apprentices.

Those in religious orders were also active homosexuals: "A certain Minorite of Toulouse, son of the nephew of Master Raymond de Gaudies, left the order because, according to the monk's own accusations, its members indulged in the sin of sodomy." [42]

Arnaud, who shed this light on medieval homosexuality, was above average in education. He could read and write and in a time when it was rare, he owned books.

He was not brought to the Inquisition because of his homosexual conduct, but because he pretended to be a priest. He heard confessions, said mass, and was thus in a state of mortal sin. While his sexuality was met with some understanding, his sins against the church were unforgivable. This was true despite the obviously lustful, rather than romantic, nature of his sexual activities.

Bestiality is not mentioned in the records of Montaillou; neither was rape considered a serious matter there, except (like the taboos applied to marriage) in the case of close relatives. This attitude toward rape is indicative of Christianity's low regard for women. The Christian church could quote St. Paul to reinforce the authoritative demanding attitude toward women:

I wish, then, that the men pray everywhere, lifting up pure hands, without wrath or contention. In like manner, I wish women to be decently dressed, adorning themselves with modesty and dignity, not with braided hair or gold or pearls or expensive clothing, but with good works such as become women professing godliness. Let a woman learn in silence with all submission.

128

For I do not allow a woman to teach, or to exercise authority over men, but she is to keep quiet. For Adam was formed first, then Eve, and was not Adam deceived, but the woman was deceived and was in sin. Yet women will be saved by childbearing, if they continue in faith and love and holiness with modesty.[42]

The reluctance of early European tribal societies to overly concern themselves with sexual matters beyond a point required the Christian church leaders to find a suitable rationale for them to enforce their religiously–biased sex–negative attitudes. They then had canon law to bridge the gaps left by Roman law and social customs. "Natural Law," as evidenced by animal behavior and the presumed instinctive moral attitude expected of all people, served as the basis of canon law: "Natural law" was to be considered God's law; the law of Jesus Christ.

In the twelfth century, St. Aelred, for example, seems to have accepted the natural occurrence of homosexual conduct in nature, yet he used animal behavior to exemplify the church's negative attitude toward sexuality in general: "More sordid, if not morally worse, than those involved in vanity and worldly pomp are those in whom there is scarcely anything left whom obscene lust has not transformed into animals." [43]

As John Boswell noted, the church's attitude during the Middle Ages may have been sex–negative, yet their approach had not criminalized homosexuality. The "sin against nature" in the view of Peter Lombard, written in the twelfth century, was confined to heterosexual conduct, and illicit sex between married couples.[44] It is only after the twelfth century that we see sodomy made a civil crime, and only during the Reformation did the viciousness of religious men come to be directed toward homosexual conduct. A historian looking at the data still extant from the Middle Ages has to be cautious to evaluate its significance relative to life and attitudes as they may have been then, especially when dealing with homosexuality.

The fortuitous preservation of records by inquisitors or civil authorities provides but a glimpse of what was going on. Keeping that in mind, we can only interpret the scattered remnants by applying principles of common sense to reach a conclusion. Nevertheless, trial records and the personal journals of observers make it clear enough that human sexual expression and gratification, including homoerotic lust, were constant issues. It is not the sparseness of data that should influence our judgment, but the fact that data exist at all. Homosexual conduct, and sexual conduct in general, has seldom been a topic for popular discourse. Also, the fact that Europe suffered a decline in literacy and education during the centuries of Christian dominance which followed the decline of Rome is a major consideration. Records are very limited on all subjects, so we would not expect to find much data. The existence of a homosexual neighborhood in Paris in the thirteenth century has been reported, and it was probably not unique: "In 1270, the poet Guillot, in his *Dit de rues de Paris*, cited the rue Beaubourg as a favorite trysting place in Paris; on the rue des Marmouzets the poet himself had been served by prostitutes." [45]

Although the following is an isolated anecdote, it is noteworthy that the recognition of homosexual feelings as "natural" could still be found among the peasants in remote and rural parts of England as late as the late 17th and early 18th centuries despite the influence of the church. David Rollison analyzed the contents of a series of letters written to an absentee land owner and his heir by the local representative covering the years 1665–1744. Letters dated August and September, 1716, relate certain "outcries and abominable facts" describing an act of sodomy committed by a tenant, George Andrews, with a young "foreigner" from Gloucester, Walter Lingsey. Lingsey had traveled from his village to seek work in the fields during harvest. He managed to find employment as a servant for a time with the local churchwarden.

As Lingsey reportedly told the story to authorities, it was on the night of August 2, 1716, when he failed to go home. Instead he was out at midnight "sitting or lying on Bucklemore Bridge." George Andrews approached him and took his hand, and "began to fondle it" while paying him compliments about the softness of his skin. After a few "such niceties," George placed his hand inside Lingsey's pants and suggested that they go to Andrews' house where it would be more comfortable. In agreement, they went off together, entering the cellar where they drank ale, "nothing to excess."

From the cellar they went to the bedroom, since it was "too late to go home." There Andrews "threw Lingsey upon his belly, and then thrust his yard into his body, and after he got off desired him to acquaint nobody with what was done to him." [46]

130

Because of the allegations being made in writing to the absentee landlord, the two men were accused and brought to trial in the village. Sodomy was then a capital offense. Andrews "had been infamous for these practices formerly." By September, "The country (was) full of outcries on the abominable fact charged against the farmer." It seems that "the country" was satisfied of George Andrews' guilt. Interestingly, it was the active partner, and not the passive recipient, who was the butt of reproach.

Responding to Andrews' guilt, the local people had a fascinating way of dealing with the behavior. They had a kind of street theater which was devised to "shame... the abominable fact." There had to be a "mock groaning."

What this meant was that a street party would be organized by a man who was expert in such proceedings. People were called upon to provide food and drink. One man "got a sack of malt, and made some very good ale;" several others took up a collection and bought "some younts [sic] of meat and other belly timber." A certain blacksmith was called in because he had recently organized a similar affair in his home parish. A youth was hired to play the fiddle and be accompanied by another who made music "with a key and tongs in consort." There was costume wearing and cross–dressing. The word had gone out to villagers and farm hands in the surrounding area: the "crime" was to be reenacted in the main street on September 22, 1716. Lingsey was dressed as a woman. One Rolfed Luckinton dressed as a midwife and assisted Lingsey in having a baby, fashioned of straw. They called it a male child and then pretended to christen it in the churchyard. They called it "George Buggarer or Buggary, charging the godfather to see it was brought up in the same religion or profession." A case was brought against the villagers as well as the two men who were accused of sodomy. But the village people simply did not testify and nothing could be proven. Thus the matter had to be dropped.

What this shows is a popular acceptance of homosexuality and a complete disregard of both church and state authorities, regarding the official negative attitudes. Obviously, this phenomenon is indicative of a general relaxed attitude toward sexuality in general, rather than overt support for homosexuality *per se*. Aside from the ribald context of "buggary," the sexual behavior of people, other than adultery, seems to have been one of healthy disinterest. Not unexpectedly, Lingsey, an unmarried youth, apparently not only worked as a farm hand but also as a household servant. As Alan Bray points out in his book, *Homosexuality in Renaissance England*, it was common in 17th century England and America to have young unmarried boys and girls as domestic servants. Bray cites a study by Edward S. Morgan covering the Puritan Middlesex County of Massachusetts. There were apparently advantages for unmarried homosexual servants, since their presence in the household would arouse no suspicion. Furthermore, bastardy was a far more noticeable problem which did attract the local justices. Illegitimate children were an unwanted economic burden on the community. Homosexuality became an attractive alternative.[47]

Section 3

SODOMIA

The power and influence of the Roman Catholic Church have been major factors in shaping attitudes toward homosexuality down through the ages. Its hostility toward human sexuality in general has been an endless source of misery for people living in the Western world. To study the depth of the church's negative obsession toward homoeroticism is to trace the development of the legal theory which criminalized homoaffectionalism. The works of P. Ludovico Maria Sinistrari are an excellent source of insight into that theory: in particular, his book *De Delictis, Et Poenis Tractatus Absolutissimus* (A Definitive Critique of Crime and Vengeance), Chapter XI, entitled *Sodomia*, published in Latin at Rome in the year 1754.

He wrote his books a century earlier in the seventeenth century but very few copies are extant or available. Translations are difficult to find, and those are rarely found in public libraries. A serious difficulty with the translations is the use of obtuse reference to the subject matter discussed. For example, rather than refer to anal intercourse, "preposter copulation" is used. "His yard" is inserted into the anus, not "his penis"; "preposter vase" is used to describe the anus, and a lesbian is referred to as a tribade (from the Greek, "she who rubs").[48]

Interestingly, the chapter on sodomy follows Sinistrari's exposition on effeminacy which he entitled Chapter X: *Mollities*. The issue of effeminacy as separate from sodomy is important to notice. Attitudes toward "softness" or "unmanliness" have been observably viewed separately from homoerotic sex *per se*. This was especially true in the ancient world and in the early Middle Ages. St. Anselm, for example, often complained about the unmanliness of king's courtiers in twelfth century England and spoke out about their "mincing steps" and "curly hair," yet he seems to have been homoaffectional, if not homoerotic, in his personal taste.

This raises the issue of who is truly homosexual, the passive catamite or the aggressive sodomite? The ambivalence raised by the question is demonstrated by recorded testimony of persons who submitted to, rather than were tempted into, performing the role of the sodomite aggressor, thereby engaging in the self–deception of passive virtue by being penetrated.

133

Sinistrari is described on the frontispiece of his book as a member of the Order of St. Francis. Specifically, he was of the Order of Reformed Minors of the Strict Observance of St. Francis. He was born at Ameno, Italy, on February 26, 1622, and attended the University of Paris where he became Professor of Philosophy. Apparently a gifted speaker, he was also well built and attractive. His gifts, handsome face, and athletic appearance made him a popular guest at the tables of men in high places. Furthermore, Sinistrari was a courteous man who was well liked by his peers. Most of all he was intelligent. His many talents attracted attention in Rome, where he was called to be consular to the Supreme Tribunal of the Most Holy Inquisition. The Inquisition was operated by the Holy Office, directly under the Pope. The Holy Office, which included judges, officials, and the necessary personnel to conduct the Inquisition, was created by Pope Paul II in 1542. The system was perfected under Pope Sixtus V at the end of the 16th century.

Since the Pope was ultimately the head of the Inquisition, it was he who selected the cardinals who ran it. Its jurisdiction extended throughout the Catholic world.[49]

Sinistrari was appointed as a coadjutor to one Claude Pertuyse, who had already spent about thirty years in the post. Later in his life, Sinistrari acted as theologian to the Cardinal Archbishop of Milan, Federico Caccia. He died at age 79 in the year 1701.

Although reprinted in part, his complete works were apparently not collected and published in full until they appeared in three volumes during the years 1753–1754. What he produced is a clear and definitive epitome of the church's position on homosexuality. It is from the *Complete Works* of 1754 that Chapter XI, *Sodomia*, is presented here. There was more than one view on sexual morality at the time and in the century preceding 1754, but the views expressed by Sinistrari were those espoused by the Papacy. That makes them especially noteworthy.

Sinistrari's work is a fascinating epitome of canon law as it defined the Catholic Church's thinking regarding sodomy. It defines the guidelines recommended to the Inquisitors of the Holy Office who tortured and maimed thousands of people in the name of God. Sadism had found its way into civil law in the Western world.

It is necessary to be keenly aware of linguistic devices when dealing with church material. To translate the title word by word may seem straightforward enough, yet words like *delictis* and *poenis* have various connotations which shade their use. *De delictis* can be translated as concerning "crimes" or "offenses," for example, and *de poenis* may be translated as concerning "punishment" or "vengeance." The choice here is to translate them as "crime" and "vengeance" to reflect the obvious purpose of the church's treatment of unrepentant sinners, which is vengeance rather than remedial punishment.

Although Sinistrari's works are of a much later period than we have been analyzing, they are indicative of the thinking of the Catholic Church as formulated over a period of centuries regarding sexual conduct, sodomy, and the role of women as sex objects. Similar to Sinistrari in tone and attitude toward women are the writings of Heinrich Kramer (Henricus Institoris) and Hames Sprenger, "Malleus Maleficarum" (The Witch Hammer), dating from about 1486.[50] Again, Kramer's work reflects attitudes developed over the previous centuries.

What these works reveal is the ugly, distorted disdain for women which is so prevalent in anti–homoaffectional writings. While there is no reason to expect male rejection of females as a necessary concomitant aspect of homoaffectionalism, it does manifest itself in a perverse way among those who also condemn male homosexuality. The phenomenon is particularly apparent among the early church fathers. It became exaggerated as the church developed its policy of "celibacy."

St. Paul makes it clear in his writings that women are subject to their husbands: "... let wives be subject to their husbands... paying honor to the woman as to the weaker vessel..." (I Peter 3:1–2, 8–9). Even the definition of a virgin in the Apocalypse is curious: it is a man who was "not defiled by women; for they are virgins...." Thus, licit or illicit, sex with a woman "defiles."

The more we look at the Bible the more it is apparent that moral confusion has resulted from the popular tendency to rely on ancient authority based on old–time religion. Ultimately, authors like Sinistrari and Kramer relied on the authority of the Bible and interpretation of the Bible. We hardly have to consider Augustine of Hippo, Thomas Aquinas, or other thinkers of the Middle Ages who were constricted in their reasoning by the scholastic system; conformity to predefined religious tenets ordained by the church was truth by definition. Thus, before we scrutinize Sinistrari and Kramer, we should look again at some of the Biblical sources.

In Matthew 19, discussing divorce, a man is permitted to set aside a wife for "immorality," and a man would commit adultery if he married a woman who had been "put away." The anti–feminine stance is quite clear. As for marriage, "Let him accept it who can." In Acts 15, there is a clear inference against engaging in sexual intercourse with women as a prerequisite to being blessed by the Holy Spirit. The anti–marriage theme is found in I Corinthians 7: "But I say to the unmarried and widowers, it is good for them if they so remain, even as I. But if they do not have self–control, let them marry, for it is better to marry than to burn (in Hell)."

With a strong anti–feminist bias evidenced by the Bible, it is not surprising to find the writings of the Inquisitors perfecting the theme. Kramer in *The Malleus Maleficarum* engaged in extreme, perverse male homoaffectionalism which degraded women as evil incarnate. In "Question VI," concerning witches who copulate with devils, he asks the question, "Why is it that women are chiefly addicted to evil superstition?" [51] The very question begs for the answers. In his discussion, Kramer simply assumes women are "so fragile a sex" they are prone to evil and immorality. "Women," he concludes, "know no moderation in goodness or vice; and when they exceed the bounds of their condition they reach the greatest heights and the lowest depths of goodness and vice... when they are governed by an evil spirit, they indulge in the worst possible vices." [52]

Kramer goes on a vicious tirade against women:

Now the wickedness of women is spoken of in Ecclesiasticus XXV: There is no head above the head of a serpent: and there is no wrath above the wrath of a woman. I had rather dwell with a lion and a dragon than to keep house with a wicked woman. And among much which preceeds and follows about a wicked woman, he concludes: All wickedness is but little to the wickedness of a woman. Wherefore St. John Chrysostom says on the text, It is not good to marry (S. Matthew XIX): What else is woman but a foe to friendship, an unescapable punishment, a necessary evil, a natural temptation, a desirable calamity, a domestic danger, a delectable detriment, and evil of nature, painted with fair colors! [53]

Sinistrari's analysis of church laws for use by Inquisitors at Rome in the seventeenth century contains the same kind of condemnation of women as found in his predecessors. However, he goes a bit further and suggests that women might have been the original culprits who caused men to engage in sodomy:

The practice of sodomy was caused by barren women, some make this preception, motivated, as it happens, by the writings of St. Paul to the Romans, Ch. I, v. 26, which speaks of the punishment prescribed by God for Philosophers, who had knowledge of God, yet did not glorify him as God. Indeed, their women changed from natural use to that which is against nature. Such lewdness was first invented by Philaene, and it affected that ill–famed poetess, Sappho, who invented sapphistic poetry, as declared by Cornelius of Lapid in Epistles to the Romans... on the other hand this is not considered true, if before the time of the writer Philaene, we read in the scriptures of the ruination of Pentapolis, who was infamous because of this, as it is exposed in Genesis, Ch. 19. There, the true issue concerns the nefarious sin with men; wherefore it is possible that female sodomy began long after, with the Greek Philaene.[54]

Thus by the end of the Renaissance we see the phenomenon of male homoaffectionalism manifesting itself in a perverted form, which glorifies male dominance in a religiously–inspired patriarchal society. There is an irony in this: for the very men who so adamantly denounced male homoaffectionalism when manifested in homoerotic behavior nevertheless respond to homoaffectionalism to glorify the dominant male as the only suitable leader of church and state. They degraded women concomitantly.

NOTES

1. New American Catholic Edition, The Holy Bible (New York: Benziger Bros., Inc., 1961), I Cor. 7:3–5; 7:7–8.

    Reluctantly Paul agrees to permit sex in marriage: "Return together again lest Satan tempt you because you lack self–control. But this I say by way of concession, not by way of commandment. For I would that you all were as I am myself," that is, celibate.

2. Robert M. Grant, Augustus to Constantine (New York: Harper & Row Publishing, 1970), p. 12. He notes (p. 271) that only unmarried Christians could be baptized in the Syrian church during the second century.

3. Derrick S. Bailey, Homosexuality and the Western Christian Tradition (London: Archon Books, 1975), p. 3.

4. Bailey, p. 65.

5. Bailey, p. 66.

6. Bailey, p. 66.

7. Bailey, p. 67.

8. Bailey, p. 68.

9. Bailey, p. 68.

10. Bailey, p. 69.

11. Bailey, p. 72.

12. Bailey, p. 72.

13. Grant, p. 271.

14. Katherine Fisher Drew, trans., The Lombard Laws (Phila.: University of Pennsylvania Press, 1973), p. 8.

    "The value fixed for a freeman's life was known as his 'wergeld' or 'man value'. The amount varied, depending on whether or not a man were Roman or German or whether he was a member of the clergy or not. But even if he were German, the 'wergeld' might also vary from man to man. Among some of the barbarians... the 'wergeld' varied according to the social status of the individual... among some... the 'wergeld' for all social classes was the same but varied according to sex and to age."

15. Pierre Rich, Daily Life in the World of Charlemagne (Phila.:

University of Pennsylvania Press, 1978), pp. 11–12.

16.   Henry Osborn Taylor, The Medieval Mind (London: Macmillan & Co., Ltd., 1938), Vol. II, p. 262.

17.   Taylor, p. 263.

18.   Taylor, p. 271.

19.   Taylor, p. 271.

20.   Taylor, p. 271.

21.   Taylor, p. 272.

22.   Taylor, p. 272.

23.   Taylor, p. 272.

24.   Katherine Fisher Drew, The Burgundian Code (Philadelphia: University of Pennsylvania Press, 1972), p. 27.

25.   E. A. Thompson, The Visigoths in the Time of Ulfila (Oxford: Clarendon Press, 1966), pp. v–vi.

26.   Taylor, p. 295.

27.   Taylor, p. 299.

28.   Thompson, pp. xxii–xxiii.

       The Codex Argenteus was written with silver ink on purple parchment. It disappeared for about one thousand years following the destruction of the Ostrogothic kingdom by Justinian. It reappeared at the monastery of Werden on the Ruhr near Essen in the middle of the sixteenth century. From there it was taken to Prague where it was to pass to the Swedes in 1648. They took it to Stockholm. Queen Christina used it to pay off her debts in 1654. It went to Holland in 1665. Count Magnus Gabriel de la Gordie, a Swedish nobleman, bought it. In 1669 he gave it to Uppsala University. It is still there, in the library.

29.   Edward Westermark, Christianity and Morals (reprinted, Freeport, N.Y.: Books For Libraries Press, 1969), pp. 363–373.

       Vern L. Bullough, Sexual Variance in Society and History (Chicago: University of Chicago Press, 1980), p. 348.

30.   Bullough, p. 349.

       He cites the Visigothic law found in MGH, Leges, Karl Zummer, ed. (Hanover and Leipzig: Hahn, 1902), et al.

31. Tacitus, Complete Works (New York: The Modern Library, Random House, Inc., 1942), "Germany," Sec. 12, p. 714.

    Well preserved bodies of men executed and thrown into bogs in Denmark seem to prove Tacitus was right. The tannic acid in the peat has a remarkable property of preserving bodies. One victim found at Gravballe had had his throat slit.

    Bamber Gascoigne, The Christians (London: Granada Publishing, 1978), p. 66.

32. John Boswell, Christianity, Social Tolerance and Homosexuality (Chicago: University of Chicago Press, 1980), p. 183.

33. Emmanuel le Roy Ladurie, Montaillou (N. Y.: Vintage Books, 1979), pp. 141–142.

34. Ladurie, p. 142.

35. Ladurie, p. 142.

36. Ladurie, p. 144.

37. Ladurie, p. 144.

38. Ladurie, pp. 144–145.

39. Ladurie, p. 145.

40. Ladurie, pp. 146–147.

41. Ladurie, p. 147.

42. I Timothy, 2:8–15.

43. Boswell, p. 303.

44. Boswell, pp. 227–228.

45. Stephen Murray and Kent Gerard, "Renaissance Sodomite Sub–Cultures" (unpublished draft dated June 22–24, 1983).

46. David Rollison, "Property, Ideology and Popular Culture in a Gloucestershire Village 1660–1740," Past & Present (Oxford No. 93, November 1981), pp. 70–98.

    I am particularly indebted to Kent Gerard at the University of California, Berkeley, for calling these data to my attention.

47. Alan Bray, Homosexuality in Renaissance England (London: Gay Men's Press, 1982), p. 47.

48. P. Ludovico Maria Sinistrari, "Sodomia," De Delictis, Poenis Tractatus Absolutissimus, Romae, MDCCLIV. In Domo Caroli Giannini

Librorum Sanctitatis Suae Provisoris in Platea Capranicensi, pp. 230–246.

The translation was by Paul D. Hardman. An English version was published by Collection "Le Ballet de Muses" in 1958 with an introduction by the Rev. Montague Summers and printed in Paris.

49. Solange Alberro, La Actividad Del Santo Oficio De La Inquisicion En Nueva España 1571–1700 (Mexico: Instituto Nacional de Anthropologia e Historia, 1981), p. 11.

50. Heinrich Kramer, et al., Malleus Maleficarum, trans. Rev. Montague Summers (New York: Dover Publications, Inc., 1971), p. vii.

51. Kramer, p. 41.

52. Kramer, p. 42.

53. Kramer, p. 43.

54. Sinistrari, trans. Hardman, p. 233.

CHAPTER VIII

THE MAMLUKES

Islam, like the Byzantine Empire, was the direct heir to the legacy of Rome and ancient Greece. For many centuries, the main repository of ancient learning, mathematics, and philosophy was in the Near East and North Africa. Given the important role of male bonding, homosexuality, and homoaffectionalism as a cultural stimulant in the ancient Near East, it is not surprising to find that it would continue being important in the Islamic era. Islam, at least as far as male sexuality was concerned, has been characterized as a "sex–positive religion."[1] One of the most significant expressions of homoaffectionalism in Islam was the governing institution of the Mamlukes.

First we should look for the origins of Islam and the social attitudes in which it grew. This will bring us back to the Byzantine emperor Justinian and the promulgations of his legal code in 529 A.D. As we had previously noted, the persecution of homosexuals under the new code was concomitantly enforced along with persecution of Jews in the empire. Justinian's suppression of the Jewish population of the island of Jotabe at the mouth of the Gulf of Akaba sparked hostilities with the Persian Empire, which came to the aid of the Jews.[2] By 602 A.D., a great war began between Byzantium and Persia which was to consume the energies and resources of both powers until the year 628 A.D. Muhammad was born in the year 570 A.D. and began to preach about 613 A.D.[3] His militant followers were able to take advantage of the weakened imperial giants and as a result could sieze vast portions of their empires for Islam.

Muhammad's new religion also used the Bible and the traditions of Abraham from the Old Testament. He declared himself the latest prophet and wrote the Koran to replace the Bible. Despite this linkage with the god of Abraham, or perhaps because of it, Islam was feared and hated by Christians. Islam presented a powerful challenge to Christianity that was both military and ideological.[4] Mecca, where Muhammad was born, had already become a religious center as well as a trading center. His parents were of the powerful Qurayah tribe, and according to Adb-al-Rahman Azzam, his immediate family on his father's side were Hashemites and thus part of the ruling oligarchy which ruled Mecca and the neighboring tribes.[5] His family was important, but not rich. As a youngster he tended sheep, then later engaged in business. He became an economic success at age twenty-five, when he married a rich older widow. They lived together until she died twenty-five years later; she bore him four daughters and two sons. Only his daughter Fatima produced heirs[6] and her descendants later introduced factionalism into Islam. They were to be the Fatimid faction which was in control of Egypt after the tenth century when the Mamlukes were introduced there. It is with Egypt and the Fatimids that we shall begin to observe homoaffectionalism in the Arab world, particularly among the Mamlukes.

In translating the word "Mamluke," William Poppen accepts the explanation of Taghri Birdi that *mamluk* means "one owned"; "a slave"; "a white slave," its plural being in the Arabic form *mamalik*. Obviously the extra schwa vowel in the middle of the word results from the blending of the singular and plural of the Arab word when anglicized. The antithesis of the word *mamluk*, Poppen notes, is *malik*, which means "possessor" or "king" when applied to a member of the military elite or to a sultan. It indicates that the state of a purchased slave boy is originally *mamluk*; manumission can be inferred as the *mamluk* advances by promotion to the title *malik*. The classification "slave" should not be confused with the low caste of blacks in subjugation in the pre–Civil War southern United States. The Mamlukes may have been purchased and bound to a master; they were still high in the social order, trained to be leaders, warriors, and rulers. The Mamlukes were the ruling military caste. They were not of any one race, especially at the beginning of the system when there were a large number of Turks among their ranks. Later, after the collapse of the Fatimid dynasty in 1171 A.D., they were primarily Circassians or Georgians. All were purchased as slave boys and then carefully trained for military and civil duties by their masters.[7] It was a unique system, amazing and extremely successful if we may judge by the extent of their power and the longevity of their empires. Their loyalties were not to wife, home, and country but rather to their master, trainer, and benefactor, the man who bought them and gave them everything.

It should be noted at this point that this study has been confined to Mamlukes who were not Mongols. While Mongol Mamlukes played an important role in the Islamic world, they involve a separate set of facts which should be studied independently.

Muhammad, as we noted, left no male line. He had powerful cousins, the Umaiyids, who stretched the empire from the Atlantic to China in the years that followed. By 750 A.D., however, they were challenged by other cousins, the Abbasids, who established their capitol at Baghdad. While the earlier Umaiyid empire was characterized by military conquest, that of the Abbasids was noted for its splendor.[8] As with the ancient Romans, splendor brought wealth and fostered decadence. The Abbasids were no longer interested in fighting if they could hire mercenaries to do it for them. Thus they began an expansive trade in slave soldiers acquired from the nomadic Turkish tribes who were inhabiting the steppes to the north, in what is now Russia. These were tough men of great prowess who were seemingly invincible.

Using such mercenaries, the Abbasid khalif Mutasim (832–842 A.D.) soundly defeated the Byzantine army. Mutasim is described as "a man of dominant personality" to whom his mercenaries were "devoted."[9] While the word "devoted" means nothing by itself, it begins a pattern of strong personal attachment which comes to typify the relationship between Mamlukes and their masters. Weakness was not to be tolerated, however, and when a series of weak khalifs attempted to succeed Mutasim, they were deposed by Mamluke guards. Not unlike the Praetorian Guard of ancient Rome, the palace Mamlukes found they could install or depose their rulers. The realization of this power saw the fragmenting of the empire. The various provinces became centers of power controlled by Mamlukes.

In the meantime, the Islamic world developed extensive trade routes from China to Spain. Wealth attended the great China and India trade as it passed up the Persian Gulf to Baghdad. But not unlike the modern states of Iraq and Iran in the same area, religious fundamentalism got out of hand and disrupted the trade. The merchants sought and found friendlier routes through Egypt, which became a flourishing new center for trade. Before then, Egypt had been a secondary province. Its new ruler was the former slave Ibn Tulun (868–884 A.D.),[10] who was a just and capable administrator. The reorganization of Iran and Syria in 905 A.D. did not induce the trade routes to return to Baghdad. About this time Dailamite tribesmen from south of the Caspian Sea overran western Persia, and by the year 945 A.D. they had taken Baghdad. This provided an opportunity for another branch of Muhammad's cousins to bid for power. For the most part, since 656 A.D. it had been the Abbasids who had held power. Now the descendants of Muhammad's daughter Fatima and her husband Ali made their move for the khalifate at Baghdad. Their supporters were called the "Shia," or party. The Shiites siezed power in North Africa and founded the Fatimid dynasty there in 972 A.D.[11] Thus we have the Umaiyids in Spain; the Fatimids in Egypt; and the Abbasids in Iraq.

In 1055 A.D. powerful tribes of Seljuk Turks broke into the Abbasid Islamic empire from the north and took Baghdad. Soon the crusading Christians were storming in from the west. Essentially they were both barbarian hordes invading a cultured world. Fortunately for the Christians, they arrived in 1097 A.D. after the death of the powerful Seljuk sultan Malik Shah. The historian John Bagot Glubb is convinced that, had the sultan still lived, the Crusaders would never have been able to enter Syria.[12] The Christians, however, did hold Syria from 1097–1291 A.D.[13]

Egypt, then under the rule of a former Turkish slave, Ibn Tulin, brought the country under the influence of the khalifs at Baghdad. The khalifs were considered the successors to the Prophet and ruled from Baghdad as religious and temporal leaders. They had for many generations utilized thousands of slaves for both military and civil service. The slaves served as bodyguards and as the force used to keep rebellious Arabs in line. These slaves were Mamlukes. The same practice was adopted in Egypt during the Fatimids. Thus, when the sultan Saladin declared the end of the Fatimid khalifate in 1171 A.D., Mamlukes were well entrenched in the system. He united Egypt and Syria in 1187 A.D. to create a new unified empire. When the Saladin dynasty became extinct in 1252 A.D., it was the Mamlukes who took the throne and established a dynasty of their own.[14]

The writer Alan Moorehead asserted that the Egyptians were not quite so decadent as the West has liked to imagine. They were particularly conservative and their rulers, the Mamlukes, were no less so.[15] In keeping with Islamic tradition, the Mamlukes were generally "abstemious," their meals being rather simple.[16] Moorehead, like others, takes notice of the origin of the Mamlukes as being purchased as children, and in the latter period, primarily from Circassian and Georgian tribes. He reviews their training in horsemanship as warriors and their eventual absorption into the ruling oligarchy. Specifically, he calls attention to the fact that the Mamluke boys were taught to regard marriage and family as fatal to their caste. To marry an Egyptian woman, for example, was to suffer degradation. They were to pride themselves on the fact that they were selected for special training and to be the beneficiary of their master, whom they would succeed.[17] "Without relatives, without children, their past was a blank."[18]

What we have here is a unique phenomenon in history: young boys were purchased, then trained to be the companions and the eventual heirs of a master who truly cared for them. They in turn devoted themselves to the master, and all his endeavors, with a remarkable degree of loyalty. Devotion and loyalty, however, were not accorded to weak masters. Loyalty was ruthlessly earned by forceful deeds by the master. Loyalty was not directed toward the state nor to any other leader who might seek support. The bond between the Mamlukes themselves and their masters can in fact best be described as homoaffectionalism.

The extent to which homosexuality was involved has been alluded to by many writers, though few chose to be specific. Islamic writers at the time did not concern themselves with the sexual conduct of their subjects, since homosexual activity was so commonplace.

Later writers continue to dwell on the wars and political intrigues and focus on mayhem more than on the details of private lives. However, European writers allow themselves to be shocked and thus, even when they would prefer to avoid the issue, they cannot resist moralizing in passing. It is essential to scrutinize secondary sources and then search out primary sources for confirmation. The writer John Bagot Glubb is a useful source since he relied on his own translations of original source material from Islamic writers like Ibn Taghri Birdi, Maqrizi and Ibn Iyas.[19] For the same reasons, the author Sir William Muir proves useful.

In reading the European sources, whether primary or secondary, it is necessary to keep in mind that we are dealing with an alien culture which was despised and misunderstood by Europeans and subject to bowdlerization. To compound the problem, the Islamic writers used an annalistic approach to history, and concentrated more on the wars, biographies, and obituaries of great men, with little information regarding their sex habits.[20] Indeed, some of the practices which seemed to have attracted the attention of Europeans were not considered unusual enough to warrant historical discussion.

The fact that the primary source writers generally used annalistic techniques in writing their chronicles also precludes much in the way of background, or detailed personal reporting. However, it is possible to use secondary sources to find the clues to data bowdlerized in the translation of the primary sources, limited though they may be. One of the less inhibited writers in this area is Allan Edwardes, the author of *The Jewel in the Lotus*.[21] Edwardes also included a section on "Eastern Sex Habits" in a book by R.E. L. Masters and Edward Lea called *Sex Crimes In History*.[22]

Edwardes provides very few citations for his statements, but he quotes a certain nineteenth century Dr. Jacobus regarding "the ferocious lust of the African Arabs...," concluding:

> The Arab is the greatest sodemist [sic] in the whole world... Woe betide any handsome young man who falls into the hands of Bedwawin [sic] rapists. They will commence by robbing him of all he has, not leaving him even a shirt. What follows need not be described, but they take turns abusing his anus and penis, and sometimes even his mouth![23]

Edwardes explains the Arabic term *el-lewati* ("the men of Lot") as referring to the Biblical Lot who lived in Sodom, and identifying them as members of sex clubs of "fanatic homophiles." The root word in Arab *luti* is given as the source of the word "loot," which has been associated with theft, pimping, and prostitution, especially involving sexual assault. Again quoting the unidentified Dr. Jacobus, Edwardes recounts "the personal testimony of a dozen or so Moslem merchants and travelers who were robbed and raped by the 'Luti'." The Arabic expression *shallehhuh tishlihh* is then described as a common expression which is translated literally to mean "to rob or strip" or "to make one undress oneself," with the connotation that the victim would be stripped, robbed and sodomized.[24] These data are included here to suggest the prevailing attitude in that part of North Africa where the Mamlukes lived and ruled. Noting this, it is essential to understand that the followers of Muhammad were no less "moral" than Christians, they merely had a different attitude regarding sexuality. The Koran does not condone or specifically condemn homosexuality *per se*. Its position is not much different than the Hebrew or Christian Biblical texts. While excesses are considered wrong, Islamic belief permits everything to be seen as

God's will and in a sense preordained. Essentially the Koran allows for human weakness with a greater degree of forgiveness and thus tolerance than does modern Christianity. The very expression in Arabic *Mashallah* ("It is God's will") enables the Muslim to ward off self–condemnation. Thus no matter how reprehensible an act may be, it would not have occurred if it were not the will of God. Conscience then becomes an intellectual exercise and not a religious deterrent to sin. The belief seems to assert that while religious and civil authorities may condemn and punish human conduct, only God may ultimately judge the actor.

In the late nineteenth century Sir Richard Burton made a name for himself by shocking the sensibilities of the Victorian world. He wrote "scandalous things" about the sex habits of Arabs and others in the so–called Sotadic Zone, where passions ran high. While it is sometimes difficult to separate fact from fiction in Burton's writings, we should note that he delved deeply into Islamic homosexuality.

Edwardes, however, does quote Burton frequently in citing the repugnance of Middle Eastern people for menstrual and hymenal blood. This, Burton suggested, may account for the attractiveness of boys to Muslims. Since they are "clean," there is a religious aspect suggesting that homosexual relationships are pure and fraternal. As another rationale for endemic homosexuality in the Muslim world, Edwardes focuses on circumcision, comparing the sex habits of men who are and are not. While his logic is unconvincing, he does make a point regarding Islamic circumcision which may have some bearing on the gratification possible as a result of the method used in circumcising boys. According to him, all the integumental flesh was torn from the penis shaft, thus reducing gratification to the friction of the glans. This method also reduced the size of the penis, which made vaginal sex less satisfying to men and sodomy more satisfying.[25]

Concentrating more on the Egyptian *felaheen* or peasant, Edwardes notes that they were encouraged to enjoy every variety of sexual gratification. As youths they engaged in "excessive genital manipulation and sodomy."[26] If we ignore Edwardes' value judgment "excessive," it is possible to confirm aspects of his conclusions from a study made by the Egyptian anthropologist Hamed Ammar. In the 1950s, Ammar studied an especially remote region where customs and habits had not been altered for centuries.

This was in Aswan Province, Egypt.[27] He studied three broad social groups: boys and girls up to age 12 or 13 (jahhal); unmarrieds (fityan); and both men and women who were married. He noticed that there was no free mixing of male and female adults, and for youngsters it was considered "impolite" for them to sit with men. Young boys were permitted to act as serving boys to men; the very young wore skullcaps while the older unmarried youths wore turbans. They would act as messengers for men at social gatherings and also pour libations. The unmarried young men would also wear a special gown, a "tab," and carry a staff. There was no mixing with women even at the social gatherings; it was "unthinkable."

Women and girls lived in an almost completely separate sphere around the home. There was much separation by gender. While women could adorn themselves with ornaments, men did not. Distinctions were made even in little things. For example, only men were permitted to cut hair. Women were expected to draw out their words as they spoke; men were not. Men could point with their index finger; women had to use the middle finger. When expressing shame, surprise, or regret, a woman would slap her face with her open palm; a man would express the same emotion by slowly clapping his hands. Men and women refrained from looking into each other's faces. Only age relieved the elderly of obeying these customs.[28]

Sexual behavior was equally regulated and distinguished for men and women. Sex–related customs were also quite different. Circumcision, for example, for boys occurred when they reached the age of from three to six years, as part of an elaborate ceremony. For girls, circumcision, which was a kind of mutilation, was performed when the girls were about seven or eight years of age, in private and with the father showing no interest.[29] Nothing in the Koran calls for circumcision, which came from pagan days as part of Arab tradition. The circumcision of girls was more of an attempt to curb the sex drives of the girls when they reached maturity, thus insuring women's pre–marital chastity.[30] Sexually provocative, demonstrative behavior, even by a wife, and certainly intimate physical behavior by a wife, was totally discouraged in public, and there was apparently very little contact at home during the day. The men would leave for the day after being served meals. Women ate only with other women. A wife could not eat with her husband until she bore him a child that lived. A wife was not even allowed to address her husband by his name, but rather as "lord" or "husband." Sons were expected to show deference to their fathers, and never sit in his presence while he was standing, and were never to sit with him.[31]

It was the husband who ruled the family and regulated the social activities of his wife. Sexually, the wife was expected to be submissive to her husband. She also had to be respectful and absolutely faithful. Preference went to the husband in all things; even food had to be served to the husband before the children. The wife was expected to open doors for her husband, pour his bath water, and tend to his needs. Despite this description of the relationship between a man and his wife, the husband treasured his wife. She headed his domestic household, kept his keys, and managed his financial affairs and guarded the family legal documents.[32]

In the village, a child's sex organs were openly discussed, being referred to as *bulough*. A girl's menstruation was noted. Boys reaching maturity were a topic of conversation: "he whose sweat has become odorous" or "he unto whom life has entered." At that point boys were given greater freedom. Girls, on the other hand, were more tightly restricted, especially as they developed breasts. Breasts and sex organs were hidden after puberty as a source of shame. Sexual conversation between male and female youths was strictly forbidden as a taboo subject. Sex talk with parents was also forbidden.[33] Sex became a source of fear and as the prohibitions mounted a new bio–social phenomenon was observed: a greater dependence on adults.[34] While there was no word for masturbation, it was the custom in the village for the adults to manipulate the genitals of infant boys. Relatives would fondle the children while admiring them. Jokes about homosexuality were also common in the village.[35] Boys were highly prized in a family. A man with seven male children was highly respected, whereas a girl child was actually feared as a source of shame to the family. Religion was used to modify any expression of disappointment over having a girl child, since it was a sin to show disappointment.[36]

Ritualistic cleanliness was important. Sand or soil could be used in the absence of water to cleanse oneself from sexual pollution. Both a man and his wife were required to cleanse themselves in a prescribed way to free themselves of sexual pollution. It was not for sanitary or medical reasons, but religious ones, that they cleansed

150

themselves. Disease, they believed, was the result of either a failure to fulfill a religious duty or failure to give a promised offering to a saint's memory.[37] The evil eye also caused illness. They thought that it was ultimately God who afflicted or cured disease.[38] To ward off the evil eye, blood had to flow. To protect a baby, a ram would be killed and the baby passed over the flowing blood seven times to assure that the life of the animal was taken in exchange for the life of the baby. This tradition, they believed, was supported by the prophet Abraham.[39] Blood was shed at marriages, and before going on a pilgrimage.[40]

There are other sexual and religious customs which would relate to the Mamlukes. Wielding power had a strong tradition. "If one wields power, one must be forceful, otherwise one is not respected." Indeed, a compassionate administrator would be called effeminate names.[41] The use of such names had nothing to do with sexual proclivities; it was being like a woman in attitude that was derided. This did not mean that a man could not be charitable and show mercy or hospitality. It was strongly believed that "he who is hospitable will never suffer in this world."[42] This tradition was so strong that it was forbidden to sell milk or bread. Selling these basics would bring shame to the seller; bread and milk were to be given freely to the needy.

The traditions and habits of the Egyptian *felaheen* or peasants also reveal insights into the attitudes of the Mamlukes who ruled them. Edwardes concluded, based on observations confirmed by Richard Burton, Gordon Pasha, and Colonel James Neill and other European officers:

> Not a few of them eventually destroy their manhood and become strict, neurotic pederasts. Satyriasis and nymphomania were common among them; erection and nocturnal and other emissions through reflex action were over common... 'Thrust your finger into the fundament of a Toork [Egyptian] and he will pollute his raiments. Brush past him from the fore and his carnal implement stab thee ere ye can run away.'"

Then Edwardes quotes an old saying: "the Toork would much rather defecate than have intercourse with a woman, for the inestimable pleasure derived there by."[43] Continuing in this vein, Edwardes contends that the bag–trousers *shirwaul* and the typical gown *tobe* as worn in Egypt concealed the constant erections of the men. Edwardes, in classic nineteenth century attitude, described the Turkish soldiers in Egypt as "effeminate" because they showed erections on parade. He declared that at first it was "humorous, then disgusting, then utterly depressing." [44] This attitude among European observers toward the Muslim world is frustratingly common. To them at first blush, sexuality is titillating, but bold confrontation becomes "depressing." However, it is this very defect which makes it possible to glean some measure of truth. These writers could not resist moralizing, and thus commenting, on the subject which might otherwise go unrevealed. Others, like Burton, could not resist scandalizing their readers.

Edwardes describes the common practice among Egyptian men of organizing in a circle to engage in what he calls "round–robin sodomy." An impressive sight, he contends: "fumbling and chaffering with their buttocks laid bare." Resorting to an unnamed "Arab philosopher," Edwardes asserts that it was said that "the Toork is insulted if, in the least, ye do not tickle his hinder parts," then he goes on to admire the reputed "size of his penis (and) his insatiable capacity for 'sotadic' love." [45] He declares that the Arabs and others in the Eastern world "held an uncanny, perhaps instinctive reverence for the phallus... a vigorous, fecundate symbol of power." [46] Edwardes then quotes from Lord Godfrey Elton's book, *General Gordon*, in which Gordon refers to Egyptian soldiers as "effeminate brutes," again reflecting European sexual bias, equating homosexuality with effeminacy. He quotes Gordon ten years later in 1885: "as far as my experience goes... all Turks and Circassians in Egyptian employ are emasculated."

Although the Mamlukes as a class became extinct after the eighteenth century, it should be noted that it was the Circassians who made up the main numbers of the later Mamlukes. [47] To make the point even stronger, Edwardes quotes another unnamed source regarding the nineteenth century Egyptian ruler Mohammad Tewfik Pasha Khedive: "he is a hateful passive; and his yawning fundament has endured the uncircumcised prickles of sundry unbelievers." [48]

Not content with applying European standards to Mamlukes, whether Turk or Circassian, Edwardes took notice of the sodomitic behavior of Sudanese Negroes whom he described admiringly as "virile as a bull." [49] In a very patronizing way he accuses the Islamic conquerers of brutalizing blacks:

152

The witless Negro, taken unawares and deluded by false traditions, became sorely depraved. Naive, he fell an easy prey to the wiles of alien men who lusted after their statuesque body. Guided by the worldly Turk, the Sudanese native abandoned his free and unassuming mode of life and plunged headlong into the fetid slough of Western degradation... he came to learn and practice every vice known to mankind... with a shortage of Negresses, he adopted sodomy. The Turk, insanely jealous of the Negro's strength and masculinity, sought gleefully to seduce him into decay. And blacks, like inquisitive children, fell victim." [50]

Obviously racist nonsense, this is the kind of information which has been disseminated by historians regarding the Mamlukes.

Without going too deeply into black African history, it seemed appropriate to test the views of Edwardes and others regarding African blacks and same-sex conduct. Anthropological studies among the Zulus revealed that when a man kills another he may not mix freely in society until he undergoes a process of fortification against certain diseases. To achieve this the person must live entirely apart from his village, and may not take up residence again until he has sexual intercourse with some female not of his own tribe, or in the case of necessity with any boy.[51]

Lesbianism was also discussed in the Zulu source, referring to "the case of a woman who marries a wife. These cases are rare but they are known." In one case there was an old woman whose relatives were killed by disease. She had a lot of cattle and took a young girl as a wife by courting her and paying the bride price or *lobolid*. When children were wanted, the older woman hired an unrelated man as a "bull" to impregnate the wife. Although the man was paid for his services, the legal father was the woman who hired him.[52]

Focusing again on the Turks, Edwardes quoted from popular pornographic verses: "Avoid the Turk, for he either eats you out of love or, in a rage tears you to pieces." Edwardes cites ample quotations from undisclosed sources: "Ogres, satyrs, and anus-bruisers, the lot of them. The Turk is a dog. There is no two ways about it. He worships the devil. The Turk would deign to take my tool in mouth." According to Edwardes, the common signal used to solicit a man for sodomy was to insert the thumb between the index finger and the middle finger. Quoting "Russian sources," Edwardes accuses the Turks of killing a man on the battle field and taking "full sexual advantage of the anal spasms." Again quoting the source: "It is, to be sure, effendi, a most devilish matter of expert timing."[53] As noted previously, Edwardes suggests that there is a play on the name of Lot, of Biblical fame, in Arabic, used to describe sexual behavior. The word in Arabic *el lyte* is used to describe a "pillaging" male whore; a band of such men were referred to as *Lewwautee*, which also means "professional sodomist." Accordingly their favorite motto is given as "the penis, smooth and round, was made with the anus best to match it; had it been made for vulvas sake, it would have been formed as a hatchet."[54] Edwardes contends that the word "gink" comes from the Arabic, which is given as a word for transvestites who were expert sodomites. The word for "fig" in Arabic also was given a sexual connotation, and was slang for "anus." The very act of inserting one's finger into one's anus was said to imply approval. Burton was given as the source for that contention.[55]

While it is difficult to corroborate Edwardes' stories through English sources, nevertheless there are more scholarly references which lend credibility to what he suggests regarding rampant homosexuality among the Mamlukes. The staid Victorian historian Sir William Muir makes reference to the subject despite his obvious distaste for the topic. In the pages of his book *The Mameluke or Slave Dynasty of Egypt* will be found such comments as "the Vizier, a pervert, still suspected of Christian tendencies, was attacked by a great body of Mamlukes."[56] In another section of his book, Muir describes the twenty year old who became Sultan Abr Bekr in the year 1341 A.D., as follows: "This youth... misguided by the youths with whom he spent his nights in dissipation."[57] Again he wrote about one Ahmed, in the year 1342 A.D., as "now twenty-four years of age, and still living a life of shameless self indulgence." Muir continues in this tone, disapproving of conduct that has broad sexual overtones.[58] Muir concluded that Ahmed had "a dissipated and cruel reign."[59] Muir follows the history of the period after Ahmed's death, and takes notice that two of his brothers came into power as youths, and each was slain in his turn. One of the brothers, at age fifteen, was referred to by Muir as an "abandoned youth." Muir found the year of the brothers, 1345 A.D., to have been "a time of debauchery, worse, if possible than anything that had gone before."[60] Muir also identified another "pervert" as a vizier in August of 1351 A.D.[61]

The history of Egypt, and the Islamic empires generally, had been a long series of intrigues, murders, and problems created by those seeking power through the rule of hereditary sultans supported by various factions of Mamlukes. Until the year 1346 A.D., the Mamlukes in control of Egypt were Turks. That year, however, the regent was a Circassian Mamluke who was ambitious to see that Circassians took power. The first move was made about 1347 A.D., but the time was not ripe; the Black Death was spreading over the land killing people by the tens of thousands. The plots and intrigues of the Mamlukes are not of principal concern in this context. By the 1350s, the Circassian Mamlukes had a firm hold on the throne, and as was their custom, replaced themselves by purchase. Al Mahmoodi, for example, came to the throne in November 1412 A.D. and assumed the title Al Mueyyad, which meant "the victor," when he became sultan. He was originally purchased from a Circassian dealer by the emir Berkuck. From courtly page boy, he rapidly advanced to "Emir of one thousand."[62] His was a classic rise from purchased slave to ruler. He was a Circassian totally different in race from those he would rule, put in place by a predecessor who was himself purchased as a slave. Thus by the bonds of homoaffectionalism, a system of governance was established and perfected which successfully ruled a mighty civilized empire for centuries.

An exhaustive and definitive study of Mamluke chronicles was undertaken by the historian Donald Presgrave Little. He asserts that there are really only three important primary sources covering the earlier Mamluke periods. Reviewing these, however, is to go through a maze of annually recorded wars, slaughters, victories, and obituaries. The translators do not write very much regarding the private sexual habits of the subjects. As we have seen, the sources indicate that the Arab world was much more tolerant of private sex habits than the Christian world.[63] Little gives an excellent insight into the formal structure of the relationship between the Mamluke and his master. The loyalty of a Mamluke was firstly to his *usted* or master, who was the last to purchase him and the one who ultimately freed him. His second duty was to his comrades, his *husdasiya*, who were purchased or served with him in slavery and were freed by the same master.[64] While this system was based on homoaffectionalism and created solidarity within the group, it was also the root source of dissention with reference to those outside the group. Thus while the ruling sultan could build up a cadre of loyal Mamlukes, he could not depend on the loyalty of the Mamlukes of his chieftains. According to the thirteenth century historian al-Amir Alam ad Din Sangar Ibn Abd Allah as-Suai, a duty of loyalty is owed to the son and family of the master: "The mamluk al-Amir Zain ad-Din Kitugua... is the mamluk of the Sultan and has best right to preserve the son of his *usted* and the house of his *usted*."[65] Little also cites other sources to show that loyalty was due to a son of a master, and that that loyalty had precedence over the loyalty due to a fellow Mamluke.[66] With the rise of Circassian Mamlukes and the decline of the Turks, Little notes the greater loyalty to each of Circassians.[67] This may have less to do with race than with a change in Mamluke education. Until the fourteenth century Mamluke boys were kept segregated by race while in training, thus keeping their own language and customs. At the time of al-Malik an Nasir it was realized that it was better to mix the boys together and avoid racial divisions, making them unified in their loyalty to their masters. "Splendid garments, golden girdles, horses, and gifts in order to astonish them" were considered more important; "If the mamluk sees prosperity fill his eye and heart," according to Nasir, "he will forget his country and prefer his *usted*."[68]

These male/male endearments were also extolled in Islamic literature. Islamic poets were fond of idealizing youths and their physical appeal. The poet Ibn Sara of Santarem wrote (in the thirteenth century):

See, his beard is sprouting yet,
Beauty's fringes delicate;
Delicately through my heart
Passion's thrilling raptures dart.[69]

Hafiz of Shiraz was the pen name of Shams Ad-Din Muhammad, a contemporary of Chaucer in the fourteenth century. His love poems about youths are famous and are credited with influencing the Shi'a sect of Islam, which developed a concept of romantic love which has in turn been credited with influencing romanticism as it spread into Europe in the Middle Ages. This was a romanticism inspired by homoaffectionalism.

The Sufis included "good fellowship" and comraderie among their

156

theories of discipline. Al-Kalabadhi makes this point in a review of literature of the Khalifate period (632–1050 A.D.). "Love is an inclination of the heart," wrote Al-Junayd. "Love is concord," wrote another. "Love means preferring what one loves for the person whom one loves." For the Sufi: "Love is a pleasure." [70] Consistent with that philosophy, the poet Hafiz of Shiras wrote:

> At dawn's first breath the nightingale said to the opening rose: 'Less of the jilt, please, plenty like you have blossomed in this garden.' Laughing, the rose replied: 'The truth won't vex me but no lover says harsh things of the one he loves.'

Hafiz also wrote the following:

> With locks dishevelled, flushed in a sweet drunkenness, his shirt torn open, a song on his lips and wine–cup in hand. With eyes looking for trouble, lips softly complaining. So at midnight last night he came and sat at my pillow. He bent his head down to my ear, and in a voice full of sadness he said: 'Oh, my old lover, are you asleep?' [71]

By 1243 A.D. a Spanish Moor, Ibn Said al-Andelusi, had compiled an equally erotic anthology of poems.

From the vantage point of the Islamic empires, the onslaught of Crusaders from Europe must have appeared as barbaric invasions, certainly as barbaric as the invasion of the Mongols. Islamic writers have tended to use the word "Frank" to describe "any European," and particularly a Christian Crusader. Some Muslim writers even equated "Frank" with the term "heathen." [72] Yet with one difference, for the Christians, like the Jews, were people of the Bible. The rude, semi–literate Christian hordes which penetrated the Islamic world during the Crusades became reacquainted with ancient culture in the process. It is in these cultural encounters that we can trace the influence of homoaffectionalism. It was in the growing awareness of the ordinary Crusader that cultural exchanges must have been affected upon returning to Europe. They encountered male bonding, homosexuality, and homoaffectionalism.

Without laboring the obvious, the influence of Islamic culture on the West has been quite considerable. The Christian Crusaders of the eleventh and twelfth centuries brought back more than a taste for spices and silks from "the Holy Land." They rediscovered ancient learning, mathematics, and philosophy. They also encountered open homosexuality and manifest homoaffectionalism. In addition, they discovered the pleasures of taking a bath.

The reinstitution of the bath house as a social phenomenon in Europe has had an enormous impact on sexual freedom. The very name "Turkish bath" indicates the source of the cultural change. The new awareness of homosexual pleasures and secular attitudes toward the subject cannot be ignored. Wayne Dynes and Warren Johansson covered the subject in an unpublished study which noted that bath houses had become "secular cathedrals" in the East, where previously Christians had been strongly discouraged from enjoying such body pleasures. By the twelfth century, bath houses had been established in Europe and had achieved a reputation of being "notorius places of sexual daliance." [74] In the fourteenth century, both Chaucer and Langland were using the word "stew" to mean both bath house and place of prostitution. The same notion appears somewhat later in the use of the term "bagnio," according to Dynes and Johansson. This is particularly important since initially, in the twelfth century, public baths were restricted to men. This meant that any sexual contact at bath houses would have to have been homosexual.[75] Clearly then, the Islamic tolerance of homosexuality was influencing Europeans.

At the end of the eleventh century the English monk Eadmer quotes his master St. Anselm, complaining that:

"At this time it was the fashion for nearly all the young men of the Court to grow their hair long like girls; then, with locks well–combed, glancing about them and winking in ungodly fashion, they would daily walk abroad with delicate steps and mincing gait. Accordingly, Father Anselm [Archbishop of Canterbury] made these things the subject of a sermon delivered at the beginning of Lent... Those whom he could not recall from this degradation he suspended from reception of ashes and from the blessing of his absolution." [76]

The English king, William Rufus, rebuffed Anselm on the issue. But Anselm wrote back to the king, decrying:

"That most shameful crime of Sodomy... but lately spread abroad in the land, has already borne fruit all too abundantly and has with its abominations defiled many. If it be not speedily met with sentence of stern judgment coming from you and by rigorous discipline on the part of the Church, the whole land will, I declare, become little better than Sodom itself. I beseech you, let us two make a unified effort, you with your power as king, I with my authority as Archbishop, to establish some decree against it such that, when published up and down the land, even the hearing of it will make everyone that is addicted to such practices tremble and be dismayed." [77]

To which the king replied, "Enough, say no more about it." While it may be too far–fetched to state that King William Rufus was directly influenced by the cultural impact of Islam, it nevertheless demonstrates the attitude of the king and the cultural climate at the time, which would make the acceptance of new ideas from the East more understandable, at least in England.

Whatever the impact of Islamic culture may have been on Europe in the Middle Ages, the homoaffectionalism found among the Mamlukes can be clearly seen in their institutions as a factor influencing the Crusaders. The colorful lifestyle of the Mamlukes came to an abrupt end, once attacked by Napoleon in 1798 A.D. While the institution may have lasted a bit longer in the remainder of the Turkish empire after that, the Mamlukes never had the control or influence which they enjoyed in Egypt. Unfortunately for the Mamlukes, they had not kept up with the modern techniques of warfare and they were simply no match for cannon.

The history of the Mamlukes is probably the best example in world history of an all–male society which successfully perpetuated itself as a governing body, generation after generation, and century after century. This continuity would not have been possible except for the homoaffectional relationship between master and the boy whom he would educate to succeed him. It was a strategy for governing, and for living, in the context of a culture which accepted homosexuality as a natural part of human existence.

NOTES

1. Vern L. Bullough, Sexual Variance in Society and History (Chicago: University of Chicago Press, 1980), p. 205.

2. H. W. Haussig, A History of Byzantine History (New York: Praeger Publishers, 1971), p. 105.

3. John Bagot Glubb, Soldiers of Fortune (London: Hodder & Stoughton, 1973), p. 42.

    Abd-al-Rahman Azzam, The Eternal Message of Muhammad, trans. Caesar E. Farah (New York: Mentor Books, 1965), p. 27.

    This author contends that the exact date of Muhammad's birth is disputed, but "it is agreed" to be around 570 A.D.; he cautions readers to question all dates of famous men in the Arab world.

4. Wilfred Cantwell Smith, Islam in Modern History (New York: The New American Library, 1957), p. 109.

5. Azzam, p. 29.

6. Azzam, p. 30.

    Fatima was the mother of Hasan and Husan by her husband Ali, the fourth Khaliph; their descendants are known as Ashaf.

7. Glubb, pp. 7–10.

    The name "mumluk" according to Glubb has only two syllables in Arabic, and therefore should not be spelled "mamaluke" as is so often done. However, different authors do use various spellings: "mumluk"; "mameluke"; "mamlouk"; and "mamlook." William Poppen in his translations of the XV century historian Abu-L-Mahasin Ibn Taghri Birdi used the spelling "mameluke" when he explained the origin and meaning of the word in his History of Egypt 1392–1469 A.D. (Berkeley: University of California Press, 1954), p. v.

8. Glubb, pp. 21–23.

9. Glubb, p. 23.

10. Sir William Muir, The Mameluke or Slave Dynasty of Egypt (London: Smith, Elder & Co., 1896), pp. 1–3.

11. Glubb, pp. 24–26.

12. Glubb, p. 32.

13. Muir, p. xiv.

Muir recommends the *Geschichte des Chalifen,* by Dr. Gustav Weil, the latter half of the third volume and the beginning of the fourth, for information on the rise of the Mamlukes.

14. Abu-I-Mahasin Ibn Taghri Birdi, History of Egypt 1382–1469 A.D., trans. William Poppen (Berkeley:University of California Press, 1954), p. v.

     According to Donald Presgrave Little (see footnote 20), page 87, Abu I-Mahasin Gamal ad-Din Yusef ibn Tagi Birdi [sic] died in the Muslim year 874, which is circa 1469–1470 A.D., and was a high–ranking Mamluke's son. Thus he is assumed to have important connections at the court of Sultan Gaqmaq (1438–1453 A.D.) with whom he had a close friendship. An excellent scholar, he is ranked second only to al-Maqrizi as a historian of Islamic Egypt and the Mamluke court. Donald Presgrave Little, p. 87.

15. Alan Moorehead, The Blue Nile (New York: Harper & Row, 1960), p. 69.

16. Moorehead, p. 74.

     This author does not provide footnotes in the text itself; he does list his sources however. For the chapter covering the Mamlukes he cites: W. G. Brown, *Travelers in Africa, Egypt and Syria 1792–1798* (Cadell & Davis, 1806) which he describes as "first class." For customs and manners, he cites: Edward William Lane, *Moslem Egyptians* (Ward Lock, 1890).

17. Moorehead, p. 72.

18. Moorehead, p. 74.

     This is a quotation from Shafik Ghorbal, The Beginning Of The Egyptian Question (Routledge, 1928).

19. Glubb, pp. 9–11.

     Glubb noted that there were very few books on the Mamlukes in English: he recommended Sir William Muir's *The Mameluke or Slave Dynasty,* above.

20. Donald Presgrave Little, An Introduction to Mamluk Historiography (Montreal: McGill–Queen's University Press, 1970), p. 100.

     The XV century Islamic writer Ibn Taghri Birdi provides evidence of this practice by breaking the rule; instead of adopting the usual annalistic form, he deals with each ruler chronologically for a period of years. He was uniquely innovative.

21. Allen Edwardes, The Jewel in the Lotus – A Historical Survey of the Sexual Culture of the East (New York: The Julian Press, 1959).

This book has an introduction by Dr. Albert Ellis and contains an extensive bibliography; however, the author does not include footnotes or citations with the text.

22. R. E. L. Masters, Edward Lea, Sex Crimes In History (New York: The Julian Press, Inc., 1973), p. 185 et seq.

The segment delineated as Appendix A was written by Allen Edwardes, "A Historical Survey of Sexual Savagery in the East"; it relates stories and a number of quotations from sources not identified; the data is very interesting but it demonstrates the need for more scholarship in the area of non–Western culture relating to sexual habits.

23. Allen Edwardes, A Historical Survey of Sexual Savagery in the East (in Masters and Lea, above), p. 200.

The author known as "Dr. Jacobus X" was included in the book The Vice, which also contains Burton's essay, "Sotadic Zone" (Atlanta: M. G. Theris, 1967). The book also includes a piece by John Addington Symonds used as an introduction. Jacobus' segment is called "Untrodden Fields of Anthropology." Jacobus, according to unpublished research by Wayne Dynes of Barnard College, New York, was also known as Sutor, which was a pen name. He is identified as the author of the book L'Amour Aux Colonies (Paris: Liseux, 1893). In referring to himself, the author of that book asserts that he was a military surgeon who had served in Indo–China until 1860; in French Guiana until 1870; in Senegal and New Caledonia until 1878; then he spent six weeks in Tahiti before retiring to France in 1893 after "serving on five continents." The book was reprinted in English in Paris by Charles Carrington in 1896.

Burton's "Sotadic Zone" first appeared as an appendix in the last volume of The Arabian Nights. A great deal of miscellaneous erotica was included in the essay while propounding a theory that there was an identifiable region about the world which fostered homosexuality. Burton concludes that "pederasty" is natural and prevalent among the Arabs, contending that the Sufis, particularly, were heirs to the traditions of ancient Greek pederasty.

24. Edwardes, p. 200.

25. Edwardes, The Jewel in the Lotus, p. 205.

Edwardes tends to make overly broad statements:
"Psychological inversion was rare in the pure Arab; environmental factors alone determine his sexual outlets," on page 205. While the reader must be cautious, Edwardes is useful in spotting the endemic

162

nature of homosexuality. Typically Edwardes concludes, "the Turk and the Persian were atavistically tempered to voluntary and involuntary homosexuality, but not the free Arab of the desert." Burton cites the Koran, Chapter iv, 20, "and if two (men) among you commit the crime, then punish them both," and he concludes that this is a prohibition against sodomy. Even if this were to be true, the penalty is limited to being reproached, being insulted or scourged; it is not a capital offense.

26.   Edwardes, p. 207.

27.   Hamed Ammar, Growing Up In An Egyptian Village (London: Routlege & Kegan Paul, 1954), p. 48 et seq.

28.   Ammar, p. 49.

29.   Ammar, p. 49.

30.   Ammar, p. 119.

31.   Ammar, p. 121.

32.   Ammar, p. 52.

33.   Ammar, p. 50.

34.   Ammar, p. 183.

35.   Ammar, p. 192.

36.   Ammar, p. 105.

37.   Ammar, p. 96.

38.   Ammar, p. 74.

39.   Ammar, p. 78.

40.   Ammar, p. 91.

41.   Ammar, p. 92.

42.   Ammar, p. 80.

43.   Edwardes, p. 207.

44.   Edwardes, p. 207.

   The use of the word "fundament" in the quotation is typical of XVIII century English usage, still found in XIX century texts; it means "anus," and may be found in court cases, both civil and military, dealing with sodomy.

45.   Edwardes, p. 208.

46. Edwardes, pp. 208–209.

   Edwardes uses the word "sotadic" taken from Sir Richard Burton's essay on the so–called "Sotadic Zone" in which Burton suggests that there is a zone about the world where human sexual passions tend toward homosexuality.

47. Edwardes, p. 208.

48. Edwardes, p. 210.

49. Edwardes, p. 211.

50. Edwardes, p. 211.

51. This reference was found in the Human Relations Area Files, Inc. on the Zulu under the code number 838. The file is located at the University of California in Los Angeles. The citation is listed as: 1: Krige, E–4,5 1965 FX 20 Zulu; there is an additional internal reference to: Stuart, "History of the Zulu Rebellion," p. 88. Also see: Wayne Dynes, "Homosexuality in the Sub–Sahara," Gay Books Bulletin (New York: Gay Academic Union, 1983), Spring/Summer, pp. 20–21.

52. Human Relations Area Files, Inc., Zulu, Code 588, 3: Vilakazi, E 1–4,5 (1956–1957), 1962 FX 20 Zulu.

53. Edwardes, pp. 212–213.

54. Edwardes, p. 213.

55. Edwardes, pp. 214–215.

56. Muir, p. 75.

   Muir uses the word "perverts" but does not explain his reason, nor does he discuss homosexuality.

57. Muir, p. 87.

58. Muir, p. 88.

59. Muir, p. 90.

60. Muir, pp. 90–91.

61. Muir, p. 94.

62. Muir, p. 95.

63. Muir, p. 62.

64. Little, p. 95.

65. Little, p. 125.

66. Little, p. 125 ff.

67. Little, p. 127.

68. Little, p. 127.

69. Alistair Sutherland and Patrick Anderson, editors: Eros: An Anthology of Male Friendships (New York: The Citadel Press, 1963), p. 136. (The poem appears there in its entirety.)

70. James Kritzeck, editor: Anthology of Islamic Literature (New York: New American Library, Inc., 1964), pp. 109–113.

71. Sutherland, p. 128.

72. Sutherland, p. 132.

73. The American Heritage Dictionary of the English Language – New College Edition (Boston: Houghton Mifflin Co., 1979).

   The term "saracen" is defined: 1. A member of a pre–Islamic nomadic people of the Syrian–Arabian deserts. 2. An Arab. 3. Any Moslem, especially of the time of the Crusades. The name "Arab" is the word used by the inhabitants of Arabia which is translated to mean "island of the Arabs." The use of the name "Arab" is discussed by Carl Brockelman, History of the Islamic Peoples, trans. Joel Carmichael and Moshe Perlman (New York: Capricorn Books, 1960), pp. 1–12.

74. Wayne Dynes, Warren Johansson, "The Public Bath as a Cultural Phenomenon" (New York: unpublished typescript, September 20, 1984), p. 2.

   They quote A. Martin, Deutsches Badewesen in Vergagenen Tagen (Jena, 1906). They also quote Heinz Grotzfeld, Das Bad im Arabisch–Islamischen Mittelalter (Wiesbaden, 1970), pp. 88–91.

75. Dynes, Johansson, p. 2.

76. Eadmer, Historia Novorum In Anglia, trans. Geoffrey Bosanquet (Philadelphia: Dufour, 1965), p. 48.

77. Eadmer, The Life of St. Anselm, Archbishop of Canterbury, trans. R. W. Southern (Oxford: Clarendon Press, 1979), p. 50.

165

CHAPTER IX

MILITARY HOMOAFFECTIONALISM

Section 1

Before Christianity

In this chapter, the broad spectrum of the homoerotic male nature, as it has impacted upon military history, will be epitomized by selecting outstanding individuals as examples. In some cases the evidence is overwhelming. In others, the evidence will be limited. In all cases, the coverage will be relatively brief, for it would require volumes to cover the subject more completely. The reader is encouraged to read other sources and keep in mind that the subject matter is often suppressed and is very difficult to obtain. Indeed, it is remarkable that so much evidence is still available. The quality of source material is always a factor, and even primary sources suffer in translation. Where the evidence is ambivalent, the reader must evaluate the conclusions drawn. Nevertheless, the subject matter must not be ignored, for it is obvious that deliberate attempts have been made down through the centuries to bowdlerize the records.

In some examples the individual may have escaped much notice in the past. This is particularly true of American heroes who will be included. More details will be given in their cases. Others like Alexander the Great are so well documented as to almost preclude additional proof.

The purpose is not to prove actual sexual conduct; it should suffice to show manifestations of close male bonding of an intimate, homoaffectionate, nature. Then, it will be shown that the individuals influenced military history and ultimately world history. The examples will also question the stereotypical portrayal of masculinity in history.

Male bonding, which is encompassed in the word "homoaffectionalism," is most evident in an all–male military environment. The norms of military life preclude the notion that homosexuality equates to effeminacy. As a matter of fact, what is considered "effeminate" and what is considered "masculine" is simply a reflection of the cultural norm of a particular society. Manifestations of homoaffectionalism down through the ages may vary, but they do so in keeping

166

with the prevailing culture.

For example, any astute reader of Homer will notice patterns of male bonding, like that between Achilles and Patroclus, which may not seem overtly homoerotic. To cover the lack of sexual details and still recognize the bonding, some historians have opted for the word "heroic" when discussing the Homeric period and the relationships.

John Boswell, in contrast, makes the point that when other historians fail to see the erotic nature of the relationships, "most Greeks" would have disagreed. Greeks like Plato saw it as obvious that Achilles and Patroclus were warrior–lovers.[1] Plato makes the ancient Greek point of view quite clear on the subject in *Symposium* [178-179]. Plato has Phaedrus observe that Love is "a mighty god, and wonderful among men." The personification "Love" is given the masculine gender in the text, and is described as "the oldest of the gods."[2] Plato authenticates his contentions by evoking Hesiod and Acusilaus.

Then Phaedrus makes a direct reference to military life:

I know not any greater blessing to a young man who is beginning life than a virtuous lover, or to the lover than a beloved youth. For the principle which ought to be the guide of men who would nobly live that principle, I say, neither kindred, nor honor, nor wealth, nor any other motive is able to implant so well as love. Of what am I speaking? Of the sense of honor and dishonor, without which neither states nor individuals ever do any good or great work. And I say that a lover who is detected in doing any dishonorable act, or submitting through cowardice when any dishonor is done to him by another, will be more pained at being detected by his beloved than at being seen by his father, or by his companions, or by any one else. The beloved too, when he is found in any disgraceful situation, has the same feeling about his lover. And if there were only some way of contriving that a state or an army should be made up of lovers and their loves, they would be the very best governors of their own city, abstaining from all dishonor, and emulating one another in honor; and when fighting at each other's side, although a mere handful, they would overcome the world. For what lover would not choose rather to be seen by all mankind than by his beloved, either when abandoning his

167

post or throwing away his arms? He would be ready to die a thousand deaths rather than endure this. Or who would desert his beloved or fail him in the hour of danger? The veriest coward would become an inspired hero, equal to the bravest, at such times; Love (the god) would inspire him. That courage which, as Homer says, the god breathes into the souls of some heroes, Love of his own nature infuses the lover. Love will make men dare to die for their beloved–love alone; and women as well as men.[3]

The same theme is found in Plutarch's *Lives* in his piece on Pelopidas. Pelopidas was a participant in the battle of Leuctra in 371 B.C., and there confronted the Sacred Band of Thebes. "According to some," Plutarch writes, the Sacred Band was formed by Gorgidas. It was a chosen group of three hundred men. Their primary duty was to protect the citadel. Thebes provided for all their needs and for their exercise. Plutarch continues:

Others say that it was composed of young men attached to each other by personal affection... a pleasant saying of Pammenes is current, that Homer's Nestor was not well skilled in ordering an army, when he advised the Greeks to rank tribe and tribe, and family together, so that tribe might aid tribe, and kinsmen kinsmen aid; but that he should have joined lovers and their beloved.

For men of the same tribe or family little value one another when dangers press; but a band cemented by friendship grounded upon love is never to be broken, and invincible; since lovers willingly rush into danger for the relief of one another. Nor can it be wondered at for they have more regard for their absent lovers than for others present; as in the instance of the man who, when the enemy was going to kill him, earnestly requested him to run him through the breast, that his lover might not blush to see him wounded in the back...

Gorgidas distributed this Sacred Band all through the front ranks of the infantry, and thus made their gallantry less conspicuous; and not being united in one body, but mingled with so many others of inferior resolution, they had no fair opportunity of showing what they could do... but then he decided that brave men, provoking one another to nobler actions, would prove more serviceable, and more resolute, where all were united together.[4]

The Sacred Band of Thebes is a classic example of an army built around pairs of homosexual lovers. As Boswell points out, "it turned out to be an extraordinarily successful experiment." However, the golden age of the overtly homoaffectionate army may have passed by the time Philip II of Macedon reportedly gave his panegyric on the Sacred Band of Thebes, after the battle at Chaeronea in 338 B.C. The world of his son Alexander, later to be known as the Great, needed a different kind of army, one too large and too diverse to segregate bands of lovers.

That the Spartans were considered to have been formidable warriors hardly needs documentation. That they lived in a military society is also well known. Boys were separated from their mothers at an early age to be trained by men. Ordinary work was performed by serfs (helots) belonging to the state, thus leaving the boys free to train as soldiers. Male bonding in Sparta was formalized and recognized as part of the culture and customs of that society.[5]

Spartan warriors provide one of the best examples of an army composed of lovers. Their system may be used to support Plato's contention that such soldiers fight more valiantly than others when joined with their lovers in battle. The battle of Thermopylae (meaning Hot Gates), in the years 480 B.C., provides an excellent example of the phenomenon. Perhaps it should be noted here that Plutarch, while making no special reference to Sparta, asserted (*Erotikos*, 752 AB) that Greek homosexuals "who claim that sensuality plays no part in their affairs, do so because they are ashamed of themselves for fear of punishment. They have to have some excuse for approaching goodlooking boys, so they make a show of friendship and virtue." However, it should be remembered that Plutarch was writing about five hundred years after the fact, and was obviously reflecting the prevailing sense of guilt regarding sex which the Romans had introduced. (See above in Chapter 4: "A Sense of Guilt.")

The Spartan King Leonidas, with his band of lovers, held the pass at Thermopylae long enough to bring about the ultimate defeat of the Persian army led by Xerxes. They lost the battle itself, but the Greeks won the war, which altered the course of history.

Robert Flacelière, a military man and a scholar, has written a convincing, well documented account of the military foundation for

169

homosexual love among the Greeks, in his book, *Love in Ancient Greece.*

He notes the many kinds of male love, including the love of a man, the love of a boy, and romantic love. He cites Hector's love for Andromache; Alcibiades temptation of Socrates; and many others. The author dwells explicitly on "the extraordinary fact, so amazing at first sight, that many of the ancient Greeks lavished all their sexually–rooted affections upon boys. For they considered members of the other sex inferior beings, lacking all education and refinement, good for nothing but to ensure posterity." [6]

Flacelière notes that the Greeks used the word *philia* to describe a broad spectrum of affectionate sentiments involved, and suggests that the English word "friendship" is a very imperfect translation to describe the affection. He also notes that in Athens, laws were enacted, probably in the time of Solon (who was made Archon in 594 B.C.), which were intended to curb the excesses of pederasty. [7] It should be noted that the word *paiderasteia*, which was the object of those laws, was used to refer to both disinterested affection and to physical, homosexual relations. It would have meant homoaffectionalism. In English, its derivative, "pederasty," has come to mean sexual inversion. Of course, it would be an error to assume that all Greeks practiced homosexuality; and probably it would be accurate to conclude that it was more common among the military and the leisure classes. In any case, the Greeks manifested no guilt or shame regarding homosexual sex.

Plutarch (*Erotikos*, 761 D) is credited with the statement: "It was chiefly warlike peoples like the Boeotians, Lacedemonians and Cretans who were addicted to homosexuality." Ephorus contended that a male lover in Crete would declare his feelings to the relatives and friends of his beloved. With their consent, the boy was carried off for three days. After the three days the boy was returned and was then given a military outfit by his lover. Interestingly, this custom appears later in Sparta: when a man took a woman for his bride she had to dress as a boy for the occasion and endure the simulated abduction.

In Crete it was considered shameful for a wellborn boy not to have a lover; those with lovers received great respect. The same attitude found its way into the Constitution of Sparta, according to Xenophon, who reports that men and boys were paired off in an actual marriage. [8] Plutarch, again in his life of Lycurgus, goes on at great length about the relationship of men and boys. Even in their marriages to women, usually to mature women, the relationship with men was preserved. As in Crete earlier, the bride was ritualistically abducted, dressed as a boy, and subjected to sexual intercourse only in the dark where the participants might not even recognize each other. Then after the event, the groom returned to his male friends. The couple could have children before they actually saw each other.[9] With all of this, there was in Athens, apparently, a sense of modesty, extolled to suggest virtue in conduct. Aristophanes titillates his readers in *The Clouds* with lines that describe how Athenian boys were cautioned to sit in such a way so as not to be shocking by exposing their genitals to spectators:

And every one's thigh was forward and high as they sat to be
　　　　　　　　　　　　　　　　　drilled in a row,
So that nothing the while indecent or vile the eye of a
　　　　　　　　　　　　　　　　　stranger might meet;
And then with their hand they would smooth down the sand
　　　　　　　　　　　　　　whenever they rose from their seat,
To leave not a trace of themselves in the place for a vigilant
　　　　　　　　　　　　　　　　　lover to view.[10]

However, it is doubtful that general morals produced such refined behavior as depicted by Aristophanes. For example, there were rules of conduct regarding male prostitution. Boys in Athens who sold their favors and who were free citizens could get into trouble and could be charged, convicted, and barred from public service and other honors. However, this is a topic beyond the scope and purposes of this book.

The Greeks set the standards by which homoaffectionalism was established in the ancient Mediterranean world. The impact of that phenomenon left its mark on the military. As noted above, however, the impact became lessened after the time of Alexander the Great.

Any attempt to be exhaustive in covering the impact of homoaffectionalism in the military over the past two thousand years would require volumes. To demonstrate the endemic nature of the phenomenon, a group of selected personalities will be discussed.

171

Alexander the Great

Alexander, later known as the Great, was born in 356 B.C. and died in 323 B.C. In those thirty three years he flashed like a comet and impacted on history. He was a military genius, a homosexual, and he altered the course of history in the wake of his military prowess.

As the son of Philip II of Macedon, Alexander inherited "the first large territorial state with an effectively centralized political, military, and administrative structure to come into being on the continent of Europe." From the very beginning legends arose regarding his birth. Reports circulated that the temple of Artemis burned down on the night of his birth. It was also said that his mother, Olympias, was penetrated by a thunderbolt the night before her wedding and that fire spewed forth from her womb.[11]

According to Theophrastus, Alexander's parents began to worry about his lack of interest in heterosexual sex when his childhood was ending. They engaged a beautiful Thessalian courtesan named Callixeina to try to help him. His mother, reportedly, begged him to have sexual intercourse with women. Apparently he remained indifferent. Despite these concerns, there was nothing effeminate about his conduct when he assumed his duties as Regent in his father's absence. Indeed, he appears to have been quite aggressive in behavior and leadership. He had an appetite for power.

Various historians have described Alexander; some have seen him as effeminate, but those are obviously subjective opinions, and apparently based on what they see in supposed portraits and statues of him. Green puts together a credible picture of him based on ancient sources: he was rather below average in height, with a muscular, compact body. He had blond, unruly hair, fair skin, and a ruddy complexion. Curiously, he had one brown eye and one that was grey-blue. Even more unusual, he is depicted as having widely–spaced, sharply–pointed teeth. Reportedly he was a fast runner and he walked with a fast gait, and had a habit of tilting his head slightly upward and to the left side. There was "a hint of leashed hysteria behind the melting charm."[12] According to Plutarch the best portrait statues of Alexander were by Lysippus, who was reportedly the only artist officially permitted to produce Alexander's image. Other artists did create likenesses, Plutarch points out, and he noted they were reportedly made with "great exactness." They too depicted the tilt of his head and his "melting eyes." [13]

Plutarch discusses Alexander's education and his relationship to Aristotle, who greatly influenced his life as his teacher. He also confirms their falling out in later life.[14] Alexander was apparently not the easiest person to get along with. He had many clashes with his father, Philip. Indeed, if Philip had not been murdered by one of his own catamites, Pausanias, there might have been a struggle for the throne. Alexander was twenty years old when his father was murdered.[15]

Alexander had a number of favorites, but the two that seem to have been the most important to him were Hephaestion and Craterus. According to Plutarch, it was Hephaestion who always emulated Alexander and followed his changing customs and affectations. The two favorites were, at times, openly jealous of one another regarding the affection of Alexander. On one occasion they began to have a duel. Alexander broke it up and chastised both of them for their lack of sense.[16]

Alexander's conquest of Persia and the lands to the East are well known. His relationship with his apparent lover, Hephaestion, is legendary. An excellent bibliography of his life and time is to be found in Peter Green's book, *Alexander of Macedon, 356–323 B.C.*

Gaius Julius Caesar

Gaius Julius Caesar was born on 12 July, 100 B.C. and assassinated on the 15th (the Ides) of March, 44 B.C. He was of a patrician family which liked to trace its ancestors to kings and gods. In his case he claimed descent from Venus, the goddess of love. Like most well born Romans he was given three names: Julius was the clan name; Gaius was his praenomen, or given name. However, since his father was also known as Julius Gaius Caesar, the father was referred to by adding Maior (senior) to the end of his name and the son added Minor (junior). In any case the father is referred to as Gaius and the son as Julius.

As with Alexander the Great, there is an abundance of source material on Caesar. His career made its mark on military history and history in general. In dealing with the material it is necessary to be aware that those who wrote about him often had their own agenda, and many of his contemporary writers were his enemies. Others, like Suetonius, were fascinated with gossip. For example,

Marcus Bibulus, who wrote about Caesar, seems to have resented Caesar's self aggrandizement, which is borne out in some of the gossip Suetonius relates.[17]

Plutarch, who wrote about a hundred years later, may have been more objective. They agree on his family background and his achievements. All report on his troubles with Sulla who was dictator of Rome during Caesar's youth. Sulla objected to Caesar's marriage to Cornelia. Cornelia was the daughter of Cinna, who, four times Consul, wielded a great deal of power in Rome. When she died prematurely, he married Pompeia. That marriage ended in divorce after he accused her of adultery. Later he married Calpurnia, the daughter of Lucius Piso, who was to succeed him as consul. For Caesar, marriage was not particularly a romantic enterprise, it was a power play.[18]

The first notable homosexual affair to attach to Caesar involved the king of Bithynia, Nicomedes III (c. 110–74 B.C.). Caesar may have first met Nicomedes in Rome when the king came to seek the help of the Roman Senate against an invasion by Mithridates. Caesar was a young boy at that time. In any case, it was to be his first military venture to be assigned to the domestic retinue of Marcus Thermus, the praetor, and to go to Bithynia. Thermus sent Caesar to levy a fleet from Bithynia. While there he lived with the king. He is said to have over–stayed his visit. This gave rise to rumors that Caesar was in love with the young king. He added to the rumors by making a brief return visit to Bithynia before returning to Rome.[19]

One contemporary poet, Calvus Licinius, wrote suggestive things about Caesar. Less scandalous then some was his quip about king Nicomedes: "*Bithynia quicquid, et paedicator Caesaris, umquam habuit*"; the quip asserts that Caesar was seduced by the king of Bithynia and had sex with him. This portrays a passive image.

Noel I. Garde, in his book *Jonathan to Gide*, cites a ribald song sung by Caesar's soldiers during his triumph after the conquest of Gaul. The words transcribe in plainer English as "Behold now triumphant Caesar, who brought Gaul under him; but he is not sharing the triumph with Nicomedes, who brought Caesar under him." Again, this is a passive image of Caesar.

It must be remembered that Caesar's sex habits were discussed by his political enemies like Dolabella and Curio the Elder. Dolabella harped on Caesar being a royal concubine; Curio the Elder

174

referred to him as a harlot; Bibulus called him "queen." Even Octavius, later known as Augustus Caesar, is quoted by Marcus Brutus as describing "Pompey as king, and Caesar as queen," explaining that Octavius was given to "jest and scoff overly broadly," thus taking the edge off the remark.

Hardly in jest, one Gaius Memmius referred to Caesar as a "cupbearer" and a "catamite," meaning someone passive in having sex with a man. Not to be outdone or ignored, the famous Cicero wrote that "Caesar, who was descended from Venus, lay down upon a bed of gold, arrayed in purple; and so his maidenhead (rectum) became defiled...." Obviously, Cicero was no friend of Caesar.

Suetonius quotes gossip when he writes that "Caesar used to go (about) in his purple studded robe, trimmed with a jag or fringe at the sleeve hand, (and that) he also wore a girdle over it, and that (was worn) very slack and loose." To comprehend the maliciousness of this remark, it is best understood when related to an admonition made by Sulla that was well known in Caesar's time: "Beware of the boy who went girdled so dissolutely." It referred to boys who had sex with men.

Notwithstanding, Caesar was a great military genius. He was highly respected and much admired. His detractors made fun of his appearance and cast aspersions, but they could not lessen his effectiveness. His military and political career have become legend. His extensive conquests created a new order in Rome. It was he who laid the foundation for the empire he never got to rule. He codified Roman law, reset the calendar, and has inspired generations of people down to the present.

Caesar had a flair for the dramatic. "On one day of his Gallic triumph, he rode along the Velabrem [a street in Rome] and was almost shaken out of his chariot when an axle broke. Undaunted, he climbed into the Capitol by torch light. He had forty elephants bearing branches and candlesticks...." So reports Suetonius. He gave the people spectacle and they loved him for it.

His detractors took pains to note his high pitched voice; still he became a great orator, and used his talents successfully to sway the people of Rome.

Suetonius has left a good description of Caesar. He was tall, bald, and had a clear white complexion; his eyes were black, lively and quick. He was healthy, though in later years he was "given to faint and swoon suddenly." Special attention was paid to the fact that he was very neat and clean.

In his personal habits, even his enemies conceded that he was modest and temperate. They had to admit that Rome flourished when Caesar emerged as a political and military force.

Fables attached themselves to him, a fact that all researchers must notice. For example, the famous quote "veni, vidi, vici," attributed to Caesar to impress generations of Latin students with his military prowess, was actually part of a display carried by supporters of Caesar on the occasion of his Pontic triumph. The words mean "I came, I saw, I conquered," but not in the sense they are taught. The words referred to Caesar's ability to understand a dispute and settle it quickly without excessive violence or loss of life; by his wisdom and display of force he brought peace.

His death was dramatic and worthy of Caesar. He was murdered by his "friends." They murdered him to protect the integrity of the Roman Republic. What they got was anarchy, civil war, and the founding of an empire that pretended to be a republic.

Tiberius

Originally named after his father, he was called Tiberius Claudius Nero. However, as fate and politics would have it, his mother, Drusilla Livia, became the wife of Octavius (later to be known as Augustus Caesar). This all took place after the murder of Julius Caesar and after the defeat of Marcus Antonius at Actium in 14 A.D. The boy was then renamed Tiberius Julius Caesar. He was born on 16 November, 42 B.C.[20]

Whether it was Augustus' idea or the work of Tiberius' mother, Augustus required Tiberius to give up the wife of his choice and marry Augustus' daughter Julia. This obviously moved Tiberius closer to the source of power.[21]

Augustus may not have liked Tiberius much, but he was impressed with his military prowess and openly praised his "thoroughly conquering the tribes between the Rhine and the Elbe."[22] Tiberius first saw military service on an expedition to Cantabria as a military tribune. After that he took over the army in the East and restored the kingdom of Armenia, bringing it back under Rome's sway. Later he successfully governed Gaul as regent.[23]

Tiberius was not in Rome as Augustus lay dying. Suetonius and Tacitus relate the accepted tale that Livia kept the death of her husband secret long enough for Tiberius to return to Rome. Then a will was produced in which Tiberius was named by Augustus as his heir. In any case, he had the power and the wits to seize the opportunity, and had himself declared the heir to Augustus. While Augustus may have avoided the use of the title Emperor and ruled as *Princeps*, Tiberius actually came to rule as Emperor while still using the fiction of shared power with "the people and Senate of Rome." [24]

Tiberius may have encouraged the fiction of the power of the Senate, but he had only limited respect for the Senators. Again according to Tacitus, Tiberius is quoted as saying of the Senators: "How ready these men are to be slaves." He was disgusted at their abject abasement. [25]

He had no doubt about the role the Emperor ought to play, and it was not one of acting general in the field. As a good soldier, he used diplomacy whenever and wherever it was possible, saving the lives of his troops. He did not believe that the Emperor ought to run off to the battle fields and endanger the state. He had been to war in Germany at least nine times and found that diplomacy was as effective as the army. [26]

Tiberius is not presented as a particularly lovable character. He apparently hated flattery and obsequiousness, whether out of modesty or mean spiritedness; as Tacitus put it, the fact remained that he was a difficult and complex personality to comprehend. He was accused of living in profligacy, especially when he went to live voluptuously on the island of Capri for eleven years. In discussing Tiberius' conduct, Tacitus informs his readers that his "purpose is not to relate at length every notion, but only such as were conspicuous... or notorious for infamy." [27]

Despite his self indulgence, he tended to necessary business. During the rule of Augustus, the so–called *Lex Papia Poppaea* was promulgated. The law was intended to enforce penalties against those who chose celibacy as a life style. It was a time in Rome when people were loth to get married. So Augustus decided to tax and penalize those who refused to have families. Tiberius removed the excesses of that law. [28]

Nevertheless, Tiberius was "whispered against" by the people and was always the center of interest. His notorious private life gave the population a lot to talk about. Suetonius is full of detailed gossip about Tiberius' sex life which reads like pornography.

However, it should be borne in mind that those histories of Tiberius, Caligula, and Nero, which were written while these men were in power, were probably falsified, or when written shortly after these men died, the histories were written under the irritation of hate. What does reveal itself in the texts is that Tiberius was homosexual and a powerful military leader. He died at age 78.[29]

Publius Aelius Hadrianus

The family of Hadrian originated in Spain. He claimed that his family had settled in Hadria, and derived their name from that town; it was later that they moved to the ancient town of Picenum which had become a Roman colony. His father was Aelius Hadrianus who used the surname Afer, and was a cousin of the Emperor Trajan. His mother was Domitia Paulina, a native of Cadiz, Spain. Hadrian was born in the Roman colony of Italica, near Seville, on 24 January, 76.[29]

When his father died he was only ten years old, and thus became the ward of his cousin Marcus Ulpius Trajan, the future Emperor. During his early years he was "deeply devoted" to Greek studies and was called "Greekling" by some. At age fifteen he entered military service. Hadrian was well treated by Trajan who advanced the lad's career, first as a public official and then as tribune of the Second Legion. Later, he was sent to the province of Lower Moesia. There he served as tribune of the Fifth Legion, the Macedonica.[30]

His cousin Trajan, who was governor of Germania Superior in the year 96, was then adopted by the Emperor Nerva. It was Hadrian who was dispatched to convey the army's congratulations to Trajan. He was then transferred to Germany. When the Emperor Nerva died in October, 97, Hadrian wished to be the first to inform his cousin. Despite attempts to delay him, he succeeded and enhanced his standing with the new Emperor. Already there were rumors being spread about his sexual conduct, and he was anxious to keep Trajan's good will.[30] Whatever the problem was, Hadrian was reconciled with Trajan by the good offices of L. Licinius Sura. It was at this time that Hadrian married Vibia Sabina, the daughter of the Emperor's sister. Hadrian advanced rapidly in military rank and as tribune of the plebs. During the first of the Dacian wars, Hadrian accompanied Trajan "on terms of considerable intimacy" and "falling in with his habits." He was richly rewarded by the

Emperor. During the second war in Dacia, Trajan appointed him commander of the First Legion, and he won great distinction for remarkable deeds. Because of this, Trajan presented Hadrian with the same diamond ring given to him by the Emperor Nerva. This gesture followed a precedent established by Augustus Caesar, which suggests that the receiver of the ring was the designated successor.[31]

On 9 August, 117, while serving as the governor of Syria, he learned that he had been adopted by the Emperor. Then on 11 August, 117, he was informed that Trajan had died and that he was to ascend the throne. Of course, the sources are not at all clear regarding the succession. There were rumors that there had been a plot which put Hadrian on the throne. Whatever the facts may have been, the most important fact is that Hadrian became Emperor, at which time he announced his intention to follow the policies of Augustus and the earlier emperors and limit the empire of Rome to its "natural" boundaries. He thus set out on a world–wide peace policy to avoid rebellions.[32]

Having established Hadrian's homosexuality and his prowess as a military man in Chapter IV, it should be noted that his sexual conduct has upset scholars down through the ages. Fortunately, there are sources other than documents to cover his activities. There are monuments, inscriptions, and coins. Writers like Royston Lambert have used these alternative sources to great advantage. The point they make, with others, is that the relationship between Hadrian and his lover Antinous leaves little doubt that the emperor was probably exclusively homosexual.

In his book *Beloved and God*, Lambert heads his first chapter the "Scandal Of The Centuries." The book and the scandal involve the Greek youth Antinous. The powerful story culminates with Antinous' death by drowning in the Nile while on a trip there with Hadrian.

The aftermath affected the whole world. Hadrian had statues of Antinous erected everywhere. They were so beautiful that, for centuries after, artists used Antinous as the standard for male beauty. Then came the apotheosis of Antinous. Hadrian had the Greeks deify him. Temples were built, rites were created and a cult grew around the legend of Antinous.[33]

What is significant in this deification is the fact that it took place just as Christianity was in its formative state. Here we have the lover of Hadrian equated with Osiris, and assimilated with the Hellenic equivalent, Dionysus.[34]

179

The deified Antinous follows the cult of Osiris: he lives, dies, and rises again. He is associated with the verdure–producing Nile which brings fertility and fecundity. His Spring feast, like Easter, celebrates his rebirth. What we appear to have is the deification of a man like Jesus as the Christ figure. Antinous comes complete with the lamb over his shoulders as "the good shepherd." All this because he was the lamented lover of Hadrian.

The Christian cults then began to arise in the empire. There was no lessening of homoaffectionalism, but it began to be attacked by the guilt–ridden Romanized Christians, to whom all pleasures became suspect if not sinful.

Section 2

After The Fall

To cover the two thousand years which follow after the advent of Christianity, an overview will be used to illustrate the point already made in great detail up to this point: homoaffectionalism played a dominant role in military life.

A useful place to begin is outside the Roman world among fiercely non–Christian peoples, the Vikings. It was they who dominated the seas during the 8th and 9th centuries. It was they who pushed into the coastal and river towns of the north and left a permanent mark on the civilization which developed in Europe, including England and Russia. They were Old Norse, the men of legend who roamed the Atlantic and the North Sea, finding their way to Iceland and the New World long before Columbus.

The term "Viking" is an Old Norse word describing the sea rovers from the Scandinavian countries. The word conjures up images of rustic, savage men plundering and looting civilized communities.

No doubt they did plunder; everyone who could, did, in those early days. It was a way of life and they were rather good at it. However, they were not Christians. That alone earned them "bad press." If you consider that among those who were pillaged by the Vikings were the Christian monks, and it was the monks who kept the chronicles of the times, then it is understandable that we know more about the evils of the Vikings than any other characteristic.[35]

Of all the "wickedness" with which the monks had to contend, being raped by a Viking must have been a most disquieting experience. Male domination was a part of the world of the Vikings; it was a basis of leadership among them.

Any one could rape a women, they reasoned, but it took a real man to rape a man, especially a warrior. That ethos seems to have been their basic outlook on sexuality. Sexuality produced a "pecking order." Whether in fact or through symbolism, when a warrior challenged a rival he evoked sex. He would use expressions like those old Anglo Saxon invectives we still use today. He might use an expression like the modern "screw you," or even blunter terms. What he was saying, and felt, meant: "I can and will mount you and I can and will penetrate your anus."

A Viking warrior making such an assertion was putting his rival on notice that the rival was considered to be at a lower status than the man making the challenge. It is important to keep in mind that homosexual conduct was not the issue, and certainly not sexual desire as affection. All young men who associated with warriors could expect to be seduced. It was part of their education.

In temperament, the Vikings were like the Dorians who had swept down from the north to invade Greece a thousand years earlier. They apparently believed in the nobility of loving boys. The norm was for younger boys to be seduced by mature men. Their culture and customs developed independently of the Judaic and Christian ethos. Their sexual proclivities have been depicted on the walls of caves from the end of the ice age to the pottery of later ages. Early pictolyths reveal a phallus–dominated society.

Theirs was a harsh, hostile environment. The land was difficult to cultivate. Survival depended on each man's ability to hunt, find food, or take what he needed from others. Leadership required the ability to dominate others and defend the clan. Of course, custom mitigated the harshness of the system. Their gods condoned their customs, blood feuds and sexual dominance included.

The harshness of the land led to use of the sea. Life on board ships was conducive to their homosexual activities. They would spend months at sea, especially if they went south to the Mediterranean. They had been visiting the Mediterranean for at least two thousand years before the Christian era.

Their biggest impact came after about the year 600 A.D. when they perfected the use of sails. For years they had been successful world traders; then they became the scourge of the seas and plundered widely.

It is inherent in our culture to resist the idea that great and powerful warriors would engage in homosexual activities. It is difficult to find documented materials in the language of the Vikings, but it can be confirmed through the accounts of victims and in the study of their language. Linguistic evidence is powerful, and this is supported by pictolyths and artifacts.

People obviously develop words to suit their culture. Accordingly, Old Norse is a language which is rich in words describing sexual matters. Couple this with the oral tradition and the contents of legends and you have a clear picture.

Martin Larsen, the Norse philologist, pointed out the significance of the word *argr*, which was in common use. It was one of the crudest terms of verbal abuse to be applied to a man. It indicated that a man had submitted himself beneath his status and as a woman. The accusation implied a most serious breach of Icelandic and Norwegian law.

The term was not a "put–down" of homosexual conduct; rather it was a condemnation of a leader who submits to sex in a passive role with a subordinate. This is especially true where the accused holds his position by being "dominant." Dominating a man sexually was honored as a sign of power to be boasted about. Submitting to a superior person was not considered demeaning—it was expected.

Even the gods were involved. There is a tale which relates a problem experienced by the god Thor. Thor losses his hammer, and to get it back requires stealth. He must disguise himself as a bride. However, the prospect of dressing as a woman concerns him: "The gods may call me *argr*. He complains of this and fears the loss of face. He fears that the other gods may think that he had been mounted and his anus penetrated.

In another situation, Odin's powerful warriors fought over the use of Gundmundr. Sinfjotli asserts that, in Valhalla, the warriors were successful in seducing and "winning the love of Gundmundr" and that they penetrated him.

The concept may seem ambivalent, but not if you keep in mind that there was nothing wrong in having sexual relations with a junior. There was stigma only if the person being seduced presumed to be a leader, who should have been in the dominant role.

The phallus was a powerful symbol for the warriors. Things of power or importance were given phallic qualities. The word to plow a field was phallic; the word to fertilize it was phallic; even the prows of ships were phallic. To this day we speak of "mowing" down the enemy, or "plowing them under." We still use common four letter, sexually charged, words to express dominance in anger.

By the time of the Norman conquest of England in 1066, the Norse had barely been Christianized. Their attitudes and customs were not yet overly burdened by Christian morality. It is not surprising to find so many of the early descendents of the William the Conqueror to have been actively homosexual.

Richard Coeur de Léon

King Richard, known as the Lion Hearted, was born on 8 September of 1157, in the royal palace at Oxford, England. He was the son of Henry II and Eleanor of Aquitaine. His grandparents were the Empress Matilda, whose own grandfather was William the Conqueror, and Geoffrey, Duke of Anjou.[36]

The homosexual affairs of his father and those of his predecessor, King William II, known as "Rufus," are well documented.[37] Henry II was a particularly capable warrior;[38] he is one of the selected examples of great military men who will be briefly listed in this section. The reader may wish to read further on the individuals included here.

As the eldest surviving son of Henry II, Richard was invested as Duke of Normandy at Rouen in July of 1189, and crowned King of England on 3 September that same year.[39]

It was the age of romantic love, of the troubadours, and it was an age of change. England was being exposed to a higher degree of culture and greater civility. The conquering Norman nobles were introducing new ideas. The dark ages were giving way to light, but there were evils yet to come. It was the age when homosexuality became heresy.

Richard was a product of his age. He was a Plantagenet, a descendant of "demons"; he was the stuff of myth and fable. Both his parents were fabulous characters who left their marks on the times. What his father could not obtain by war and politics, his mother could through wit and cunning.

To understand Richard, it is necessary to keep in mind that his great grandfather conquered England; his father was also a powerful war lord and law giver; his mother was one of the best educated, most cultured, and richest women in the Christian world. Theirs was an omnipresent family in world affairs.

His mother, as a potentate in her own right, had first married King Louis of France, and went on Crusade with him. Reports have it that she led her own army in triumph into Jerusalem, bare breasted like an Amazon.

Once she spotted Henry II, she wanted him. In short order she divorced Louis and married Henry, the future king of England. Morals at the time were freer than they were to be at later times. People were still rather tolerant of the sexual habits of others.

However, change was at hand. Hate mongers were busily preaching against the habits of the nobles and princes of the church.

Richard, like the rest of his family, had a penchant for excess. It is that characteristic, more than any other, which enabled historians to declare that he was overtly homosexual. He could not resist the opportunity of confessing his sins in public. He confessed with a flourish at Messina in Sicily in August, 1190, while setting out on Crusade. He was demonstrative and ostentatious.

While waiting in Sicily, Richard decided to put on a spectacle. He was going to demonstrate that he was the mightiest of the lords; richer than all others; and leader of the Crusade. He planned to "up-stage" his one time lover, Philip Augustus, king of France. Philip Augustus, in contrast, entered Messina modestly and without ostentation or fanfare.

Richard arrived to the blare of trumpets and the noise of swords hitting their buckles. The sun gleamed from the highly polished shields and armor of Richard's army. The clamor brought forth the people from the towns for miles around. Whether Philip Augustus realized the propaganda ploy or not can not be known, but he defused the effect by not reacting to the display. He simply kissed Richard and thus established his equality with him before the multitude.

The two kings knew each other very well. Theirs was a strange love–hate relationship. One contemporary wrote that there was "such a mutual delight and affection between them that their love for each other could never be dissolved or violated." Their love was recorded and transmitted in the "Annals of Roger of Hovedon," which were translated by Railly in 1853.

Richard and the Crusaders were still in Messina about Christmas time. Having bullied the country and extorted from its rulers, he engaged in more showmanship. This time he would publicly confess his overt homosexuality. He contended that he was worried about his soul. Thus he assembled all the clergy with the aid of his army. Once he had them all in the chapel of Reginald de Moyac in Messina, he made his dramatic appearance. Barefoot, carrying scourges made of bundles of branches, he entered as a penitent seeking forgiveness for his sins.

His embarrassing revelations regarding his sexual practices made the clerics uneasy. Surrounded by his army, they were asked to absolve him of his sins. What could they do?

185

One eye witness was suitably impressed, and wrote: "He became a man fearing God and doing good and did not return to his vice." The continuing saga of Richard proved that the witness was much too optimistic. In fairness, however, Richard did appear to have been sincere when he confessed, and repented.

There were strong forces developing in the world at that time to oppose homosexuality; Richard must have been aware of John of Salisbury, who was Archbishop of Chartres when he died in 1180. John of Salisbury's *Polycraticus*, in Book III, excoriates rulers who practice homosexuality. From this period on, homosexuality was to be attacked as a crime for the first time in France.

As another precursor of things to come, there was a report of a time when "there came a hermit to King Richard and, preaching the words of salvation to him, said: 'Be thou mindful of the fate of Sodom, and abstain from what is unlawful: for if thou does not a vengeance worthy, God shall overtake thee'." The text goes on to report that the king "despised the person of his advisor," and that Richard "was not able to readily withdraw his mind from what was unlawful." This occurred only five years after his public confession at Messina.

In 1195, when Richard became seriously ill and he feared for his life, he was warned that the illness was a "manifest sign of God's wrath." Typically, Richard repented again. However, once recovered, he went back to his usual sexual practices. Once again he was attacked by a preacher.

The preacher, Fulke de Neuilly, confronted Richard: "I warn thee, O King, on behalf of Almighty God, to marry as soon as possible thy three shameless daughters, lest worst befall thee..."

"Hypocrite!" Richard responded, "To thy face thou liest, inasmuch as thou knowest that I have no daughters whatever."

"Beyond doubt, I do not lie, because, as I said, thou hast three most shameless daughters, of whom one is Pride, the second Avarice, and the third Lust."

Prophetically Richard responded: "Listen, all of you, to the warnings of this hypocrite, who says that I have three shameless daughters, namely Pride, Avarice and Lust, and recommends me to get them married. I therefore give my pride to the Knights Templar, my avarice to the Monks of the Cistercian Order, and my lust to the prelates of the church."

Richard did marry, but he never really lived with his wife.

Berengaria, his widow, was denied her rights and had to appeal to the Pope to make good her claim. No one would believe that Richard slept with her.

Richard was only forty-two when he died. He accomplished much during his life. He was a multifaceted personality who was loved and hated, loathed, and detested; and also revered and respected. He was a powerful military leader and he was homosexual. He lost his life in an endless war against his boyhood lover, Philip Augustus, King of France; he was killed while besieging the Castle of Chaluz, on 7 April, 1199.[39]

"I have lost the staff of my age, the light of my eyes," wrote his mother, Eleanor of Aquitaine. She was one of the few who mourned his passing.[40]

Jacques de Molay

Jacques de Molay may or may not have been homosexual; he is included here because he was the Grand Master of the Knights Templar. As such he was accused of sodomy and heresy among other crimes, as were all the Knights Templar. He and they as a group were condemned and convicted. His own fate was to be tortured and burned at the stake in March, 1314.[41] His background and early life are only incidental to his fate as the last Grand Master.

The Order of the Knights Templar was founded by Hugh de Payens in 1128 as a military order to protect the routes used by the Crusaders to invade the Holy Land.[42]

At the very Council of Troyes, where the Order of Knights Templar was formed, homosexuality was common enough to be the basis of ribald humor. One contemporary felt no reluctance to announce that all the friends and admirers of St. Bernard were there to support the formation of the Order, except the Bishop of Orléans, whom he described as a succubus and a sodomite.

It was a time when women, in general, were considered personifications of evil and carnal lust. The cult of the Virgin Mary, while seemingly glorifying woman, in fact ritualized the endemic anti–feminist attitudes.

As it was organized, the Templars were accountable only to the Pope and answered to no other. They were a military and financial success. As a result, over the years they amassed extensive land holdings throughout the Western World and their castles became the repository for vast hordes of gold and other valuables belonging to Kings and Princes. Paris became the center of their financial empire. They began their acquisitions with a major donation of land in 1127.[43] Their vast wealth became the focus of the greed of Philippe IV of France, known as The Fair (le Bel).

Philippe was always in need of money. Obtaining cash in the year 1307 was not easy. The story of the destruction of the Knights Templar and the grab for their gold is a shocking tale which has been covered in great detail by others. What is of interest here is the fact that Philippe IV used the alleged homosexuality of the Knights Templar to institute civil law, for the first time, against homosexuals. He combined homosexuality with heresy, treason and simony, and then claimed the right to protect the interest of the Church by seizing the lands and valuables of the Templars. He presumed a color of right under Church law by claiming to act on behalf of the Pope.[43] The story is sordid. It became the bases for subsequent civil proscriptions later in history. Thus one of the most powerful and successful military forces of the Crusades was destroyed by a homophobic individual who was King of France. The legacy of homophobia fostered by Philippe the Fair altered attitudes, frightened people, and left its mark on the military down to the present.

Undoubtedly Henry VIII of England (1491–1545) of England took notice of Philippe's success in gaining wealth by attacking the military order of monks. Other monks would be fair game. Indeed, a letter exists in which Henry VIII gave advice to his relative, King James V of Scotland. After chiding James V for resorting to absconding with livestock when in need of cash, he advises him to seize monasteries after accusing the monks of sodomy. Henry VIII is important here because it was he who instituted civil proscriptions against homosexuality in English law and in the military codes.[44]

As might be expected, homophobic laws were introduced into the American colonies as a result of British law and custom. Thus by the time of the American Revolution, these laws were in effect, even if not enforced.

Homoaffectionalism and the American Revolution

This portion lends itself to a division among several individuals brought together by the American Revolution. This period of American history has become almost sanctified and consequently much is suppressed that ought to be known. The heroes of the War of Independence, which is a euphemistic term for revolution, are painted larger than life, uniformly endowed with nobility which transcends human weakness. Too often they seem less then flesh and blood, perhaps with the exception of Benjamin Franklin, and they are made to appear almost sexless.

The reality is that some of the key personalities were homosexually active, and they were bent on forming a monarchal form of government. Indeed, these individuals were most active in the circle around George Washington. The question of the sexual orientation of George Washington will be left to others. Despite the rumors put forth by some students of history, not enough real evidence has been found to make any definitive conclusion.

The flourishing monarchist movement within the Continental Army and the homoaffectionalism displayed by the circle around Washington has been largely ignored by historians. The extant information and rational conclusions based on recurring inference can be presented to make the point: there were homosexuals involved in the Revolution and they were monarchists. To be sure, there were also monarchists who were not homosexuals; however, those selected for this study were both, and also famous for their military prowess.

To explain the phenomenon of bowdlerizing history goes beyond the scope of this study. In the mind of some "patriot" historians, the lesson preached may have been more important than the truth. The question of the monarchal movement has been largely suppressed or ignored. The fact that George Washington was offered a crown is hardly discussed. The fable of George Washington and the cherry tree he chopped down is an outstanding example of distortion. It was the concoction of Parson Mason Locke Weems, who was a sometime clergyman; Washington, he said, confessed to his father that he chopped down the cherry tree because, "I can not tell a lie." Obviously, Weems could.[45]

Some of the myths and distortions of the revolutionary period were created for the best of patriotic reasons by Thomas Jefferson as propaganda against King George III. Others, like Benjamin Franklin and John Adams, also engaged in a propaganda war against the crown. Thus it is necessary to read the source material carefully, since it may be an interlacing of fact and propaganda, and try to discern the truth.

For many, at the end of the revolution, the only logical solution to the complex problems facing the new American nation was some form of constitutional monarchy. Among those who wanted a monarch were Alexander Hamilton; Nathan Gorham, who was President of the Continental Congress; General Baron von Steuben, Inspector General of the Continental Army; and Rufus King, a prominent member of the Continental Congress. The list could be extended.

The plan was to ask Henry, Prince of Prussia, to be King. He was the brother of Frederick the Great, King of Prussia. Henry was a military leader of importance. He was also homosexual, as we shall show. His brother, King Frederick, who was only an incidental player in the Revolution, was also homosexual, and one of the greatest military geniuses of the time.

Baron von Steuben, a friend of Henry, Prince of Prussia, and well known to Frederick the Great, played a key role in the homosexual and monarchist group around George Washington.

In dealing with Steuben, the researcher is confronted with many problems. Not only was he involved in the monarchal movement, which historians seem to want to suppress, but he was apparently homosexual, a fact historians have avoided. To make matters worse, Steuben and his family tended to lie about their own lineage and background. The 19th century German–American historian Frederick Kapp produced one of the best biographies of Steuben in 1859, but was misled on certain points. James McAuley Palmer had to refute the genealogy reported by Kapp, after gaining access to German archival material produced by the German historian Kalkhorst. Nevertheless, the basic facts remain.

Based on oral information provided to Kapp by John W. Mulligan, who was probably Steuben's lover, it was before the adoption of the present U.S. Constitution that a circle of friends around Steuben questioned the form of government being considered. It was proposed to have the President of the United States vested with authority like the princely powers of the Dutch monarch. Steuben was asked to approach Henry, Prince of Prussia,

190

and invite him to take the high office.[46] There is ample evidence of this extant in the Library of Congress, and in books which have collected and collated the correspondence of the prime players, such as Rufus King, Thomas Jefferson, John Q. Adams and Henry Clay.[47]

The formation of the Society of Cincinnatus was part of the monarchal scheme. Incidentally, that society may be looked upon as the first veterans' organization. Granted that it was restricted to officers and gentlemen, nevertheless it is a precursor. It is not only a precursor of veterans' organizations but seems to have influenced the formation of Tammany Hall as a political society in New York. This is germane here only because some of those who were the originators of the Society are the subject of this study.[48]

In 1784, George Washington became alarmed at the outcry against the Society and, as President of the Order, persuaded their general meeting in Philadelphia to recommend the renunciation of all political activities and the hereditary aspects. Hamilton was urged to support the changes, but he would only agree to the hereditary rights of the eldest sons being changed.[49]

Alexander Hamilton

It was declared by his biographer, John C. Miller, that in an age which produced such men of stature as George Washington, John Marshall, James Madison, Thomas Jefferson, William Pitt, and Napoleon Bonaparte, Alexander Hamilton was the greatest of these "choice and master spirits of the age." His contributions to the formation of the United States were enormous. At the same time he was controversial. Born out of wedlock, he was subject to derision by his enemies. John Adams referred to him as "that bastard brat of a Scotch peddler." [50]

Hamilton was born in the British colony of Nevis on 11 January, 1757, and was shot to death by Aaron Burr, in a duel, on 12 July, 1804. His father was a Scottish merchant from St. Christopher; his mother was Rachel Fawceet (Faucette). His mother was married to someone else when he was born. Her legal husband was a Dutch (German?) landholder in St. Croix named John Michael Levine (Lavien). His parents did not stay together, and although his father lived until 1799, Hamilton was virtually an orphan. His mother died in 1769.[51]

Bowdlerized histories of Hamilton's life paint his mother as a paragon of virtue accepted by society despite the fact that she bore an illegitimate child while married to another man.[52] Others are not so kind. According to the bill of particulars for a divorce filed by John Lavien, and referred to by John C. Miller in his biography of Hamilton, Lavien described his wife as no better than a prostitute. However, in fairness, it must be borne in mind that she endured a loveless marriage and was forbidden to remarry under Danish law, which applied, since she was the offending party.

As a youth, Hamilton was employed in the general store of Nicholas Cruger, in Christianstadt. Then with the aid of his aunts and friends, he was sent to New York to be educated in the fall of 1772. He went to King's College, now Columbia University, the following year. It was there he became active in the politics of the day.

Eventually he came to the attention of George Washington who engaged him as his secretary. Then, on 1 March, 1777, Washington made him an aide-de-camp with the rank of Lieutenant Colonel. In a few months, Hamilton had become de facto Chief of Staff. Washington was impressed with him and "he became a trusted advisor." He helped with the enormous work load of organizing and systematizing army procedures. Indeed, he wrote an army reorganization plan 28 January, 1778, and then wrote a organizational report on the Inspector General's Office which was accepted by Congress 18 February, 1779. Additionally he wrote a comprehensive set of military regulations for the Continental Army.[53]

Hamilton detached himself from Washington, and had a quarrel with him. He wanted to command troops and see active duty. Washington finally gave him a regiment in the corps led by LaFayette. At the siege of Yorktown he "commanded (a) brilliant attack." After the war he studied law and became an attorney. He served in the Continental Congress from 1782 until 1783. He was disenchanted with the Continental Congress and supported a stronger form of government.[54]

Having covered the rather routine aspects of Hamilton's life it is essential to review the evidence of his homosexuality and thus relate him to this study. Perhaps the best way to accomplish this is to let him speak for himself. The following letter, which will be quoted in pertinent part, was written by Hamilton when he was twenty-two years of age. It was written to his friend Colonel John Laurens, who was a few years older than Hamilton. Laurens was the son of the President of the Continental Congress, Henry Laurens. The dating of the letter was made by scholars, based on internal evidence: April, 1779.

Cold in my professions, warm in my friendships, I wish, my Dear Laurens, it might be in my power, by action rather than words, to convince you that I love you. I shall only tell you that 'til you bade us Adieu, I hardly knew the value you had taught my heart to set upon you. Indeed, my friend, it was not well done. You know the opinion I entertain of mankind, and how much it is my desire to preserve myself free from particular attachments, and to keep my happiness independent of the caprice of others. You should not have taken advantage of my sensibility to steal into my affections without my consent. But as you have done it and as we are generally indulgent to those we love, I shall not scruple to pardon the fraud you have committed, on condition that for my sake, if not for your own, you will always continue to merit the partiality, which you have artfully instilled into me.

Note here that Hamilton switches to the royal "we" from time to time; this practice is found in many of his letters and is not intended to indicate the plural.

The letter went on to discuss events of the day. Hamilton commented on Laurens' appointment as an aide-de-camp to Washington, and wrote that Congress was wrong to delay Laurens' appointment to the rank of Lt. Colonel. Hamilton then brought up the subject of marriage. He expressed his resistance to it, but the need for it, and recommended it to Laurens:

And now my Dear as we are upon the subject of wife, I empower and command you to get one in Carolina. Such a wife as I want will, I know, be difficult to be found, but if you succeed, it will be stronger proof of your zeal and dexterity. Take her description—she must be young, handsome (I lay stress upon a good shape), sensible (a little learning will do), well bred... chaste and tender (I am an enthusiast in my notions of fidelity and fondness), of some good nature, a great deal of generosity (she must neither love money nor scolding, for I dislike equally a termagant and an economist). In politics, I am indifferent what

193

side she may be of; I think I have arguments that will easily convert her to mine. As to religion a moderate stock will satisfy me. She must believe in God and hate a saint. But as to fortune, the larger stock the better. You know my temper and circumstances and will therefore pay special attention to this article in the treaty. Though I risk going to Purgatory for my avarice; yet as money is an essential ingredient to happiness in this world—as I have not much of my own and as I am very little calculated to get more either by my address or industry; it must needs be that my wife, if I get one, bring at least a sufficiency to administer to her own extravagances. NB You will be pleased to recollect in your negotiations that I have no invincible antipathy to the maidenly beauties and that I am willing to take the trouble of them upon myself.

If you should not readily meet with a lady that you think answers my description, you can only advertise in the public papers and doubtless you will hear of many competitors for most of the qualifications required, who will be glad to become candidates for a prize as I am. To excite their emulation, it will be necessary for you to give an account of the lover—his *size*, make, quality of mind and *body*, achievements, expectations, fortune, etc. In drawing my picture, you will no doubt be civil to your friend; mind you do justice to the length of my nose and don't forget, that I --------. [The last portion of this last sentence is not legible in the original. Whether Hamilton goes on to note the size of anything else is a matter of conjecture.]

After reviewing what I have written, I am ready to ask myself what could have put it into my head to hazard this *jeu de folie*. Do I want a wife? No—I have plagues enough without desiring to add to the number the greatest of all; and if I were silly enough to do it, I should take care how I employ a proxy. Did I mean to show my wit? If I did, I am sure I have missed my aim. Did I intend to frisk? [sic] In this I have succeeded, but I have done more, I have gratified my feelings, by lengthening out the only kind of intercourse now in my power with my friend. Adieu Yours. [The word "intercourse" is obviously a double-entendre.][55]

Hamilton also wrote to Laurens 11 September, 1779; his tone was petulant, like that of a slighted lover:

I acknowledge but one letter from you, since you left us, of the 14th of July which just arrived in time to appease a violent conflict between my friendship and my pride. I have written you five or six letters since you left Philadelphia and I should have written you more had you made proper return. But like a jealous lover, when I thought you slighted my caresses, my affection was alarmed and my vanity piqued. I had almost resolved to lavish no more of them upon you and to reject you as inconstant and an ungrateful_____. But you have now disarmed my resentment and by a single mark of attention made up the quarrel. You must at least allow me a large stock of good nature. [Note again the use of the royal "us" in the first sentence. The rest of the letter discussed business of the war. The blank space was left in the original.][56]

Laurens' letters were less romantic, but like Hamilton he used very informal forms in closing and not the standard "Your Most Obedient Servant" and such forms generally in use at the time. A typical closure for his letters may be seen in his letter to Hamilton dated 18 December, 1779:

I am sorry to write you just as I am on the wing. Be so good as to thank Tilghman for his letter; inform him from Mr. Mitchell that his habiliments are making. My Love as usual. Adieu.[57]

In closing a letter assigned the date July, 1782, Laurens wrote:

Adieu, my dear friend; while circumstances place great distance between us, I entreat you not to withdraw the consolation of your letters. You know the unalterable sentiments of your affectionate Laurens.[58]

When Laurens was killed, as the war ended, Hamilton notified LaFayette. The letter was dated 3 November, 1782: "Poor Laurens, he has fallen a sacrifice to his ardor in a trifling skirmish in South Carolina. You know truly I loved him and will judge how much I regret him."[59]

Hamilton did marry, and as he indicated to Laurens, he married a rich woman. He allied himself with one of the richest and most powerful families in New York. He married Elizabeth, the daughter of General Philip Schuyler on 14 December, 1780. He had eight children.

When Hamilton decided to marry Elizabeth Schuyler, he was apparently worried what would happen if they had a falling out after marriage. He had seen what had happened to his mother. Thus when he became engaged he wrote to Elizabeth and sent her what he called "a set of sober questions of the greatest importance." The question he wanted answered was whether she was willing to "share every kind of fortune" with him. "Be assured, my angel, it is not a diffidence of my Betsy's heart, but of a female heart, that dictates the questions. I am ready to believe everything in favor of you, but am restrained by the experience I have had of human nature, and of the softer part of it." [60]

In his biography of Hamilton, Flexner asserted that Hamilton's feelings for Laurens "included hero worship." He also concluded that "where Hamilton was intellectual, Laurens was physical." That author reviewed Hamilton's passionate correspondence not only with Laurens but with LaFayette and contended that they raised "questions concerning homosexuality." [61] There is no question that he was homoaffectionate. Regardless of the status of homosexuality and the law in the eighteenth century, at Hamilton's social level it was not an issue. Flexner quoted from letters to LaFayette to make his point: "Before this campaign, I was your friend agreeable to the ideas of the world;" he goes on, "My sentiment has increased to such a point the world knows nothing about it." [62]

Various descriptions of Hamilton indicate that he was tall; however, he was apparently 5 feet, 7 inches. He was very erect, as one source put it "remarkably erect"; quick and energetic in his movements, with a clear ruddy complexion; reddish brown hair and deep blue eyes. His eyes were called intense and severe, but his mouth was kindly and winning. Over all he seems to have had captivating traits, charm and grace. He was always a hard worker with a "marvelous capacity for concentration." However, after reading his letters and considering his actions and responses to situations, it is likely that he was also irascible and hot–headed and had a quick temper. [63]

It was his hot head and temper that led to his end. He had opposed Aaron Burr, who was running for public office in New York state. Burr took exception, bad feeling followed and ended in a fateful dual. Hamilton was shot and wounded by Burr and died slowly and painfully on 12 July, 1804.[64]

Frederick II

Frederick II, called The Great, was King of Prussia from 1740 until 1786. He was the older brother of Henry, Prince of Prussia, whom the American monarchists wanted to make King of the United States. Both men were military leaders, both were homosexual. Both were linked to Baron von Steuben, the Inspector General of the Continental Army and one of the coterie around George Washington.

For those who wish to read more about Frederick the Great, there are a number of books but only a few go into his homosexuality. As usual, historians have tried to avoid the subject; some even try to deny that he was. Nancy Mitford's biography of Frederick the Great is one of the few which covers the subject adequately.[65]

Both Voltaire and Mirabeau knew Frederick well, and both wrote their opinions and observations from personal experience. Mirabeau was a professional gossip. In 1789, he published his "Secret Memoirs of the Court of Berlin"; the work appeared in two volumes and were originally entitled *Histoire Secrète et Anecdotes de la cour de Berlin*.[66]

In reading the English translation, edited by Oliver H. G. Leigh and printed in 1901, you will have the added problem of an author being coy or devoid of a proper word to be used about the subject. For example, when referring to a lesbian, he had no words in his vocabulary to cover the subject, without an explanation, which he avoids. He used the Greek word "Tribade," that is, "she who rubs." The word lesbian had to wait until later in the 20th century. When he was confronted with male homosexuals, and he wanted to use a derisive term, he employs the word "Gitons." Unless the reader is familiar with Gaius Petronius' *Satyricon*, the meaning of "Gitons" might be missed. The word is derived from the name of the young lad called Giton, who was the catamite and slave of one of the heroes of the story.[67]

Frederick was the son of Frederick William I of Prussia; his grandfather was the Elector Frederick III. In 1701 the grandfather got the permission of the Holy Roman Emperor to style himself King of Prussia. Frederick's father was a strong willed tyrant toward the young Frederick. Reacting to his son's homosexual affair with

Lieutenant Katte, he had Katte beheaded on an especially built scaffold erected outside young Frederick's window. He was only 18 years old at the time and had to watch his lover die. Frederick was stripped of his rank and titles and imprisoned for two years by his father. He had his spirit completely broken but it did not change his sexual orientation.

Frederick learned to play the game. He became an ardent student of military drill and procedures. He agreed to be married to a woman selected for him by his father. Eventually he was brought back into court and reinstated as Crown Prince. He had beaten his father at his own game. He became the perfect Prince and military man.

His grandmother was the daughter of King George I of England, but there seems to have been very little family life and support for young Frederick, except from his sister Wilhelmina. His brother, Prince Henry, was much younger than he. Although Henry was also homosexual, there was no apparent closeness between the brothers.

To give some idea of the type of gossip Mirabeau wrote in his letters concerning homosexuality, the following examples will show his style:

In discussing the King's generosity to certain people at court, Mirabeau noted in a letter dated 20 November, 1786, that whereas the king appeared to give little to his greatest favorites publicly, "yet there are indications that he bestowed great secret largess; (and) that he had secret reasons for conferring such on some persons." Of course the word "favorite" is routinely used by historians and others wishing to infer something else. It is a word like "minion," used for the same reasons. For example, in the same letter, Mirabeau notes that "Brederic, late a lackey to Prince Henry, became a kind of favorite" of the King. He had been "the Prince's well–beloved groom." All these remarks have a malicious tone when read in context. The same letter went on to show how Prince Henry picked up bed partners. Mirabeau wrote that the Count of Brandenburg requested permission of him (Prince Henry) to be present at a particular banquet the Prince was giving for soldiers; Prince Henry gave permission, then, after caressing the "child" (he was actually a young man), said to him, "It is difficult, my little friend, to converse with you here, but ask your father leave to come to my palace, and I shall be glad to see you." Mirabeau went on to comment: "thus artful are his politics." [68]

On 18 November, 1786, Mirabeau noted King Frederick's loyalty to those who supported him while he was still the Crown Prince and subject to his father's wrath. One who benefited when Frederick came to the throne was Count Alexander Wartensleben. The Count had been an officer of the guard, assigned to watch the Crown Prince Frederick. Frederick's father wanted his son spied upon. The Count refused and was arrested and thrown in the prison at Spandau. Mirabeau wrote that Frederick and the count enjoyed "that intimacy (which) will not admit of secrets."[69] The same letter went on about Prince Henry, too, commenting about what the military men thought of the Prince: "they know that the 'Gitons' [flagrant homosexuals] have been, and will always continue, with him..." In a foot note on the word "Gitons," as used in this letter, the editor declared that "this word has a meaning too offensive to be translated."[70]

Throughout Mirabeau's correspondence there are repeated instances where he remarked on the obscene language used by the King in gatherings of intimates. On 19 December, 1786, Mirabeau took notice that the king was brought to laughter by "the obscene jests of Prince Frederick of Brunswick."[71]

Mirabeau quoted Frederick directly from a letter wherein the King, in his old age, was giving advice to his nephew and heir regarding homosexual orientation: "I can assure you, from my own experience, that this Greek pleasure is not a pleasant one to cultivate."[72] Sir Richard Burton who cited this letter in his own work noted that it is reminiscent of a much quoted comment attributed to Voltaire. According to the anecdote, Voltaire and an Englishman agreed upon having a homosexual "experience," and they found it satisfactory. Some days later, when the Englishman wanted to do it again, Voltaire caustically replied: "Once a philosopher; twice a sodomite!"

Voltaire, who had been a long time correspondent of Frederick, may have had a crush on the Prince and later King. In any case, he was a guest of the King's at the palace. He was well aware of Frederick's sexual orientation. At one point when Voltaire decided to leave Prussia and return to France, he gathered some written materials produced by Frederick which were of a ribald, homoerotic nature. These were written by the King under the title "Le Palladion." Frederick wrote other homoerotic works, but "Le Palladion" became the center of a touchy situation. Frederick had

Voltaire arrested and detained in Prussia until the incriminating manuscript was safely back in the King's hands.[73]

Despite the quarrel, Frederick and Voltaire remained friends; when Voltaire died, Frederick gave a memorial address to the Prussian academy, where he noted that the enemies of Voltaire would sink into oblivion while Voltaire's fame would grow from age to age. On another occasion Frederick said, "I was born too early, but at least I have seen Voltaire." [74]

Frederick the Great was one of greatest military geniuses of all time. Not only did he lay the foundation for the powerful Prussian military machine which dominated Europe until World War I, and which was the basis of Adolf Hitler's aspirations, he directly influenced the development of the Continental Army and subsequent U. S. Army. He was the personal teacher of General Baron von Steuben, the one individual who created a "modern" army for George Washington.[75]

Baron von Steuben

Friedrich Wilhelm Ludolf Gerhard Augustin, Baron von Steuben embellished his own name late in life to enhance his career. He changed his name to Fredrich Wilhelm Augustus Heinrich Ferdinand. In America he was known as Frederick William Augustus von (or de) Steuben. His grandmother, who was the Countess Charlotte Dorothea von Effern, married below her status; she married Herr Augustin Steube. However, she knew the importance of status, so she and her husband changed the name to von Steuben about 1708. Steube was a part time preacher, known to be sexually aggressive. His father had been a tenant farmer. As luck would have it, Augustin Steube got to preach in Castle Schmalkalden and in the Palatinate, and by age twenty-seven became pastor of the Reformed Church of Leimer. That was the year he married Charlotte Dorothea, 1688. Thus began the family that produced Baron von Steuben.[76]

The only career open to a poor but socially aggressive family was the military. Now with a "von" in their name, the officer corps was open to young Steuben. His father had also been a soldier, which brought the youngster into contact with soldiers and their life from his earliest years.[77] As his career advanced, Steuben served in the army of Prince Henry and became acquainted with him. Later Steuben was captured by the Russians on 23 October, 1761, and with a number of officers and soldiers was honorably taken to Russia. While there he attracted the attention of the Grand Duke Peter, who was soon to be Peter the III of Russia. The attraction was undoubtedly sexual, and thus Steuben became a guest in the palace. It was this situation which enabled him to be of great service to Frederick the Great. The Grand Duke Peter informed Steuben that the Empress Elizabeth was dying, and that when he became Emperor he would make peace with Prussia. That information was transmitted to Frederick the Great to his great advantage.[78]

After the war, while Steuben is still a young man, something happened. He had to leave the Prussian service. Kapp noted in his biography that Steuben claimed, later in life, that "an implacable personal enemy" led to his leaving.[79] Kapp accepted the idea that Frederick the Great was engaging in his usual rough treatment of military personnel once their services were no longer essential, but there was more to the story. Palmer quoted an anonymous letter, dated 13 August, 1777, which accused Steuben "of having taken familiarities with young boys which the laws forbid and punish severely... that is the reason that M. de Steuben was obliged to leave Hechingen, and that the clergy of your country intend to prosecute him by law as soon as he may establish himself anywhere." [80]

Needing employment, Steuben traveled extensively after his release from the army. It was during this time that he made the acquaintance of Count de St. Germain, who became a factor in his going to America some years later. While in the company of Prince Frederick of Wurtemburg, Steuben was introduced to the Prince of Hohenzollern-Hechingen. With the warm recommendation of Prince Henry, Steuben was offered the office of Grand Marshall of the Prince's court, which he accepted. There he became a most intimate confident of the Prince and remained with him for ten years. It was after that, while seeking a higher post with the Emperor, that Steuben's "implacable personal enemy" made the accusation regarding the misconduct with boys.

It was while serving Hechingen that Steuben attained the rank of Baron (Freiherr) and became a knight of the Margrave of Baden's Order of Fidelity. After that, his employer suffered financial reverses and Steuben had to look elsewhere. In 1776 he tried to enter the French army; that failed, as did a later effort to join the Austrian army. He continued to try other places. While in Baden, Steuben met a man who knew Benjamin Franklin and suggested that Steuben might find a use for his talents in America. Letters were sent to Franklin and others by his new friend. Fortunately, Steuben's professional reputation was well known. The French court was now involved and, as it happened, Count de St. Germain was the French Minister of War. It was he who recommended him to Beaumarchais, who, in turn, was responsible for giving secret aid to the American colonies. To assure a suitable reception of Steuben, it was agreed to send him to America as a "Lieutenant General." [81] He was sent to the American colonies complete with a male secretary and an aide-de-camp.

After his arrival at Valley Forge he was put in charge of training an army. He introduced systems and procedures learned from the Prussian army. He also became deeply involved in the politics of the day and, when the war was over, joined with the monarchists, suggesting that his long-time friend Henry, Prince of Prussia, be considered to be King of the United States. That became the plan. [82]

During this time Steuben met the youth, John W. Mulligan. The lad was hired as his secretary. They lived together, until Steuben died, on close and intimate terms as evidenced by the few letters left. Most touching of all the documents is the letter written by Mulligan to Benjamin Walker, on 29 November, 1794, to tell him that Steuben had died "on Tuesday morning last." [83]

It should be noted, despite the mountain of documents and correspondence produced by Steuben, that almost none of his personal correspondence with John W. Mulligan is to be found. The negative evidence suggests that it may have been deliberately destroyed. The facts regarding his sexual orientation are few, but the conclusion may be drawn that he was homosexual. For the purposes of this study, he is important as the military link to the great tradition of Prussian army of Frederick the Great. He laid the foundation for the United States Army which was built on that tradition.

Section 3
The 19th Century to the Present

With the 19th century there was a marked change in the approach of the public toward homosexuality. In the past, "the love that dare not speak its name" was hampered by a limited vocabulary and a lack of non–pejorative words to discuss the phenomenon. To this point, for this study, the word homoaffectionalism has been used to cover certain aspects of male bonding, which may or may not have involved homoerotic sexual expression. Proof of actual sexual contact was more elusive in most cases, and the word "homosexual" did not exist until Dr. Karoli Maria Benkert (1824 – 1882) created it.[84] The creation of the word in 1869 was a response to the word "Uranian" invented by Karl Heinrich Ulrichs (1825 – 1895).[85] The term usually used in the Prussian sanctions was "unnatural tendencies." The word "Uranian" was utilized by Dr. Magnus Hirschfeld (1868 – 1935), but it soon gave way to the less pejorative word. The usual words used were "sodomite" or "pederast," primarily based on religious usage and Greek history. In Germany, words like "Knabenschaender" (boy lover) were in vogue. As we advanced to Charles Darwin, the "natural order" of things became involved and a perversion of that nature produced a "pervert."

While England and the United States tried not to discuss the subject and France decriminalized the conduct, Germany went through the agony of change and confrontation. The original, antihomosexual, Prussian Paragraph 143 of the Penal Code of 14 April, 1851 became Paragraph 152 of the North German Confederation. A rough copy of the Code is reproduced in Magnus Hirschfeld's *Jahrbuch Fur Sexuelle Zwischenstufen*, vol. 7 (1905), pages 3 to 66. It found its way to become the more infamous Paragraph 175, which was used by Adolf Hitler to exterminate homosexuals.

The repression in Germany produced a highly organized sexual liberation movement. Hirschfeld published a book entitled *The Uranian* in 1903; he also started an international movement which ultimately led to sexual reform in England, though long after his death.

It was the military victory over the French in the Franco–Prussian War that led to the spread of antihomosexual sentiment, beginning with the establishment of the Second Reich at Versailles in January of 1871. The absorption of the Southern German Kingdoms introduced Paragraph 175 throughout the Empire.

The French Constituent Assembly decriminalized homosexuality in 1791, while Louis XVI was still King. Later it was confirmed in the adoption of the Code Napoleon in 1813.

In Prussia, those convicted of "unnatural indecency" were burned at the stake until as late as 1794. Lesser penalties were imposed between 1794 and 1851. There were many attempts to lessen the penalties. Between 1837 and 1968, prison was the usual penalty.

On 16 October, 1929, after the successful passage of a reform bill in a committee of the Reichstag, Paragraph 175 was to be repealed. Then came the collapse of the American stock market, with its world–wide impact. The Nazis come to power and Paragraph 175 remained and was expanded.

Fortunately, Hirschfeld, who was a Jew, was out of the country when the Nazis burned his Institute in Berlin. They burned thousands of books, research papers, and photographs. Ernst Roehm led the attack.

As irony would have it, it was Ernst Roehm who established a private militia to support Hitler. Roehm was homosexual. He created the S.S., the Brown Shirts. Then he was killed on Hitler's orders, along with about 400 others, accused of homosexuality and treason to Hitler, in June of 1934.

In his book *Hidden Heritage*, published in 1980, Byrne R. S. Fone makes a modern plea on behalf of the word "Uranian." He also discusses the origin of the word "Lesbian" and the term "Daughters of Bilitis." Both these terms came into being in a book by the French writer Pierre Louys, called *Songs of Bilitis* (1894). Until the early 20th century, as noted above, the word "tribade" was used to describe female homosexuals.

As Fone notes, the word "gay" just seemed to appear in the United States after World War II. During World War I the term was associated with a fun–loving effervescent personality, as in a "gay blade" or in the song lyrics: "When our hearts were young and gay." There was some usage of the term "gay" during the 19th century as a euphemism applied to a prostitute. The word gradually developed overtones of sexism, because it was not gender specific and it was being applied to lesbians as well as homosexual men. Thus with the rise of feminism in the late 20th century, the word "Gay" is used for homosexual men and the word "Lesbian" for female homosexuals. In the last decade of the 20th century the pejorative word "Queer" has been adopted by militant homosexuals as a confrontational self–description.

At the beginning of the 20th century, the world was still concerning itself with the sexual transgressions of the high and mighty. On 17 November, 1906, a German weekly newspaper, *Die Zukunst*, carried an attack on the alleged group of homosexuals who were the friends and advisors of Kaiser Wilhelm. It was written by the editor Maximilian Harden, under the title "Praeludium." A week later he exposed the Kaiser's long term affair with Prince Philipp zu Eulenburg–Hertefeld. The article also implicated Count Kuno von Moltke, and accused them of "secret immorality" and "unnatural vice."[86] The scandal grew until Eulenburg left the country in 1907.

The scandal of 1907 broke on the heels of a 1902 scandal involving Alfred Krupp, also an intimate of the Kaiser. But in this case, Krupp, a manufacturer of guns and munitions, became the center of an exposé of his homosexual conduct with young men on the Island of Capri.[87]

Since World War I, more attention has been paid to homosexuals in the ranks and on board ships. Dr. Magnus Hirschfeld participated in a study which was published under the title *The Sexual History of the World War*. Havelock Ellis wrote an introductory piece and Hirschfeld wrote the Forward; it was published by Cadillac Publishing Co. in 1941, six years after Hirschfeld died. It focused on the sexual behavior of soldiers and sailors, both officers and those in the ranks. It covers such material as "sex lives of warring nations"; "at the battle fronts"; "behind the lines"; "in military hospitals"; and "in enemy prisons." The approach of the book follows the pattern of the late 19th century, and without naming names, declares that the work was compiled "in collaboration with world–famous physicians, scientists and historians." In keeping with the times, there was a warning on the opening page to tell the public that it was "intended for circulation among mature educated persons only."

This brings the study to World War II, and the current status of homosexuality and the military.

The Homosexual and the United States Military

Until World War II, there were few explicit proscriptions against homosexuals in the military service. That declaration was made by Paul Koffsky, office of General Counsel, Department of Defense, during a panel discussion on the question of "Homosexuality In the Military." When those policies existed at all, he noted, they were in the form of Medical Department regulations. In 1923 the Medical Department held homosexuality to be sexual pathology, which could be used to exclude individuals from the military service. From 1948 to 1956, the regulations provided for a medically disqualified discharge. The regulations defined the conduct as a "psychosexual condition" rendering the individual medically unfit for military service.

It was during World War II that the Army for the first time discharged a significant number of troops because of homosexuality based on several regulations. The first was Section VIII of Army Regulation 615–200, which provided for physical or character disabilities as demonstrated by the soldiers' habits, traits or misconduct. Normally, those discharges were "without honor" under Section VIII.

Koffsky continued his report by citing the second regulatory authority for discharges at that time. There was a Circular No. 3, issued in 1944, which was designed to separate "true and confirmed homosexuals" who were "not deemed reclaimable," and whose conduct was not aggravated by independent offenses. Under the Circular, depending on status, officers were permitted to resign for the "good of the service," enlisted personnel were given discharges "without honor."

By the end of World War II in 1945, greater emphasis was placed on reclamation of homosexual soldiers. Those persons could be returned to active service. In 1947 the policy became stricter. At that time if the soldier had "homosexual tendencies but had not committed any homosexual act in the service," there would be an undesirable discharge. The general discharge was given "in rare circumstances," if the soldier had a long period of service "in an honest and faithful manner." Honorable discharges were "quite rare" and were given only when the soldier had an especially meritorious military record. The policy concerning the presence of an aggravating offense accompanying the homosexuality remained the same:

the soldier would be court martialled.

In 1949, the Department of Defense which had just recently been established issued a directive setting forth policy on homosexuality. That Directive was implemented by the Army in 1950. The Directive stated that "true, confirmed, or habitual homosexual personnel, irrespective of sex, will not be permitted to serve in the Army in any capacity and prompt separation of known homosexuals from the Army is mandatory." In addition, the accused was required to report to the commanding officer any facts concerning the overt acts of homosexuality of which the soldier was aware.

By 1955, the policy was vacillating and relaxed somewhat. Some soldiers were considered to be "reclaimable" when they "inadvertently" participated in overt acts of homosexual conduct. However, "inadvertence" was not defined. By 1958, the more rigid policy was reinstituted which declared that "homosexuals do not qualify for military service."

In 1970, the separate regulations on homosexuality were revoked. "Guidance" was then incorporated into the regulations covering officer and enlisted separations. The new regulations made a distinction between "tendencies" and "homosexual acts." The term "tendencies," however, was not defined. Officers who had "homosexual tendencies" would be separated for moral or professional dereliction, or "to protect national security." With enlisted personnel there had to be a finding of a homosexual act before a finding of "homosexual tendencies" could be made. Enlisted personnel were separated for "unsuitability" if they had "homosexual tendencies."

Some litigation concerning the homosexual policies began in the years before 1980. Just before 1981, the policy was that the acts or profession of homosexuality would give rise to a presumption of homosexuality, which was rebuttable by the service member. The pre–1981 policy is distinguished from the current policy in an important respect. Under the earlier policy, a member of the service who engaged in homosexual conduct or who "displayed homosexual tendencies" was given the opportunity to convince an administrative discharge board that the member's duty performance was outstanding, and that he or she should be retained in the service.

The current (1992) policy is found in Department of Defense Directive 1332.14, issued in January of 1982. That policy Directive maintains that homosexuality is incompatible with military service.

Under the policy, individuals are excluded from the military when they engage in homosexual conduct or by their statements demonstrate a propensity to engage in homosexual conduct. Homosexual orientation requires the discharge of a service member, regardless of service performance.

To justify the new stricter policy, the Department of Defense cited the need to "maintain good order, discipline, and morale, to promote mutual trust and confidence among military personnel, to ensure the integrity of the system of rank and command, and to facilitate assignment and world–wide deployment of military personnel who often must live and work with little privacy."

Directive 1332.14 defined the term "homosexual" to include those individuals who either have committed homosexual acts, are committing homosexual acts, or desire to do so. Thus, as a general rule, either conduct or orientation results in a determination of homosexuality. The homosexual act is defined as bodily contact, actively undertaken or passively permitted, between members of the same sex for the purpose of satisfying sexual desires. Conduct or statements of homosexuality or bisexuality, either present or during current service, are the basis for separation.

The Directive provides specific standards for separation. The general rule is that homosexual orientation necessarily results in separation. Separation is required if the person has engaged in, attempted to engage in, or solicits another to engage in homosexual acts "unless there is a finding that all of the following criteria have been met:

"First, the proscribed conduct is a departure from the member's usual and customary behavior;

Second, in view of the totality of the circumstances, the conduct is unlikely to recur;

Third, the member did not accomplish the conduct by force, coercion, or intimidation while the member was on active duty;

Fourth, on a case by case basis, it is determined that the individual member's retention is consistent with the Service's interest in proper discipline, good order, and morale of the force; and

Fifth, the member does not have a homosexual orientation. In other words, that the member does not desire or intend to engage in homosexual acts.

208

The Directive provides for guidance on the characterization of the type of discharges for homosexuality, which alone do not require other than honorable." [88]

Department of Defense's Policies Attacked

The sharp political response to the Department of Defense's policy reflects the growing power of the homosexual community in the United States during the last decade of the 20th century. Three Congressmen demanded a review of the polices by the United States General Accounting Office. They were the Honorable John Conyers, Jr.; the Honorable Gerry E. Studds; and the Honorable Ted Weiss. A response to their request was issued in the form of a report dated 12 June, 1992. It was published for public consumption and information.

The report compiled and analyzed statistics on the separation of homosexuals from the military service from 1980 to 1990; it included the number of personnel by service, race, ethnics, gender, and occupational category. It set out to determine the cost of replacing personnel separated under the policy and the cost of investigation into allegations of homosexuality. It also identified and analyzed the evidence that had been developed by the Defense Department, the military services, and the non-defense sources cited to support the policy on homosexuality. It then obtained information on the general public's attitudes, other nations' military forces policies, and other organizations' views on the compatibility of homosexuality with the military and other work environments. [89]

The report found that there had been an average of about 1,500 men and women discharged annually between 1980 and 1990 in the category of "homosexuality." The discharges reached a high of about 2,000 in 1982 and a low of about 1,000 during 1990. The majority discharged were enlisted men; most were white. These discharges were routinely upheld by military courts and civilian courts.

It was found that the Department of Defense does not maintain records on the costs of investigating cases. The report had to limit its costs studies to the cost of recruiting and training.

The report found that psychiatric and psychological organizations in the United States disagree with the policy, and believe it to be factually unsupported, unfair, and counterproductive. In addition,

209

two studies commissioned by the Department of Defense have refuted the position that there is a potential security risk associated with homosexual orientation. In addition, the Secretary of Defense and the Chairman of the Joint Chiefs of Staff acknowledged that homosexual orientation was no longer a major security concern.

The report found that in recent polls the public has become more accepting of homosexuality and of homosexuals serving in the military. Some allied nations have policies similar to those of the United States, and others permit homosexuals to serve in the military. Further, it was shown that police and fire departments in several major cities in the United States have removed employment restrictions regarding homosexuals, without adverse effect on mission.

The statistics showed that, in early 1992, four of seventeen selected nations allied with the United States, or about 24%, had policies that appeared to be designed to prevent homosexuals from entering military service. Thirteen countries of the group did not exclude homosexuals. During the past ten years, at least two countries had dropped their exclusion of homosexuals in the military, and one of the four then excluding homosexuals was reviewing its policy; it expected to rescind its policy in the near future.

Among the statistical findings, it was reported that the Navy represented 27% of the active force during the period of 1980 and 1990. They accounted for 51% of the homosexual discharges, which totaled 8,638 cases. The Army represented 37% of the military forces, discharged 25%, or 4,235 individuals, for homosexuality. The Air Force with 27% of the total force accounted for 18%, or 2,993 cases discharged for homosexuality. The Marine Corps with 9% of the active forces discharged 6%, or 1,053 individuals, for homosexuality. They also found that there was a "disproportionate" number of discharges of white women from the services for homosexuality.

The report also noted that the Defense Department's policy was not based on scientific or empirical data, but rather on the "considered judgment of military professionals and civilian policy makers."

The report also listed a number of examples of expulsions for which performance was not a factor. The individuals were generally outstanding in their performance:

Leonard P. Matlovich, a twelve year veteran of the Air Force.

Claude E. Secora, a sixteen year veteran of the Air Force.

Perry Watkins, a fourteen year veteran of the Army.

Dusty Pruitt, a fifteen year veteran of active and reserve duty in the Army.

James L. Dronenburg, nine years with the Navy.

Miriam Ben–Shalom originally enlisted in Army Reserve in 1947 and served for three years. Then she enlisted along with fellow reservists; she was honorably discharged on 1 December, 1976 but refused reenlistment.[90]

Doubtless there are many others.

The response to the criticism of the Department of Defense by the General Accounting Office evoked an outcry from the religious fundamentalist community. Its most overt expression was in the form of a rejoinder entitled "Position Paper on the DoD [Department of Defense] Policy on Homosexuality." That study reiterates the discredited views found in the DoD policy and demands they be adhered to. The rejoinder was sent under a cover letter signed by Captain L. H. Ellis, CHC, U.S. Navy, The Chaplain, U.S. Marine Corps, on the letterhead of the Department of the Navy, Headquarters, United States Marine Corps. It was disseminated to other high ranking military Chaplains. The report was prepared by Commander Eugene T. Gomulka, Chaplain Corps, United States Navy, Deputy Chaplain, United States Marine Corps, and dated 20 July, 1992. That communication and the antihomosexual report were quickly attacked by Congressman Gerry E. Studds in a letter dated 25 August, 1992, sent to Captain Ellis, with copies to the Secretary of Defense Richard B. Cheney. In referring to the letter Studds wrote:

> This document rationalizes the prejudice and hate that pervades the military regarding this issue, when it should be condemning them as insensitive and unwarranted reactions. To widely disseminate this paper among the Chaplain corps, with an official Command endorsement of its contents for all Flag Officers, is an embarrassment to both the military and the religious faiths represented.[91]

Thus at the close of the 20th century, the conduct which could not "speak its name" in the previous century refuses to be silent. The United States Presidential Campaign of 1992 saw the

appearance of a candidate who sought the backing of the fundamentalist religious right of the Republican Party, which openly
condemned homosexuals and their life styles. That candidate was
Patrick J. Buchanan, who in 1977 permitted his name to be used
in the introduction of a book dedicated to Anita Bryant, a popular
singer, who had been campaigning against homosexuals in Dade
County, Florida, and in California, or anywhere else, when "needed."
The book was openly hostile to homosexuals, and was published
by the Center for Conservative Christian Studies in Tulsa, Oklahoma.
Her career was shattered as a result of her campaign, and Buchanan
lost his bid.

One of the issues which came up during the 1992 Presidential
race, and which divided the two candidates, President George Bush
and Governor Bill Clinton, concerned the status of homosexuals
serving in the military. Bush said that they should not serve, Clinton
said they should. The topic was explored, on television, by
correspondent Bruce van Voorst on 2 September, 1992, as a segment
of *The MacNeil/Lehrer Newshour* entitled "Gays in the Military." [92]

Van Voorst noted a popular movie called *Top Gun* in which a "hot
shot" pilot is depicted as the best of the Navy's aviators who were
known as "top guns." It was the image of the all American boy,
"macho in every way." Then he compared the movie character to
a real "top gun," Navy Lt. Tracy Thorne of West Palm Beach, Florida.
Thorne was a bombardier navigator on an A–6 intruder attack
aircraft. He had finished first in his class at flight school. One
fellow officer picked him as a sure thing to be an Admiral. Then
Thorne went on a television show known as "Nightline," and the
world learned that he was homosexual. Thorne was shown
declaring:

What I'm trying to do is show people that you can be gay, you
can do your job; and your friends, you know, fellow officers in
the Navy, have no problem, people that I've come out to have
no problem with my homosexuality.

Thorne then went on to describe the agony of going public and
the trouble he was having with the Navy because of it. In keeping
with the Department of Defense's policy, Thorne was recommended
for separation from the service.

The commentator noted that homosexuals serve without

discrimination in all other government agencies, including the State Department and the super–secret Central Intelligence Agency. Gays and lesbians, he noted, serve alongside the more than one million civilians in the Department of Defense. Now, it was noted, the issue of homosexuals in the military service had become part of a Presidential campaign for the first time in history.

President Bush was then shown on a television clip from one of his speeches: "I do support our policy in the military. And I will continue to support it."

Then Arkansas Governor Bill Clinton was also shown being asked if he would support gays in the military, and he was shown responding: "Here's where I'm coming from on this issue. I believe we don't have a person to waste in America. We need you all."

Van Voorst then showed the question being posed to the Chairman of the Joint Chiefs of Staff, General Colin Powell. General Powell responded:

It's difficult in a military setting where there is no privacy, where you don't get choice of association, where you don't get choice of where you live, to introduce a group of individuals who, proud, brave, loyal good Americans, but who favor a homosexual life style. And I think it would be prejudicial to good order and discipline to try to integrate that into the current military structure.

The commentator then interviewed various military personnel and got mixed answers. Then the Secretary of Defense Richard Cheney was shown making a much quoted statement:

There have been times in the past when it's been generated on the notion that somehow there was a security risk involved, although I must say I think that's a bit of an old chestnut, that the question turns more upon the need of the Department to maintain the combat effectiveness of our military units.

Van Voorst noted that the same arguments had been used to discriminate against blacks and women in the military, and that President Harry Truman ended racial discrimination with the stroke of a pen in 1942.

Going directly to the criticism of the Department of Defense's

213

antihomosexual policy in the special report issued by the Government Accounting Office, the commentator interviewed Paul Jones who headed the team which produced that study. Jones stated that:

> DoD is implementing its policy. They're expelling several thousand men and women each year based on their sexual preference, that is homosexual preference. It's costing 'em money. We found, in 1990, it cost 'em about 27 million (dollars) just in training and recruiting costs. We found there's no empirical data to support that policy.

In late October, 1992, United Press International reported that the Federal Court of Canada had struck down the Canadian military's policy against employing or promoting homosexuals, ruling that it violated the country's Charter of Rights and Freedoms. The ruling followed a constitutional challenge by Michelle Douglas, a twenty-eight year old Ontario woman, who was forced to give up a promising air force career because she was lesbian. Australia quickly followed suit, striking down its anti-homosexual policy in the armed forces.

In November, 1992, Arkansas Governor Bill Clinton was elected President of the United States. During his campaign he pledged repeatedly to lift the restriction barring homosexuals from the U.S. military service.

NOTES

1. John Boswell, Christianity, Social Tolerance, and Homosexuality (Chicago: The University of Chicago Press, 1980) p. 25.

2. Plato, "Symposium" [178–179]; Great Books of the Western World (Chicago: Encyclopaedia Britannica, Inc., 1952) Vol. 7, p. 152.

3. Boswell, p. 25.
    Plutarch, "Pelopidas" [18–20]; Great Books of the Western World (Chicago: Encyclopaedia Britannica, Inc., 1952) Vol. 14, p. 238–239.
    According to Boswell two additional sources would be Athenaeus 13.561E; and Polyaenus 2.5.1.

4. Plutarch, Vol. 14, p. 238–239.

5. Plutarch, Vol.14, p. 42.

6. Robert Flacelière, trans. James Cleugh, Love in Ancient Greece (New York: Crown Publishers, Inc. 1962) p. 66.

7. Flacelière, p. 62.

8. Flacelière, p. 68–69.

9. Plutarch, Vol. 14, p. 39–40.

10. Aristophanes, "The Clouds," trans. Benjamin Bickley Rogers; Great Books of the Western World (Chicago: Encyclopaedia Britannica, Inc. 1952) Vol. 14, p. 500.

11. Plutarch, Vol. 14, p. 541.

    Peter Green, Alexander of Macedon, 356–323 B.C. (Berkeley: University of California Press, 1991) p. 35.

12. Green, p. 54–55; p. 518.
    Peter Green provides more detailed references on Alexander's appearance on page 518 under note #36. It is particularly interesting to consider the contention that Alexander may have suffered from congenital "tortocollosis" [sic], a condition which may account for the tilting of his head. According to Webster's New Universal Unabridged Dictionary (Cleveland: New World Publishing, 1964). Second Edition, p. 1926; the correct spelling of the medical condition is "torticollis," and means "a condition of persistent involuntary contraction of the cervical muscles, producing a twisting of the neck and an unnatural position of the head..."

13. Plutarch, "Alexander", Great Books of the Western World (Chicago:

Encyclopaedia Britannica, 1952) Vol. 14, p. 542.

14.   Plutarch, p. 545.

15.   Plutarch, p. 576.

16.   Plutarch. p. 563.

17.   Plutarch, "Caesar," Great Books of the Western World (Chicago: Encyclopaedia Britannica, Inc.) Vol. 14, p. 577.

      Gaius Tranquillus Suetonius, The Lives of the Twelve Caesars, trans. Philemon Holland, (New York: The Heritage Press, 1965) p. 3–4; 16.

18.   Dio Cassius, trans. Ernest Cary, Roman History (Cambridge: Harvard University Press, 1984) Leob Classical Library, Vol. III, p. 215.

      Suetonius, p. 15.

19.   Suetonius, p. 4.

20.   Suetonius, p. 36.

21.   Suetonius, p. 34.

22.   Suetonius, p. 157.

      P. Cornelius Tacitus, trans. Alfred John Church and William Jackson Brodribb, The Complete Works of Tacitus (New York: The Modern Library, Random House, 1942) p. 78.

21.   Suetonius, p. 159.

22.   Tacitus, p. 5; 64.

      Suetonius, p. 167.

23.   Suetonius, p. 160; 167.

24.   Tacitus, p. 6.

      Suetonius, 172; 173.

25.   Tacitus, p. 37.

26.   Tacitus, p. 67; 90.

27.   Tacitus, p. 27; 178–179; 183.

28.   Tacitus, p. 115–117.

29.   Tacitus, p. 226.

30.   Aelius Spartianus, trans. David Magie, "Hadrian," Scriptores Historiae Augustae (Cambridge: Harvard University Press, 1947) vol. I, p. 3–4.

The name of the author, Aelius Spartianus, is probably fictitious. He was obviously a person with access to documents either as a librarian or secretary with a knowledge of the law. He was one of six who are credited with writing the Scriptores Historiae Augustae. These men worked during the period from 285 A.D to 335 A.D.

Their work can not be totally relied upon because of errors and, according to scholars in the field, may contain information from forged documents. It is a strange collection, but the use of public documents is also apparent. The work is useful if used with caution. The information regarding the family and origin of Hadrian are reportedly from an autobiography of Hadrian which is now lost.

30. Spartianus, p. 5–7.

The author relates an incident on page 7 which has an abrupt missing word or words: "... he became a favorite of Trajan's and yet, owing to the activity of the guardians of certain boys whom Trajan loved ardently, he was not free from........... which Gallus fostered." What ever he was not free from is what may have caused him to worry about Trajan's attitude toward him.

31. Spartianus, p. 9–11.

32. Spartianus, p. 13–15.

33. Royston Lambert, Beloved And God (New York: Viking Penguin, Inc., 1984) p. 2–8.

It should be noted that Lambert uses archaeological, documentary and numismatic sources.

34. James H. Breasted, Dawn of Conscience (New York: Charles Scribner's Sons, 1935) p. 48; 94–100.

Breasted does an extensive study of the origins of Christianity in the religious practices of Egypt and the ancient East and demonstrates the relationships.

35. The Anglo–Saxon Chronicles, trans. Ann Savage, (Great Britain: Dorset Press: 1983) p. 84–101.

The Viking invasions of England were continuous until 887 – 871 at which time King Alfred "made peace" with them.

To get a better understanding of the Vikings the following list of books can be recommended: History of the Franks, by Gregory of Tours (c. 539 to 594) translated by Lewis Thorpe, Penguin Books, 1977; The Vikings, by James Grahm–Campbell and Dafydd Kid, Wm. Morrow & Co., Inc. 1980; Phallos, by Thorkil Vanggaard, International University Press, Inc., 1972; The Norsemen, Count Eric Oxenstierna, New York Graphic Society Publishers, Ltd., 1965; Four

Thousand Years Ago, Geoffrey Bibby, Alfred A. Knopf, 1962; *The Medieval World,* Norman F. Cantor, The MacMillan Press, 1968; *Daily Life in the World of Charlemagne,* Edward Peters, University Pennsylvania Press, 1978.

36. Anglo–Saxon Chronicles, p. 274.

Amy Kelly, Eleanor of Aquitaine (Cambridge, Harvard University Press: 1950) p. 103.

37. Anglo–Saxon Chronicles, p. 226–227.

Eadmer, trans. Geoffrey Bosanquet, History of Recent Events in England (Philadelphia: Dufour, 1965) p. 48–50.

Eadmer, trans. Richard W. Southern, The Life of St. Anselm (Oxford: Clarendon Press, 1979) p. 69.

These last two works by the monk Eadmer are contemporary accounts. While both books mention the problems that existed between Anselm and king William II, known as Rufus, the formal *History* only briefly mentions their argument over sodomy.

The *Life* goes into greater detail. Anselm, who must have been at the very least homoaffectionate himself, takes issue with the King because of the rampant practice of sodomy in England at the time.

Boswell, p. 215; 218–220.

Boswell goes into more detail regarding the possible homosexual emotions of Anselm. It was at this time that the church was attempting to introduce proscriptions against homosexual conduct in England. There had been no statutes in England regarding homosexual conduct. The so-called Council of London of 1102 urged the adoption of measures to inform the general public that "sodomy" would be considered a sin. Saint Anselm, who then was Archbishop of Canterbury, wrote to the archdeacon William, prohibiting the publication of the decree and stated that: "This sin has hitherto been so public that hardly anyone one would be embarrassed by it, and therefore fallen into it because they were unaware of its seriousness." The official rationale for not publishing it was that it was drafted hastily.

39. Kelly, p. 343–344.

40. Kelly, p. 344.

41. Stephen Howarth, The Knights Templar (New York: Dorset Press, 1991) p. 15–18; 309.

Boswell, p. 297.

42. Howarth, p. 42–43.

43. Howarth, p. 278–279.

    Boswell, p. 295–298.

44. Dom David Knowles, The Religious Orders of England (Cambridge: University Press, 1959) p. 204–205.

    John Bowle, Henry VIII (New York: Dorset Press, 1990) p. 190–193; 198–199; 232–233.

    It should be noted that "Crimes Against Nature" first appear in England as statute 25 Hen. VIII, c. 6.; they were later revised and reappeared as 5 Eliz. c. 17. However, the English must have realized that imposing the death penalty was counter-productive, so unlike Philippe IV's statute, Henry VIII's made it virtually impossible to perfect the elements of the crime. The English used a similar technique established by the Church; thus the crime carried the death penalty, but the penalty was seldom used. A prosecutor had to prove actual ejaculation, and in the anus, with witnesses. The same principle appears later in the British Admiralty Codes.

45. Allan Nevins, The Historian as Detective, Ed. Robert W. Winks (New York: Harper Torchbooks, 1968.

    The story of the cherry tree first appeared in a book written by Weems entitled The Life of Washington, published in 1800, which was quoted by Nevins in his book, under the title "The Case of the Cheating Documents."

46. Richard Krauel, "Prince Henry of Prussia and the Regency of the United States," American Historical Review, Vol. XVII, p. 44–51.

    Frederick Kapp, Life of Baron Frederick William von Steuben, (New York: Mason Bros., 1859) p. 584.

    It should be noted that Steuben had denied that Prince Henry was willing to take the monarchy. When publicly asked about it he is quoted as having said: "As far as I know the prince would never think of crossing the ocean to become your master. I wrote him a good while ago what kind of fellows you are; he would not have the patience to stay three days among you." Couched in the form of jest, these remarks were obviously intended to put off any further discussion of the subject. By the time the issue was raised publicly, it was a failed, unpopular idea.

47. Charles R. King, Life and Correspondence of Rufus King (New York: G.P. Putnam's Sons, 1894) p. 644–647.

    Charles R. King was the grandson of Rufus King, and it was he who collected and collated the letters.

As late as 20 December, 1825, it was the subject of a letter written by John Quincy Adams to C. King, which expressed the hope that the issue would be laid to rest: "Henceforth Prince Henry of Prussia will suffer to sleep in peace." See page 647.

Thomas Jefferson was an adamant opponent of the monarchal form of government. He identified Alexander Hamilton, Baron von Steuben, and General Knox as the major proponents, and he accused them of forming the Society of Cincinnatus to foster their own purposes. See his comments: Lipscomb, Andrew A., "The Anas," *Jefferson's Works*, (Washington, D.C., 1903) pp. 266–271. Jefferson relates that the monarchists were disruptive at an earlier convention at Annapolis which proceeded that in Philadelphia. Even there, he contends, they had tried to create a monarchy, with Alexander Hamilton proposing a compromise which would have made the chief officer of the United States a President for life.

48. Edgar Erskine Hume, "Poland and the Society of Cincinnati," The Polish–American Review, 1935 vol. 1, No 10, p. 11–31.

This article goes into extensive detail regarding the Society. The author was the President of the Society.

Edgar Erskine Hume, "Early Opposition to the Cincinnati," American Historical Society, (American Historical Society, 1936) Vol. XXX, No. 4, p. 597–638.

The opposition to the society was based on its hereditary membership and its monarchal aspirations. Both Steuben and Washington were Presidents of the Society, Hamilton was a member. The powerful opponents included the Adamses, Jefferson, John Jay, and Elderidge Gerry. Fortunately, the Marquis de LaFayette was also opposed to the Order, for he was living in France when their revolution began. Those wishing to read more extensively in the correspondence between the statesmen of the day will find a long list of letters and their dates on pages 12 and 13 in the article "Early Opposition to the Cincinnati" mentioned above. Jefferson was particularly concerned because the Order was based on the military. He wrote a letter to that effect, addressed to Gouverneur Morris, on 10 February, 1784, in which he stated that if the Cincinnati "took well in the States, he would not care if the Revolutionary War had succeeded or not."

Just before the French Revolution, Honoré Gabriel Victor Riqueti, Count de Mirabeau, published a vehement attack on the Society entitled *Consideration on the order of Cincinnatus*. It was published in London, first in French in 1784, then in English in 1785. His brother, Colonel André Boniface Louis Riqueti, Viscount de Mirabeau, was one of the original members of the Society. It should be noted that once the Reign of Terror began in France, those who were members of the Order of Cincinnati were automatically considered worthy of execution as monarchists.

Louise Burnham Dunbar, A Study in Monarchal Tendencies in the United States from 1776 to 1801, (Urbana, Ill.: University of Illinois, 1970) p. 50; 52; 73; 95; 97.

This book is an excellent resource with an extensive bibliography and foot notes.

49. John C. Miller, Alexander Hamilton Portrait in Paradox (New York: Harper & Row, 1959) p. 146–147.

50. James Thomas Flexner, The Young Hamilton (Boston: Little, Brown & Co., 1978) p. 18.

According to the author, Hamilton never doubted that James Hamilton was his father. After his death, however, Timothy Pickering felt it necessary to investigate the matter. In 1822, James Yard, who was closely connected with the family in Nevis, confirmed that Hamilton was born on that island. Pickering noted that: "Although little if anything was publicly spoken, yet it seems always to have been understood among those who were acquainted with the extraordinary man that he was the illegitimate offspring of a Mr. Hamilton, in the West Indies." Pickering had his doubts, for he notices, in the late 1790's, that Hamilton's boyhood friend, Edward Stevens, bore a remarkable resemblance to Hamilton, a fact that had been noticed by others. It was Edward Steven's father who was among those who befriended Hamilton when he was "orphaned" by the death of his mother. There is no evidence, other than Pickering's observations, that Stevens may have been the father of Hamilton.

51. Miller, p. 4.

52. Allen Johnson & Dumas Malone, "Alexander Hamilton," Dictionary of American Biographies (New York: Charles Scribner's Sons, 1932) p. 171–179.

53. Flexner, p. 171.

Johnson & Malone, p.171; 172.

54. Johnson & Malone, p. 173.

55. Harold C. Syrett, Editor, The Papers of Alexander Hamilton (New York: Columbia University Press, 1961) vol. II p. 34–38.

The missing words in the letter clearly suggest some kind of male to male sexual banter, as Hamilton enumerates his physical charms. It was not uncommon to equate the size of a man's penis with other anatomical appendages, whether feet, or fingers or, in this case, noses. Searching literature in my own files I came upon an article written by the historian Jonathan Ned Katz and published in "The Advocate," dated 10 October 1988. Katz quotes a conclusion drawn by Havelock Ellis, in the book *Studies in the Psychology of Sex*: "The Romans firmly believed in the connection with a large nose and a large penis."

In considering the possibility that the word "intercourse" as used by Hamilton was double-entendre, the word was checked in *The Oxford English Dictionary* in the Compact Edition, published in New York by Oxford Press in 1971. In 1798 Malthus used the word "intercourse" to describe illicit sexual union. A Dr. Abernathy used the word the same way in a medical text in 1804. Obviously, the word must have been in common usage at the time of Hamilton to find its way into the literature of the day.

56. Syrett, Vol. II, p. 165–166.

57. Syrett, Vol. II, p. 231.

58. Syrett, Vol. III, p. 121.

59. Syrett, Vol. III. p. 199.

60. Flexner, p. 26.

Johnson & Malone, p. 172.

61. Flexner, p. 255.

62. Flexner, p. 316.

63. Johnson & Malone, p. 178.

64. Flexner, p. 451.

John S. Pancake, Thomas Jefferson & Alexander Hamilton (Woodbury, N.Y.: Barron's Educational Series, Inc., 1974) p. 322–323.

65. Nancy Mitford, Frederick the Great (New York: Harper–Row, 1970) p. 125.

Mitford covers his life completely. On page 125 she quotes from a letter written by Frederick to his sister, Wilhelmina, whom he adored, regarding the death of a special friend, Freidrich Rudolf von Rothenburg, who was injured at the Battle of Chotusitz in 1742.

The wound was ultimately responsible for his death in 1751. He died in Frederick's arms: "I can think of nothing but the loss of one with whom I have spent twelve years in perfect friendship."

Susan W. Henderson, "Frederick the Great of Prussia: A Homophile Perspective," Gay Saber (New York: Gay Academic Union, 1976) vol 1, No. 1, p. 46–54.

66. Honoré Gabriel Riqueti, Comte de Mirabeau, tran. Oliver H. G. Leigh, Secret Memoirs of the Court of Berlin (Washington: M. Walter Dunn, 1901) p. xii.

67. Petronius, The Complete Works of Gaius Petronius, tran. Jack Lindsay, (New York: Privately Printed for Rarity Press, 1932) p. 5; 15.

Giton is the young lad who is engaged through out the book. His name first appears on page 5, and his purpose is described in detail on pages 79 to 81. Other translators use the term "Ganymedes" after the boy taken to Olympus by the god Zeus.

68. Mirabeau, p. 212.

69. Mirabeau, p. 224.

70. Mirabeau, p. 229.

71. Mirabeau, p. 285.

72. Sir Richard Burton, "The Sotadic Zone," The Vice (Atlanta: M. G. Thevis, 1967) p. 49.

The same quotation is found in the article by Susan W. Henderson, cited above, on pages 47–48; she translates the French version found in Burton's work. The French version is as follows: "Je puis vous assurer, par mon experience personelle, que ce plaisir est peu agréable à cultiver."

73. Mitford, p. 18.

Henderson, p. 47–49.

74. Henderson, p. 42.

Henderson cites Letters of Voltaire and Frederick the Great, edited by Richard Aldington, published in New York in 1927, page 384.

75. Kapp, p. 46.

Kapp reports that the youthful Steuben was one of the original students selected to be included in the Military Academy created by Frederick the Great. He was one of thirteen original students, and was personally instructed by the King himself. The author bases

223

this information on material found in *Lebensgeschichte Friederichs des Grossen* by J.D.E. Preuss, published in Berlin in 1833 under title: *Dritter Band*, Pages 199 and 150. It was confirmed in the personal writings of Steuben available to the author as *Steuben's Manuscript Papers*, vol. xiii.

76. James Mc Alpin Palmer, General von Steuben (Cambridge: Yale University Press, 1937) p. 14.

Palmer relied on the careful research of the German historian Kalkhorst to refute the genealogy used by Friedrich Kapp, see:

Kapp, p. 38–39.

77. James McAlpin Palmer, "Steuben," Dictionary of American Biography, (New York: Charles Scribner's Sons, 1936) Vol. IX, p. 601.

78. Palmer, Dictionary of American Biography, p. 601.

Kapp, p. 42; 57.

79. Kapp, p. 61.

80. Palmer, p. 92.

81. Palmer, Dictionary of American Biography, p. 602.

82. Thomas Jefferson, Jefferson's Works, ed. Andrew A. Lipscombe, (Washington: 1903) p. 266–269.

83. A photocopy of this letter and a number of others are in the possession of the author. The original is in the possession of the New York Historical Society from which it was obtained.

84. James D. Steakley, The Homosexual Emancipation Movement in Germany (Salem: The Ayer Co., 1982) p. 10–12.

Benkert was also known by his Hungarian name, Karoli Kertbeny; he was a literary man and not a physician as some have written. The surname Benkert is German; he changed his name preferring a more Magyar sounding name.

85. Steakley, p. 6–8.

86. David F. Greenberg, The Construction of Homosexuality, (Chicago: University of Chicago Press, 1988) p. 352.

Theodore Zeldin, France, 1848–1945 (New York: Oxford University Press, 1979) Vol. 1, pp. 313–414.

Zeldin credits the omission of homosexual offenses from the Napoleonic criminal code as the achievement of the archchancellor Cambacérès, who was a homosexual; Greenberg disagrees.

Cambacérès, according to Greenberg, helped prepare the civil code and had nothing to do with the criminal code, which was prepared by a committee of five jurists. The removal of criminal sanctions reflected the philosophy of Enlightenment. It was an extension of the concept of freedom of contract between consenting adults.

87. Steakley, p. 36.

    Emil Ludwig, Wilhelm Hohenzollern (New York: G.P. Putnam's Sons, 1927) p. 29.

87. William Manchester, The Arms of Krupp (Boston: Little, Brown and Co., 1968) p. 226; 229–236; 756; 780; 813; 870.

88. Leigh Bradley; Paul Koffskyl; Cpt. Melissa Wells–Petry, "Homosexuality in the Military," West's Military Justice Reporter, vol. 30, p. CCVII–CCXI.

89. Frank C. Conahan, et al., DoD's Policy on Homosexuality (Washington: General Accounting Office, 1992) p. 10–15.

90. Conahan, p. 16–78.

91. Copies of the letters and the documents quoted are in the possession of the author. They were provided by the Congressional Office of Gerry E. Studds.

92. Bruce Van Voorst, "Gays in the Military," MacNeil/LehrerNewshour, T.V. Transcript, (Overland Park: Strictly Business, 1992) p. 12–16.

CHAPTER X

SUMMARY

The current Western attitude toward human sexual conduct and homosexual conduct in particular, as it is expressed in law, is the direct result of religious doctrine developed from misinformation and a lack of understanding of human sexuality.

By tracing the origins of the laws which have influenced Western society and the religious pressures which fashioned their adoption and transformation, it is possible to show how attitudes were altered and meanings perverted to suit religious beliefs rather than truth.

There were no apparent restrictions on same–sex relationships in the very early laws. As a matter of fact, as we have seen in the laws of the Babylonians and the Hittites, some privileges accrued to homosexuals, especially sacral male prostitutes.

It is important to recognize that there must have been a time in the evolutionary process when sexual activity preceded the awareness of its reproductive function. Our primordial progenitors, like other animals, must have gratified their lusts instinctively and copulated without giving any thought to the significance of the act at all. The fundamental fact of orgasm does not require any intellectualizing regarding the birth of children. It is reasonable to conclude that the relationship of sexual activity to childbirth was a relatively late and incidental recognition.

The instinct to gratify lust through sexual activity could have had nothing to do with what is thought of today as morality. There would have been no sense of guilt attached to the act.

Since it would seem safe to assume that nature followed a biologically beneficial adaptive process in the successful development of *homo sapiens*, then sexual preoccupation and having a larger penis than any other primate species must have played a vital role in the evolution of the species.

It is also quite evident that *homo sapiens* thrived in group living. This would necessitate the development of social behavior. Mating or even rudimentary sexual activity while living in a group requires some form of social adaptation to avoid disruption. Thus individuals regardless of brute strength had to conform to the needs of other individuals, with a degree of sensitivity not expected of other animals.

226

In prehistoric times the number of individuals living in a group for survival would have been rather limited, but not limited to close relatives. Dominant males could not have driven other males out of the group if the group were to develop successfully. Male toleration of other males would have been essential. Richard Leakey used the term "reciprocal altruism" to characterize cooperative, adaptive human behavior, and considered that particular aspect of human adaptiveness as crucial to the successful survival of *homo sapiens*.[1]

The tendency to tolerate and even like other same–sex human beings, other than close relatives, seems to be the essential element in the process of evolution which has enabled the species to survive and succeed. Leakey noticed that human beings respond to altruism and recoil from the selfish and inconsiderate. By openly manifesting moralistic aggression against "nonreciprocators," Leakey asserts, *homo sapiens* jolted the nonconformers back to reciprocating. This process relies on a sense of guilt being evoked in the nonconformers.

Rationalizing the process of group pressure through guilt must have aided in the development of religions and gods who were then created by humans. Gods must have been needed to explain the incomprehensible to the awakening human mind. Rather than assume that prehistoric *homo sapiens* was a brute devoid of sensitivities, it is more reasonable to assume that early human beings were altruistic creatures capable of sympathy, gratitude, and affection.[2]

The bonding of individuals by means of sexual attraction plays an exceptional role in the relationship between *homo sapiens* "without parallel in the animal kingdom."[3] The desire to procreate does not appear to be the instinctive urge which brings two individuals together sexually. Giving birth may be a concomitant circumstance when a male and female copulate, but it has nothing to do with altruistic instincts. Altruistic instinct leads one human to be attracted to another, regardless of gender. Altruism permits the development of affection and camaraderie. It is the essential element of civilization; it makes civilization possible. It enables humans to tolerate and have affection for other humans and makes cooperation and mutual assistance possible.

Altruism and the affection it engenders between males permits close cooperation, respect, support, and loyal attachment. This has enabled leaders to garner the support and loyalty of other males for the good of all. It is not the brute strength of the leader that earns the loyalty of the group, but a combination of traits including attractiveness and ability.

It is the phenomenon of homoaffectionalism in human behavior which best describes the civilizing component of altruism. Without male bonding and the affection it depends upon, civilization simply could not develop.

It is the awareness of homoaffectionalism as a part of the historical development of men down through the ages that has been traced in these studies. Although notice has been taken of the subordinate role of women as a historical fact, it should not be assumed that their instincts are different with regard to same–sex attraction. The major difference is the fact that society has not afforded many women the kinds of roles that it has permitted men to play in history. As a consequence, the sexual behavior of women has been judged by men, relative to other men. For the most part the sexual conduct of women has been judged as it affects men, and the rights of certain men to women as property.

The male of our species does not absolutely need a woman to gratify his sexual urges; nor do women necessarily need men to gratify themselves. Consequently, it should hardly be surprising that human beings engage in same–sex relationships. Realizing this, it should be noted that the limiting of access to women, by circumstances or social custom, would encourage men to seek alternative sexual outlets. This would be particularly true during the prolonged period of adolescence which is characteristic of *homo sapiens*.

There is no convincing evidence in nature that precludes same–sex gratification as an alternative norm. Perhaps it is a natural adaptation to limit childbirth. The alternative use of same–sex partners for men would certainly reduce tension in societies where the availability of women is restricted.

We have traced the acceptance of same–sex relationships through the earliest civilization in the Tigris–Euphrates region. From there, the pattern of homoaffectionalism can be traced down through the ages from the very beginnings of Western civilization. The homoaffectionate behavior of the main characters of the Epic of Gilgamesh exemplifies the importance of the acceptance of homoaffectionalism to the history of civilization. This story, the oldest extant legend in Western culture, is homoerotic and homoaffectionate.

228

It is particularly important also to take notice that the Epic of Gilgamesh and the relationship between the two men depicts a civilizing of human beings, Enkidu in particular. Obviously the "enclosure" over which Gilgamesh rules identifies the city of Uruk at its very earliest stage of civilization. The affection of Gilgamesh for Enkidu is the means by which Enkidu is converted from a very hairy wild man to a civilized human being.

The homoaffectionalism depicted in the Epic is the same as that described by Plato in the *Symposium*: it "compels lovers and beloved alike to feel a zealous concern for their own virtue." It is also directed toward young men or boys who have begun to "acquire some mind." Held pointed out that Greek love relationships did not end with maturity, but endured until death. Mutual sexual gratification was an important aspect of the ideal relationship.[4]

It is the Greeks who have presented the best image of homoaffectionalism. By coupling it with homoeroticism, they were able to inspire later scholars. The influence of the Greek writers was part of the enlightenment of the eighteenth and nineteenth centuries. The Greeks perfected civilization through homoaffectionalism, and then inspired modern scholars to accept homoaffectionalism as part of civilization.

As noted in these studies, early Western law tended to ignore recreational sex as long as the rights of certain men to certain women was not disrupted. Same–sex recreational conduct was also generally ignored by the state at least up until the Romanizing of Christianity. The Romans seem to have been the first people to manifest a sense of guilt with regard to sexual conduct. They enjoyed it, but then let themselves feel guilty. They developed a morbid sense of guilt which was later reflected in Christianity.

In part, the Roman sense of guilt reflects a preconceived notion regarding themselves and their progenitors. Their progenitors, it was thought, were so noble, brave, and virtuous that they would not have been so frivolous about pleasure. Sex was a pleasure; therefore, it was not to be overly enjoyed: the overenjoyment of pleasures was considered a sign of weakness.

Obviously the Romans enjoyed all kinds of pleasures to excess, but they suffered guilt as a consequence. This phenomenon stemmed from their fundamental belief in the mythical virtue of their simple ancestors who raped the Sabine women to found their race. Enduring hardships and privation was a part of their character;

229

brutality became a part of their heritage.

The Romans invented instruments of torture which were later perfected by Romanized Christians as tools of conversion. They inherited their morbid funeral customs from the Etruscans. From the very beginning, death rituals were a part of Roman culture. The killing of human beings as part of Roman funeral rites gave rise to the funeral "games" later in their history.

The ritualistic blood sacrifice and the death of a tortured deity were most suitable to the Roman temperament at the time Christianity was being formed. The need for self–effacement and even flagellation were a part of Roman culture long before the advent of Christianity.

What we have tried to show in these studies is the gradual influence on the developing legal systems of the Western world of the morbid Romanized Christians. Believing as they did that "the end is nigh" and only the soul mattered, it is not surprising that they turned against the flesh. There was no need to procreate and copulation was a pleasure; therefore, it was a sin. This became a pattern of thinking which stifled reason.

The collapse of the Roman Empire in the West stymied Christian power to some extent. The Germanic tribes seemed to have fewer problems in dealing with sexual conduct. Pre–literate German tribes were not much concerned about the sexual habits of free men. The use of women was regulated, since a woman was basically the property of some man. It was necessary for the early church fathers to distort local German customs to fit Christian morals into the German mold.

The German tribes recognized a taboo regarding the spilling of blood, but not of semen. By equating semen with blood, it was an easy step for Christians to equate the spilling of semen with the spilling of blood as an offense against God (nature). Nevertheless, it took Christianity a long time to make same–sex conduct a serious crime in Europe.

The formation of Canon Law seems to have been a Christian response to the lack of a civil law to govern personal behavior within the family and between free consenting adults. Even Roman law respected the rights of individuals within the family and generally left the regulating of personal conduct to the head of the household.

We have traced the homophobic influences of the Romanized Christian church on the legal system which developed in Europe.

At the same time we have tried to trace the resistance to that trend and explain what it is about human beings that tends to foster homoaffectionalism. The influence of Islamic culture on Europe is included to demonstrate the impact of their sex–positive religion on a reawakening medieval world. The Mamlukes were selected as the best example of homoaffectional acceptability.

Making the leap to more contemporary issues, it would appear that in the last decade of the twentieth century, the legal and political pressures exerted on the U.S. military may force the acceptance of homosexuality and permit lesbians and gay men to serve. On 25 October, 1992, the former manpower chief, Lawrence Korb, who served in the Pentagon in the 1980s, was quoted as favoring a change in policy, and believed that lifting the ban on homosexuals was inevitable. His opinions were disseminated nationally through "Newhouse News Service" by David Wood.[5] Korb was a senior fellow at the Brookings Institute in Washington, D.C., when he was quoted. He pointed out that, despite the efforts to screen out homosexuals from the military, they still served honorably, with an estimated 180,000 homosexuals believed to be on active duty. The ban on homosexuals in the U.S. military is not law, it is policy. A presidential order could change that policy.

"Tolerance and civility must be taught. Simply putting people together in the same room, whether blacks and whites or gays and straights, does not in itself help them get along. You have to teach them," said the historian, Edwin Dorn. He was also quoted by Wood. Hopefully, this book will add to that teaching process.

In these studies we have hypothesized that the ability of male *homo sapiens* to tolerate and empathize with other males gives rise to homoaffectionalism, and that that ability is the essential element which enables the species to develop a civilization. It is the tendency toward male bonding and homoaffectionalism which permits individuals to cooperate and work together for a common purpose, for the general good. Mental ability and the development of unique skills, and not just strength alone, were leadership requirements. Homoaffectionalism allows for homoerotic expression, and rationalizes homosexuality as a physiological and cultural norm. This conclusion suggests that the interference with homoaffectionalism by organized religions and the laws they inspired has hampered the development of the human race and has retarded civilization.

NOTES

1. Richard E. Leakey and Roger Lewin, People Of The Lake (Garden City, N. Y.: Anchor Press, Doubleday, 1978), p. 191.

2. Irenaus Eibl-Eibesfeldt, trans. Geoffrey Strachan, Love And Hate (New York: Holt, Rhinehart & Winston, 1971), pp. 8–32, pp. 129–169.

   Eibl-Eibesfeldt anticipated the work of Jane Goodall, whose televised researches among the chimpanzees in the wild cannot be ignored, especially their implications regarding human behavior. He dealt with a wide range of adaptive animal behavior patterns, which are common to human beings and some lower animals.

3. Eibl-Eibesfeldt, p. 155

4. George F. Held, "The Parallel Between the Gilgamesh Epic and Plato's Symposium," Journal of Near East Studies (Chicago: University of Chicago Press, 1983), 42, No. 2, p. 137.

5. David Wood, Newhouse News Service, "When Military Gay Ban Ends," San Francisco Examiner, 25 October, 1992, p. A-4.

BIBLIOGRAPHY

Alberro, Solange. *La Actividad Del Santo Oficio De La Inquisicion En Nova España, 1571–1700*. Mexico: Instituto Nacional de Anthropologia e Historia, 1981.

Aristophanes. *The Clouds*, in *Great Books of the Western World*. New York: Encyclopaedia Brittanica, Inc., 1952.

Azzam, Abd-al Rahman. The Eternal Message of Muhammad. Trans. Caesar E. Farah. New York: Mentor Books, 1965.

Bailey, D. S. *Homosexuality and the Western Tradition*. London: Longman, Green & Co., Ltd., 1975.

Beazely, J. D. "Some Attic Vases in The Cyprus Museum." *Proceedings of the British Academy* 33, 1947.

Birdi, Abu-I-Mahasin Ibn Taghri. *History Of Egypt 1382–1469 A.D.* Trans. William Poppen. Berkeley: University of California Press, 1954.

Boswell, John. *Christianity, Social Tolerance and Homosexuality*. Chicago: University of Chicago Press, 1980.

Bradley, Leigh, Paul Koffsky, Cpt. Melissa Wells-Petry. "Homosexuality in the Military." *West's Military Justice Reporter* v. 30.

Bray, Alan. *Homosexuality in Renaissance England*. London: Gay Men's Press, 1982.

Breasted, James H. *The Dawn Of Conscience*. New York: Charles Scribner's Sons, 1935.

Browning, Robert. *Justinian and Theodora*. London: Weidenfeld and Nicolson, 1971.

Buckland, W. M. *Textbook Of Roman Law*. Cambridge: University Press, 1932.

Bullough, Vern L. *Sexual Variance*. Chicago: University of Chicago Press, 1976.

Cassius Dio, Cocceianus. *Dio's Roman History*. Trans. Earnest Cary.

Cambridge: Harvard University Press, 1961.

Chavel, Charles Ber. *Commentary On The Torah.* New York: Shilo Publishing House, Inc., 1978.

Danby, Herbert. *The Mishnah.* Oxford: University Press, 1933.

Dover, K. J. *Greek Homosexuality.* London: Duckworth Company, Ltd., 1978.

Driver, G. R. and John C. Miles. *The Babylonian Laws.* Oxford: The Clarendon Press, 1952.

Eadmer. *History of Recent Events in England.* Philadelphia: Dufour, 1965.

Eadmer. *Life of St. Anselm.* Oxford: The Clarendon Press, 1979.

Ebeleing, Eric and Bruno Meissner, eds. *Reallexikon der Assyriologi und Vorderasiatischen Archaeologie.* Berlin: Walter de Gruyter. Vol. 4.

Edwardes, Allen. *Jewel in the Lotus: A Historical Survey of Sexual Culture in the East.* New York: The Julian Press, 1959.

Edwards, Chilperic. *Code of Hammurabi.* Port Washington, N. Y.: Kenikat Press, 1904.

Eibl-Eibesfeldt, Irenaus. *Love and Hate.* Trans. Geoffrey Strachan. New York: Holt, Rinehart & Winston, 1971.

Encyclopaedia Judaica, Vol. 15. Jerusalem: Keter Publishing House, Ltd., 1971.

Finegan, Jack. *Light From The Ancient Past.* Princeton: Princeton University Press, 1959.

Fiore, Silvestro. *Voices From the Clay: Development of Assyro–Babylonian Literature.* Norman: University of Oklahoma Press, 1965.

Fone, Byrne R. S. *Hidden Heritage.* New York: Irvington Publishers, Inc., 1980.

Gascoigne, Bamber. *The Christians.* London: Granada Publishing, 1978.

Gibbon, Edward. *The Decline And Fall of the Roman Empire.* London: J.

236

F. Dove, 1825.

Gide, André. *Corydon*. New York: Farrar, Straus & Co., 1950.

Glubb, John Bagot. *Soldiers of Fortune*. London: Hodden & Stoughton, 1973.

Goodenough, Erwin R. *Jewish Symbols in the Greco–Roman Period*. New York: Bollinger Foundation, 1964.

Grant, Robert M. *Augustus to Constantine*. New York: Harper & Row, 1970.

Greenberg, David F. *The Construction of Homosexuality*. Chicago: University of Chicago Press, 1988.

Grimal, Pierre. *The Civilization Of Rome*. Trans. W. S. Maguinness. New York: Simon & Schuster, 1963.

Harden, Donald. *The Phoenicians*. New York: Frederick A. Praeger, 1962.

Haussig, H. W. *A History of Byzantine Civilizations*. Trans. J. M. Hussey. New York: Praeger Publishers, 1971.

Heidel, Alexander. *The Gilgamesh Epic and Old Testament Parallels*. Chicago: University of Chicago Press, 1971.

Held, George F. "Parallels Between the Gilgamesh Epic and Plato's *Symposium*." *Journal of Near East Studies*. Chicago: University of Chicago Press, 1983.

Hirschfeld, Magnus. *Jahrbuch Fur Sexuelle Zwischenstufen*. * vol. 7 (1905)

Holmes, W. M. Gordon. *The Age of Justinian and Theodora*. London: G. Bell & Sons, Ltd., 1912.

Imparati, Fiorello. *Le Leggi Ittite*. Roma: Ateneo, 1964.

Jacobsen, Thorkild. *The Treasures of Darkness*. New Haven: Yale University Press, 1976.

Jefferson, Thomas. Jefferson's Works, Washington: 1903.

Johns, C. H. W. *Babylonian and Assyrian Laws*. Edinburgh: T. & T. Clark, 1904.

Jolowicz, H. F. *Roman Foundations of Modern Law*. Oxford: The Clarendon Press, 1957.

Jones, A. H. M. *The Decline of the Ancient World*. London: Longmans, Green & Co., Ltd., 1966.

Kapp, Frederick. *Life of Baron Frederick William von Steuben*. New York: Mason Bros., 1859.

Kiefer, Otto. *Sexual Life in Ancient Rome*. New York: Barnes & Noble, 1956.

King, Charles R. *Life and Correspondence of Rufus King*. New York: G.P. Putnam's Sons, 1894.

Knowles, Dom David. *The Religious Orders of England*. Cambridge: University Press, 1959.

Ladurie, Emmanuel Le Roy. Montaillou. New York: Vintage Books, 1979.

Lambert, Robert. *Beloved and God*. New York: Viking, 1984.

Laurisen, John and David Thorstad. *The Early Homosexual Rights Movement 1864–1935*. New York: Times Changes Press, 1974.

Leakey, Richard E. and Roger Lewin. *People Of The Lake*. Garden City, N.Y.: Anchor Press, Doubleday, 1978.

Little, Donald Presgrave. *An Introduction to Mamluk History*. Montreal: McGill–Queen's University Press, 1970.

Lombard Laws. Trans Katherine Fisher Drew. Philadelphia: University of Pennsylvania Press, 1973.

Malter, Henry. *The Treatise TA'ANIT of the Babylonian Talmud*. Philadelphia: Jewish Publication Society of America, 1967.

Marmor, Judd, ed. *Homosexuality: A Modern Reappraisal*. New York: Basic Books, 1980.

McNeill, John J. *The Church and the Homosexual*. Kansas City: Sheed, Andrews & McMeel, 1976.

Middleton, Conyers. *The Life of Marcus Tullius Cicero*. London: J. Wright, 1804.

Mirabeau, Comte de. *Secret Memoirs of the Court of Berlin.* Washington: M. Walter Dunn, 1901.

Moorehead, Alan. *The Blue Nile.* New York: Harper & Row, 1960.

Moyle, J. B. *The Institutes of Justinian.* Oxford: The Clarendon Press, 1913.

Muir, Sir William. *The Mameluke or Slave Dynasty of Egypt.* London: Smith, Elder & Co., 1891.

Neufeld, N. E. *The Hittite Laws.* London: Luzac & Co., Ltd., 1951.

New American Catholic Edition, *The Holy Bible.* New York: Benziger Bros., Inc., 1961.

Petronius. *The Satyricon.* New York: Penguin Books, Ltd., 1983.

Plato. *The Laws.* Trans. Trevor J. Saunders. Middlesex: Penguin Books, Ltd., 1980.

Plato. *The Symposium.* Trans. Walter Hamilton. Middlesex: Penguin Books, Ltd., 1982.

Plutarch. *Lives,* in *Great Books of the Western World.* Chicago: Encyclopaedia Brittanica, 1952.

Procopius. *The Secret History.* Trans. G. A. Williamson. Middlesex: Penguin Books, Ltd., 1966.

Rich, Pierre. *Daily Life in the World of Charlemagne.* Philadelphia: University of Pennsylvania Press, 1978.

Rollison, David. "Property, Ideology and Popular Culture in a Gloucestershire Village 1660–1740." *Past And Present,* No. 93.

Russell, Bertrand. *Wisdom Of The West.* Garden City, N.Y.: Doubleday & Co., Inc., 1959.

Shapiro, H. A. "Courtship Scenes in Attic Vase–Painting." *American Journal of Archaeology.* Vol. 85, No. 2, April, 1981.

Sinistrari, Ruggero. Personal communication to Paul D. Hardman, Berkeley: September 9, 1983.

Spartianus, Aelius. "Hadrian," *Scriptores Historiae Augustae*. Cambridge: Harvard University Press, 1947.

Steakley, James D. *The Homosexual Movement in Germany*. New York: Arno Press, 1975.

Suetonius, Gaius Tranquillus. *The Lives of the Caesars*. Trans. Philemon Holland. New York: The Heritage Press, 1965.

Sutherland, Alistair and Patrick Anderson. *Eros*. New York: The Citadel Press, 1963.

Tacitus, Cornelius. *Complete Works*. Trans. A. J. Church and William J. Brodribb. New York: Random House, 1942.

Taylor, Henry Osborn. *The Medieval Mind*. London: McMillan & Co., Ltd., 1938.

Thompson, E. A. *The Visigoths in the Time of Ulfila*. Oxford: The Clarendon Press, 1966.

Ulrichs, Karl Friedrich. *Vindex: Social–Judicial Studies on Sexual Love Between Men*. Trans. Michael A. Lombardi. Los Angeles: Urania Manuscripts, 1979.

Verstraete, Bert C. "Homosexuality in Ancient Greek and Roman Civilization." *Journal of Homosexuality*. Vol. 3, (1), Fall 1977.

Virgil (Publius Vergilius Maro). *The Works of Virgil*. Trans. John Dryden. London: James Swan, 1806.

Westermark, Edward. *Christianity And Morals*. Freeport, N.Y.: Books for Libraries Press, 1969.

Wright, Addison G. *Midrash*. Staten Island: Society of St. Paul, 1976.

Yates, William Holt. *The Modern History of Egypt*. London: Elder & Co., 1843.

Zeldin, Theodore. *France, 1848–1945*. New York: Oxford University Press, 1979.

INDEX

249

ABOUT THE BOOK

Homoaffectionalism is the author-coined word for the intimate associations that have developed between men throughout history. The Gilgamesh Epic, traced to 2,500 B.C., was clearly based on intimacy between two men. Some of these relationships were sexual, others not, but all have had their beneficial influences on culture and the human condition. Some societies have shown more toleration than others, frequently avoiding the entire issue in writing their laws and recording their histories. Some religions have become intransigently opposed for various reasons, but it wasn't always that way.

Although this is not an "outing" book, Hardman shows by careful analysis of historical documents and legal codes that male bonding and homoaffectionalism, which allows for homoerotic expression, has enhanced the development of the human race throughout history.

The long-avoided question of an occasional sexual component in male bonding is given a sensible non-judgmental review. Hardman has made a valuable contribution to scholarship.

—W. Dorr Legg, Dean
One Institute, Los Angeles